e4

Scotland's Historic Buildings

Also by Hubert Fenwick

ARCHITECT ROYAL
THE AULD ALLIANCE

HUBERT FENWICK

Scotland's
Historic Buildings

PHOTOGRAPHS BY THE AUTHOR

ROBERT HALE · LONDON

Robert Hale & Company
63 Old Brompton Road
London SW7

Filmset and printed in Great Britain by
BAS Printers Limited, Wallop, Hampshire

Contents

Illustrations

Plans

Glossary

AISLE: Division of church often separated by pillars from nave, choir or transepts; often a chapel containing family tombs.

APSE: Rounded or many sided end of the chancel or choir of a church.

ASHLAR: Dressed stone.

AUMBRY: Wall cupboard, often used to house Sacred Vessels in a church.

BARMKIN: Outer defence wall.

BARREL-VAULT: Semicircular roof either of stone or timber.

BARTISAN: Battlemented sentry walk.

BEE-BOLE: Opening in garden wall to contain bee-skeps or hives.

BROACH SPIRE: Spire that splays out at foot directly from tower walls.

BUT-AND-BEN: Literally, one room out and one room in.

CAP-HOUSE: Small building at top of stairs opening onto roof.

CLOSE: Building with courtyard.

CORBEL: Projection in stone or timber to support walls or beams.

CORBIE-STEPS, CROW-STEPS: Stepped gable ends.

CRENELLATION: Indentation on battlements.

DECORATED: Middle period of Gothic architecture.

DIVOTS: Sods, as used to cope thatched cottages.

DONJON: Keep, or tower of Norman castle.

DOOCOT: Dovecote or pigeonloft, either circular or rectangular and when domed known as 'beehive'.

DYKE: Stone wall usually enclosing garden.

ENCEINTE: Enclosure or outer wall of medieval castle.

FLAMBOYANT: Late-Gothic style with flame motive design.

FORESTAIRS: External stairs of wood or stone.

FREESTONE: Soft and easily-quarried stone.

GAIT: Walk or street.

GARTH: Enclosed garden or cloister.

HARLING: Sand, lime and balast rendering to rough masonry.

JAMB: Ingoe, or side support to doorway or window.
JOUGS: Metal neckpiece for wrong-doers.

LANCET: Narrow window with pointed arch typical of early Gothic period.
LUCARNE: Dormer or roof window, usually of stone.

MACHICOLATIONS: Openings between corbelled supports of parapet.
MERCAT CROSS: Market cross.
MOTTE: Mound, often artificial, upon which a timber fort was built.

OGEE: Similar to ogival, shape in which convex and concave curves combine.
ORIEL: Projecting window.
OVERSAILING: Single pitched roof replacing conical tower or turret.

PALAS: Place, Jacobean building of modest height, not a tower.
PALLADIAN: Style, based on Roman, introduced by Andrea Palladio in the sixteenth century.
PELE: Wooden palisade, later a tower of stone.
PEND: Vaulted passage.
PORT: Entrance gateway to medieval burgh.
POTENCE: Movable ladder in circular dovecote.

QUOIN: Corner stone; BUCKLE-QUOIN: in shape of buckle.

RIG: Ridge, but also long, narrow strip of land often enclosed.
ROMANESQUE: Buildings derived from Roman and characterized by the use of rounded arches.
ROOD: Screen between nave and choir of church.

SCALE-AND-PLATT: Straight stair with landings.
SHOT-HOLE: Hole for use of firearms against unwanted visitors.
SHUT-HOLE: Literally hole that can be opened or shut, usually near the door for air.
SHUTTER-BOARD WINDOW: Window with fixed upper lights, usually leaded, and opening wooden shutter below.
SKEW-PUTT: Finish to skew, or gable-coping, at eaves.
SOLAR: The upper hall in medieval castle or manor.

SQUINCH: Arched support for angle turret that does not reach ground.

STUDY: Small room in turret.

SWEPT-DORMER: Dormer window with swept-up roof.

TOLBOOTH: Jail, usually incorporated in Town House.

TURNPIKE STAIR: Spiral or corkscrew staircase.

WHEELHOUSE: Hexagonal shed containing geared wheel for threshing, animal motivated.

WYND: Narrow passage or lane between houses, also Vennel.

YETT: Iron grille or gate.

Introduction

A BOOKLET entitled 'Scotland's Historic Buildings' was recently delivered to me by an official of Edinburgh Corporation. It came with a letter to the effect that I was the owner of a building of special architectural or historic interest, details of that property and why it had been so classified. This was part of the newly delineated Conservation Area which covers most of the Georgian 'New Town', begun in the mid-eighteenth century and only completed within the last hundred years. My house is in a 'New Town' crescent dating from about 1820, which is not very old and scarcely historic, but elegant and beautiful and worthy of preservation as part of a whole street, part of a piece of urban planning which, in the second half of the twentieth century is without parallel in Scotland and has few rivals in Europe. The architecture of my house and the rest of Edinburgh's Georgian 'New Town' is neo-classical, that is to say it derives from Greco-Roman precepts and is, therefore, hardly indigenous, being a Scottish variation on a well worn theme. Yet the way in which it has been adapted, and the thoroughness of the whole plan is very local, suggesting that Doric architecture has affinities with 'doric' speech and ideals. Curiously enough, however, the picture on the outside of the booklet, 'Scotland's Historic Buildings', shows a tall house with crow-stepped gables, dormer windows, red pantiles, harled walls and small-paned windows, a more familiar idiom north of the border than Edinburgh's neo-classical splendour and possibly more in keeping with the term 'historic'.

The official booklet explains the difference between 'Listed Buildings' and 'Scheduled Ancient Monuments', the latter usually unoccupied and generally older, the former being, as mine is now, 'of special architectural or historic interest', and occupied. Current legislation is described, showing how and why certain buildings are scheduled or listed, what one may or may not do in the way of alterations or enlargements, how to obtain permission to do them and what grants are available. The arrival of the booklet marks a turning point not only in the affairs of the City of Edinburgh but in other Scottish burghs as one council after another declares its historic quarters inviolable by the developer and the vulgarian. Standardization is the rule in building now rather than the exception, which may account for the interest being shown in older structures; they usually display some of that human touch which is lacking in modern architecture; and luckily in Scotland there remain enough historic buildings standing to make looking at them worthwhile. These buildings tell Scotland's story more clearly and evocatively than any other single item in our environment. They show how our ancestors lived and worked and played and fought, raising themselves from primitive beginnings to construct some of the finest houses and streets that ever graced a civilized state. Apart from the most studiously copied specimens Scottish architecture has a character all its own, as visitors notice straight away. Berwick-upon-Tweed, for example, is as Scottish a town as exists between the border and John o'Groats, Scottish in speech and physiognomy in a manner that belies its somewhat anomalous political position. Compare it with Carlisle, at the western end of the Anglo-Scottish divide, and one recognizes the difference at once, for Carlisle is as patently English in tone and appearance as the southernmost airt in Britain.

The origins of these picturesque cultural divergencies are, of course, to be found in the separate history of Scotland as an independent kingdom until 1603, and having a separate parliament until 1707. During the centuries before that the country had developed close links with the Continent, and notably with France in the famous 'Auld Alliance', which had its climax in the marriage of Mary, Queen of Scots to the Dauphin in 1558. In Jacobean times there was much direct trade with Scandinavia and the Low Countries; and all this is demonstrated in Scotland's historic buildings, giving them a special cachet that makes them quite different to anything existing elsewhere. Scottish architecture, whether it be of churches, castles or houses, is rarely as grand as that of England but it is nearly always peculiarly Scottish, sometimes with a French flavour, as in the corner turrets and pinnacles, or

Flemish, as in the crow-stepped gables and red-pantiles. Scots architects and builders have known how to take from others what they liked or found useful and adapt it to their own purposes in a rather remarkable way. Indeed, there is something in the very make-up of most Scotsmen that is at once solid and logical, romantic and mystical. It shows in the Scottish pre-occupation with principle, on the one hand, and with legend on the other; and it certainly appears in our architecture. We do not usually slavishly copy other people but study their work, so that in the Highlands romantic castles that rival those seen in Italy or the Rhineland rise almost naturally amidst some of the most beautiful scenery in these islands; while along the east coast rows of crow-stepped, Dutch-gabled houses testify to other origins and purposes. The so-called Georgian-style buildings currently offered for sale in some parts of southern Scotland are not of this kind but 'foreign' importations, and their general acceptance north of the border suggests an appalling ignorance of the native idiom on the part of both seller and purchaser. The castles in the Highlands and the Netherlandish-looking houses of the East Neuk o' Fife, on the other hand, are Scottish by adoption and adaptation; and throughout the country, until quite recently, there survived an obvious and extraordinarily persistent architectural homogeneity. I travel a good deal, especially on the Continent, and I know of only two countries across the channel which can boast so homogeneous a native architecture within so limited a space as Scotland. They are Portugal and Holland, both small and backed by powerful neighbours, yet having succeeded in developing art forms the excellence and individuality of which have acquired international reputations.

Scotland's particular claims to fame in the cultural field are not in doubt, one has but to think of the names and fame of Messrs Ramsay, Raeburn, Scott and Burns for proof. What is not always fully realized, however, especially north of the border, is the significance of the Scottish contribution in architecture. In the eighteenth century alone we produced James Gibbs, Wren's successor and disciple; Colen Campbell, codifier of the Palladian mode in Britain; Sir William Chambers and the Adam family, who need no further introduction. Then there was Charles Cameron, who accepted the invitation of

Catherine the Great to become her architect, went to Russia and designed some of the most magnificent neo-classical palaces ever seen. These buildings are maintained by the Soviets, in fact, many of them were severely damaged during the last war and have been faithfully and expensively restored by the Communists. Their reasons for doing this may be ambiguous but posterity will be grateful just the same.

However, this book is not primarily concerned with architects, and not at all with archaeology. It is about the buildings most of us see and use either regularly or from time to time in the course of our normal lives. Some are decayed but the majority are roofed and inhabited, and those that are not are capable of restoration with the minimum of imagination and at modest cost. Churches come first in the story because they were the first stone buildings, erected in an age when laymen had perforce to live in timber huts which they burnt down at the enemy's approach. Churches, on the whole, were spared until the days immediately prior to and after the Reformation; they were built of stone to last and as fitting memorials to the faith of their creators. Castles of stone followed, many of them being made comfortable as strife with the 'auld enemy' ceased and fratricidal conflict faded away. Often such castles became the nucleus of larger buildings, romantic essays in the Scotch Baronial manner. Sir William Bruce, the first professional Scottish architect and the first in a long line which dominated 'The Mistress Art' in the late seventeenth and early eighteenth centuries, introduced the 'Italian' or Palladian style into Scotland. He used it in the rebuilding of the ancient Palace of Holyroodhouse for Charles II, which was completed in 1679. This heralded the end of the old indigenous way of doing things and the arrival of neo-classicism, the apotheosis of which came in the late eighteenth century with the work of Robert Adam and the laying out of the Georgian 'New Town' of Edinburgh.

The industrial age brought a number of revivals, mostly Gothic; some of this was sheer fun, much of it awful; but some blended in quite well with the past and the romantic Scottish background. I do not refer so much to Balmoral as to the castles designed by Adam in his later years, and to a number of amusing follies and monuments that today seem an essential part of the Caledonian scene. The industrial age also brought an important Scottish contribution in the bridges and canals of Thomas Telford, and the lighthouses of Robert and Alan Stevenson. They were consultants and engineers of the first order and each in his way created a new form peculiarly suited to the Scottish landscape. More recently our buildings have tended to reflect those of the rest of the United Kingdom and of the world at large, so that one can hardly distinguish some Scottish towns from those of southern England or North America, at least at a distance; which is a pity, since even in our own improvident age it should be possible to retain some of the more obvious traditional differences, especially those of a pleasant and individual character.

H.F.

Spring 1974

I
Religious Buildings: Early Churches and Cathedrals

THE EARLIEST buildings in Scotland, as in most countries, were defensive, the most characteristic being the large Iron Age brochs, or round towers, looking not unlike small cooling towers at a blast furnace. These survive in varying degrees of wholeness in Shetland and the north east, their nearest equivalent elsewhere in Europe being the Nuraghi, or prehistoric chief's castles in Sardinia. Christian religious edifices followed in the seventh and eighth centuries, Celtic cells and finally Celtic-inspired churches. Again, the more important remains are in the north-east of the country, in the Orkney and Shetland Islands and in the Western Isles. Little of this, however, concerns us greatly here, since none of them are roofed or used, and in this book we are chiefly dealing with functional or well-preserved buildings. Thus we come almost at once to Queen Margaret's Chapel, on the highest point of the Castle Rock in Edinburgh. Architectural historians differ as to the exact age of this splendid little shrine dedicated to the saintly Saxon consort of Malcolm Canmore. It has certainly stood for nigh-on 800 years and is still the scene on occasion of baptisms and weddings amongst the military personnel at the castle. G. P. H. Watson, writing on the Church in Medieval Scotland, in *The Stones of Scotland*, edited by George Scott Moncrieff, suggests that this is where Queen Margaret heard her last Mass, before dying in Edinburgh Castle on 16th November 1095; and some portion of this tiny Romanesque or early Norman chapel does seem to date from the eleventh century. Other writers are less precise, but all are agreed that even if Queen Margaret herself did not see the present building her sons probably did, and that it is without doubt the oldest place of worship north of the border still functioning as such.

The chapel is built of stone, a circumstance not without significance in the story of its survival, since the castle within whose defences it stands was originally constructed of timber and was burned down on more than one occasion, notably by Robert Bruce himself, in the fourteenth century. No part of the existing castle dates from before that century, and that part submerged within later structures. As we shall see, stone 'keeps' on the Norman model were rare in Scotland, and instead it was more usual to erect wooden towers in 'motte and bailey' fashion, that is, atop earthen mounds, either artificial or natural, and protected around the perimeter by wooden palisades—hence the term 'pele tower'. The few stone castles dating from before the thirteenth and fourteenth centuries were thrown down or otherwise rendered useless in the Wars of Independence, when the Scots adopted a scorched earth policy: and after Bannockburn the ties with England, which had been growing closer all the time, were severed and the country developed a national style of building that lasted well into the seventeenth century and beyond.

Until the English invasion and the depredations brought by the Reformers, Scottish religious buildings were generally spared in the sack and pillage that was meted out to many domestic and military edifices; and this more permanent, more respected position was reflected in their solid, stone construction. So far as Queen Margaret's Chapel is concerned, at least the lower parts of the masonry are of the eleventh or early twelfth century. The building has suffered a number of changes in the course of its long life and the upper parts are newer, though still Romanesque. The chapel served as a munition store for a while, but recently has been beautifully restored, and whitewashed inside, revealing the most delightful semi-circular apse which, oddly enough, has no external form, the building being a simple rectangle outside. A typical Norman arch, rounded, with chevron carving divides the minute altar space from the nave, and modern stained glass of taste has been inserted in the one authenticated window at the west end. It is, perhaps, remarkable that with all the disturbances that have occurred in the political and religious life of Scotland over the past eight centuries that this jewel has come down to us so little damaged, still a hallowed shrine, indeed, probably the most hallowed shrine of its kind remaining.

There are those, with strong nationalistic tendencies and perhaps an over-romantic view of Celtic civilization, who think the arrival in the north of the future Queen Margaret, her conversion of her husband to 'western', Roman Christianity and her attachment to Anglo-Norman political ideas was a disaster. Be this as it may, it resulted in the closer union of Scotland and England over a period of some two hundred years when the country enjoyed an era of peace and prosperity it has never repeated. During this time 'Inglis', or Northumbrian English, became the language of all but the Gaelic and Norse-speaking people of the north and west, and Scottish architecture began to resemble more and more that of south Britain: especially under Queen Margaret's most pious son, David I, who was nicknamed 'that sair sanct for the croun' on account of his founding so many cathedrals and abbeys. The whole course of our history changed after the death of Alexander III, the last king in the old line, and the demise of his heir, the ill-fated 'Maid of Norway', who died in 1290. She had been betrothed to the first Prince of Wales, the future Edward II, a union which might have changed history, though without making the lass happy, but which in fact led to years of inter-necine strife between the Anglo-Norman barons and to the direct interference in Scottish affairs of the Kings of England.

The change did not come all at once, however, and even some earlier influences survived Queen Margaret's and her sons' attempts at westernization. They included, in the historic buildings context, two remarkable Round Towers, one at Brechin, the other at Abernethy. Both survive for the same reason that Margaret's own chapel does, they belonged to religious establishments and were consequently sturdily built of stone. At Brechin a much-restored medieval cathedral stands a short distance to the west of its ancient belfry, while at Abernethy the Round Tower alone survives. Both date in their lower parts from the early eleventh century, but they have been added to in Norman times, and, in the case of Brechin, provided with a new conical roof. There is Celtic work around the door at Brechin, which is well above ground level and could only be reached by a movable ladder. This confirms the dual purpose of the towers, defensive as well as

(*left*) Round tower and reconstructed mercat cross, Abernethy, Perthshire. (*right*) Romanesque doorway and part of saddle-back tower, Strathbrock, West Lothian

religious, reminders of monastic hospitality in times of peace and refuges for the fearful during Viking raids.

Actually, Scots masons never quite gave up their affection for the rounded as opposed to the pointed arch. It crops up again and again throughout the Gothic period, and returned in full flavour at the Renaissance. This fondness may have reflected a harking back to Celtic modes, they having Italian, or at any rate Roman precedents; and it may be no coincidence that dislike of the Gothic arch was widespread in medieval Italy, the Florentines eventually discarding 'pointed' architecture altogether in the fifteenth century. There may also be some significance in the fact that our first bishop, St Ninian, went to Rome to be consecrated and founded his tiny cathedral, his so-called 'Candida Casa', or white house, at

Whithorn, in Galloway, while the Imperial legions were still in Scotland. In any event, round-arched architecture continued popular in the north long after the rest of Europe had adopted French Gothic, and as late as the thirteenth century some of our most charming Romanesque kirks were erected. They include a rather unusual assembly in a single county, West Lothian, or Linlithgowshire, where no less than four fine specimens survive, with two others partly Romanesque, and all still in use.

The best known of these, perhaps the best known of its kind in Scotland is the Parish Kirk at Dalmeny, on Lord Rosebery's estate, which is replete with small, semi-circular apse, tiny chancel and long dark nave. It is lit by few and very narrow windows, many of them with elaborate decorations around the openings, and there is a handsome Norman arch between the sanctuary and the body of the kirk. A recent restoration by Sir Robert Lorimer completed the design with a massive little tower, military-looking and a trifle stunted, but no doubt Norman in inspiration. The south door is a masterpiece of Romanesque carving and grotesque decoration, with a somewhat detached looking panel of interlaced arches in the form of blank arcading above. Not far away is Kirkliston, where the old church has been tampered with, but retains a good tower, finished with a saddle-back, or gable-ended roof in the Scots manner, and typical bell-cot at one gable. It is in this church that the memorial to the 'Bride of Lammermuir' can be seen. A few miles to the west is Uphall, which the late Ian Lindsay restored. He was the local laird and had his pew in the kirk of Strathbrock, as Uphall is properly called. Here again the saddle-back tower of the church has survived intact and is entered by a surprisingly plain but attractive Romanesque doorway. The Georgian reconstruction of the Parish Kirk at Ecclesmachan disguises the fact that it too is of Norman origin and twelfth-century features protrude from it here and there. It lies at the side of a quiet road leading north from Uphall in the direction of Abercorn which was once the seat of a Pictish bishop and is actually built under the bield of a hill upon whose summit there once was a Roman Fort. The nave of the church has been entirely rebuilt in mock Norman of the most artificial and uncompromising kind but the chancel, having been appropriated by the Hope family in the seventeenth century and subsequently adapted by them for a laird's pew and retiring rooms, has retained its medieval walls. I shall have more to say later about the Hope 'gallery' but it is worth mentioning here that beneath it are two hog-back tombstones, potent witness of the passage through the area of the Danes, and two broken portions of the Pictish bishop's cross. A rounded arch and two grotesque heads remain *in situ*, plus what is probably the only remaining Sanctus bell-cot in Scotland. This is at the crossing, where the old nave would have met the chancel and its bell would have been rung for the benefit of the sick and the old who could not attend the Mass to tell them the most solemn part of the service, the Elevation of the Host, had been reached.

Mr Lindsay published a series of 'wee bookies' about these and other West Lothian churches which is now out of print. Included was South Queensferry, where beside the original Parish Kirk, now discarded, there exists the only original Carmelite foundation in Britain whose church is still used as a place of Christian worship. The Friary Kirk of Mount Carmel, popularly known as the Priory, dating from the fourteenth and fifteenth centuries, comes slightly outwith a Norman context, though it does display many of those curious roundnesses beloved of Scottish masons, and the friars did come to the county as early as 1290. They were preaching friars, like the Franciscans, but with much older traditions going back via the Syrian church to the days of the Jewish prophets and holy men who spoke to God on Mount Carmel. They had a special dispensation from the Pope to retain their own liturgy and customs and had twelve friaries north of the border. They died out at the Reformation but their church at South Queensferry, barrel-vaulted and roofed with sturdy stone slabs, survived them because it was the property of the Dundases of Dundas Castle, who brought the friars there in the first instance.

The Knights Templar also had a priory at Torphichen, near Linlithgow, but except for part of the crossing, which it is proposed eventually to restore, their kirk has been replaced by an eighteenth-century box-kirk of the more usual type. Further afield, however, just across the Forth, is Aberdour, where the kirk of St Fillan, popular for weddings but too small for large gatherings, hides itself from the public gaze behind the walls of Aberdour Castle, former seat of the Earls of Moray. Parts of the church have obviously been rebuilt out of stones from the ruined castle, but the Norman chancel dates from 1178 and, oddly enough for Scotland, is flat-ended. Like Dalmeny, it has been thoroughly restored, though the problem of how to adapt a medieval building to Presbyterian worship has no more been solved here than in most other places. 'Stuck in the corner of Popish grandeur', is how Robert Burns described the state of St Michael's former Collegiate Kirk in Linlithgow in his day; and many Scottish churches are not much better now. Mr Lindsay, who was Scotland's leading ecclesiastical architect for many years, was very firm on this subject, and wherever he could made Church of Scotland congregations face west, instead of east, turning their backs on the non-existent altar. Another way of getting out of the difficulty was to place the pulpit half way down one wall, usually the south and run the seating longways on; but the idea of trying to fit a Calvinistic religion into the framework of a medieval one was anathema to him. As things are, both Aberdour and Dalmeny resemble low-church Anglican kirks, which, of course, they are not! Still, it is good to see such places used and well-maintained; and Aberdour has the biggest, lowest crow-stepped roof I think I have ever seen, a post-Reformation feature in the best Scottish masonic tradition.

Opposite Aberdour, from which it is reached by motor boat, is Inchcolm, Shakespeare's St Colme's Inch in *Macbeth* and sometimes known as the 'Iona of the East'. The conventual buildings on the island are amongst the best-preserved in Scotland, the reason being that while the kirk itself was ravaged and afterwards left to decay the monk's quarters were taken over at the Reformation by the Moray Lords of Aberdour, who made them the nucleus of a private residence. Thus they have remained almost till today, where they are looked after by the Department of the Environment. The Abbey of St Columba on Inchcolm is not as old as Iona, having been founded by Alexander I as a thanks offering for being saved from drowning in about 1123; while Iona became a holy place as early as the sixth century; though the present buildings,

Twelfth-century chancel with Charles II tower, Leuchars, Fife

restored like so much else in modern Scotland by Ian Lindsay, replace those erected in the fourteenth and fifteenth centuries by Benedictine monks. The followers of St Columba were driven out by the Danes, when the relics of the saint were removed to safety on the mainland; and it was not until the end of the nineteenth century that the then Duke of Argyll made the ruins over to the Church of Scotland, as Trustees, and only recently that the necessary restoration and rebuilding has been completed.

Compared to Iona, therefore, the actual buildings on Inchcolm are a great deal more authentic and include an ancient hermit's cell in which the near-drowned Alexander I is said to have sheltered after his saving from the sea. The first foundation was a Romanesque structure, which however, was greatly enlarged in Gothic times with the addition of a new, cruciform church, when the old one was made into a house. The Abbey was frequently raided by English sailors and much repair work went on, but being comparatively near to the land, and centres of population, it always recovered and the monks had a refuge nearby. Amongst the treasures uncovered by the Department are valuable thirteenth-century wall paintings, unique in Scotland, which were mercifully hidden behind plaster and other accretions when the original choir was turned to domestic use. They show clergy taking part in a funeral procession. Of the same century is the octagonal stone-roofed Chapter House, still with its stone seat around the base for the clergy to sit on, though its shape is not typical, the Scottish tradition in chapter houses being more for rectangular ones.

In northern Fife is Dalmeny's most serious rival to fame in the lovely little kirk at Leuchars, between St Andrews and Newport. Although only the chancel and minute rounded-ended apse are Norman, and the roof of the latter was capped in the seventeenth century by a Charles II tower, the church is not over-restored and is full of atmosphere. Below an eaves course composed of barbaric heads runs a band of beautiful Romanesque arcading, supported by interlacing arches springing from the ground; and this arrangement seems complemented rather than the reverse by the amusing octagonal turret with stone cupola that replaces the old roof. The kirk was founded by Baron de Quincy, whose castle stood close by. This is now reduced to a few enigmatic bumps in a field and a doocot, or pigeon-cote, the family having departed with others after the Wars of Independence, when Scots became chauvinistic and shed some of their Anglo-Norman overlords; but it does serve as an early example of how many of our first parish kirks came to be built by the barons, at their gates, or within them, either as glorified chantry chapels or full blown collegiate churches.

Not all our parish kirks were founded in this manner, of course, and in Strathearn, which runs west to east through southern Perthshire, are a number of what are loosely termed 'Culdee Churches'. Pre-dating the introduction of the feudal system they follow missions started in the eighth century by St Fillan, a somewhat shadowy figure after whom, as we have seen, the old kirk at Aberdour is named. It is difficult to disentangle him from another Fillan, whose activities seem to have been largely confined to the eastern end of Fife, who had his 'weem' or cave at Pittenweem. Perhaps they were one and the same person, a composite figure as some historians think

St Columba was! In any event the St Fillan who dwelt in Strathearn, and whose crozier-case and bell are preserved in the Museum of Antiquities in Edinburgh, was an important figure in Celto-Pictish mythology whose spiritual status survived the advent of Queen Margaret and the introduction of the feudal system and whose reliquary was paraded in front of the troops before Bannockburn. Associated with him is a series of interesting buildings stretching from Muthill and Dunning, in Perthshire, to St Andrews and Markinch in Fife. Each of these boasts a tall Romanesque tower romantically associated with the Culdees. There has been much written about those Celtic monks, left-overs one might say of St Fillan's mission, yet functioning within the Roman obedience. They seem to have been permitted a certain amount of autonomy, though, unable to proselytize, they did eventually die out. They were not rebels nor heretics, merely old-fashioned, harmless survivals of another age which a tolerant Scottish hierarchy let fade away in peace.

To label the churches at Muthill and Dunning as Celtic is misleading, since they date, at the earliest, from the twelfth

Saddle-back tower of the Paris Kirk, Dunning, Perthshire

century, when the Culdees were already of little account.
Yet, architecturally they show almost as much out-of-datedness
as their assumed begetters. The towers, which are what really
matter, are entirely Romanesque in style and display a remarkable homogeneity of design and decoration. Muthill and
Dunning have typical round-headed window openings with
columned supports, and both are saddle-backed and crow-
stepped. Muthill kirk survived until 1818, when it was wantonly
demolished and some of the stones used to build a commonplace 'God-box', out of scale and out of keeping with its
surroundings; while St Serf's, at Dunning, is still a church,
though an eighteenth-century one. The towers of both are
intact, however, and were originally detached, like Italian
campanile. Indeed, it is to Italy one seems automatically drawn
when surveying the contemporary towers at Markinch and
St Andrews. The first, like Dunning, is now attached to the
west end of a later building, but crowned with a neo-classical
obelisk that actually suits it. St Rules's, or Regulus' tower at
St Andrews, stands well preserved amidst the gravestones
and toothy remains of what was once Scotland's great and
glorious metropolitan cathedral. It may have been built
with the guidance of stonemasons from Monkwearmouth, in
County Durham, though G. P. H. Watson says the detail has
close parallels with work at Aubazine, near Limoges, in
France. The abbey church there is an Auvergnat structure
of the eleventh century containing the oldest *armoire*, or ward-
robe, in France, and its details may very well have inspired
northern English and Scots craftsmen, but not its turreted
octagonal tower. Sir John Stirling Maxwell, founder member
of the Royal Commission on Ancient Monuments and author
of *Shrines and Homes of Scotland*, includes Dunblane and Abernethy in his list of contemporary 'Culdee' towers. Dunblane
may be right, if one refers to the lower portions of it, for the
rest is in pointed Gothic and topped with a battlemented
parapet and small spire. I wonder about Abernethy? The
base is a lot older than Muthill and Dunning, or Markinch
and St Rule's towers, but the upper part may, in this case, be
of the same, Romanesque period, having been constructed
when it ceased to be a refuge from the Danes and became the
belfry of a new kirk.

At the height of its power in Scotland the pre-Reformation church counted more than 900 parish kirks, more than a hundred monasteries and convents, forty collegiate kirks and fourteen cathedrals, one of the latter, Galloway, being in the Province of York and another, Orkney, in that of Trondheim. Of this huge patrimony, particularly large for such a small country, a mere handful of buildings survive in any state of authentic wholeness, perhaps a couple of dozen parish kirks, though none of these are unrestored; about half the collegiate kirks, these being securely endowed and more adaptable to reformed use; no abbeys or monasteries and only one mainland cathedral, St Mungo's in Glasgow. Kirkwall Cathedral, in Orkney, has also been preserved, but it is a Norwegian church, the old Norse kingdom including Shetland and Orkney, the Counties of Sutherland and Western Isles and Man; and Orkney and Shetland only became part of Scotland at the end of the fifteenth century, when the King of Norway, failing to redeem from pawn the dowry he should have provided when his daughter Margaret married James III, forfeited his right to the islands. Other parts of his Scottish provinces were lost at different times, though it is interesting to note that the Diocese of Sodor, or The Isles, still survives in the title of the present bishop of Sodor and Man. The Benedictine Abbey Kirk at Iona became the Cathedral of the Isles in 1507, and only enjoyed that position for a very brief length of time. It was left to ruin at the Reformation and the existing Cathedral of the Isles is at Millport, on the Isle of Cumbrae, in Buteshire. This was built at the instigation of the sixth Earl of Glasgow in the middle of the nineteenth century. Its architect was the celebrated William Butterfield; but apart from his clever use of local material and site, and the superb panorama over the water from it to the hills of Arran, there is not much here one can call Scottish.

St Mungo's Cathedral in Glasgow, like St Magnus' in Kirkwall, was saved from destruction, though not entirely from periodic attack by iconoclasts, through the energy and foresight of the townspeople, who in Kirkwall took over the building and frustrated Knox's orders thereby. In 1972 St Magnus' was undergoing repair and an appeal went out from the burgh for financial assistance, for it is not under the care of the Department of Environment as is sometimes stated, nor even the property of the established Church of Scotland. It is and always has been since the seventeenth century the proud possession of all the people of Kirkwall. Its bishops continued to function without perceptible interruption right up to the arrival of William of Orange in Britain, and though themselves 'reformed', inhabited the former Earl's Palace. The Cathedral was restored in the nineteenth century by the town council using funds provided by the Sheriff Toms bequest, when the rather unsatisfactory modern Scandinavian spire replaced the original, lower-pitched one. Perhaps in a later restoration a simpler, bolder finish will be put to the tower commensurate with the Norman pillars and arches of the interior?

As for events in Glasgow, orders came from Edinburgh to 'ding doun' the cathedral, but again the townspeople frustrated the Lords of the Congregation and saved the building. It then survived without significant damage until the nineteenth century, when it became the property of what used to be 'Ancient Monuments', who restored it but permitted the demolition of the two western towers. Actually only one of these, the northernmost, resembled a tower and rose above the height of the nave roof. It was built with money saved in Lent from not eating butter, hence its name, the Butter Tower, and was rather similar to the one at Bourges. The other was a secular looking affair of crow-stepped gables, and served in pre-Reformation times as the consistory. It contained what remained of the archiepiscopal documents left behind by Archbishop James Bethune, or Beaton, last in the Roman obedience, who vacated his See shortly before the Reformation settlement taking with him the titles of his office and a number of other valuable objects. He was a nephew of the better known Cardinal David Beaton, who was murdered in his own castle at St Andrews, when John Knox was amongst the interested onlookers. The Archbishop thought he could best preserve his freedom of action by leaving the country until its religious troubles blew over; but they did not, and he lived in France for the rest of his long life, serving Mary Queen of Scots as ambassador and refounding the ancient Collège des Écossais, in Paris. He was offered his diocese back by the first king of Great Britain, but died in exile in 1603.

So the 'Butter Tower' and consistory were 'dinged doun' by the Victorians, with the approval of the appropriate Government body and the Church of Scotland, in order to achieve symmetry on the western façade of Glasgow Cathedral; when defunct Papal Bulls were seen burning in the street and citizens only just had time to rescue a few of them from the flames before they perished for ever. The windows of the nave were filled with bad German painted glass, which has fortunately now gone, and one was shown round the building by a uniformed, capped official, as in some ancient castle or palace. Apart from the choir, which was still used as a place of public worship, St Mungo's became another 'Ancient Monument', and is still listed as such by the Department. One good thing that was done at the time was the clearing out of the earth and rubble from the crypt, where the Shrine of St Kentigern, or Mungo was, revealing to a modern generation its marvels, for it is amongst the grandest things of its kind not only in Scotland but possibly in Christendom. Today, the site of the saint's tomb is again honoured and revered, and the early pointed vaulting that supports the floor of the choir above glistens with purity and splendour about it.

The chapter house is on the same lower level as the crypt, and is square, not octagonal, as was the usual custom in the north. Above it was the sacristy and this structure closely resembles what the old consistory was like, with its castellated roofline, domestic crow-steps and end-on relationship to the rest of the cathedral. Unless one walks round to view this end of the building, braving the sight of John Knox atop his column in the neighbouring necropolis, it is almost impossible to appreciate the original effect of the siting of St Mungos' for it was not a building standing in isolation as it now appears but part of a group that included the Bishop's Castle and the thirty or more manses of the canons and prebends. The castle survived the Reformation and was still there when Robert Adam was commissioned to design a hospital on the site, when it was demolished; while the numerous clergy houses have since been reduced to one near the cathedral, and one in the country, both belonging to the same ecclesiastical barony which was purchased by one of the last prebend's relatives and named Provand's Lordship.

This interesting house is now a museum, filled with seven-
teenth- and eighteenth-century Scotch furniture and folk
objects, and was one of the special interests of the late Dr T. J.
Honeyman. It came into history rather prominently when
Mary Queen of Scots, failing to find accommodation in the
Archiepiscopal Palace, went there for shelter instead. She was
visiting Darnley, 'this pocky fellow ... I thought I should
have been killed with his breath', shortly before Bothwell and
the Earl of Morton killed him, one by mistake the other on
purpose, in two separate plots that merged in a single explosion
at Kirk o'Fields, in 1567. Provand's Lordship thus has a link
with the notorious 'Casket Letters' one of which is said to have
been written by Queen Mary whilst in Glasgow. It would be
a pity to spoil the story by suggesting that most of the letters,
including the one referred to, were probably forgeries, or at
best edited by Morton and his friends, but this is so. Yet the
old house beside the cathedral is what really matters. It is the
oldest in Glasgow, and not only this, Provan Hall, its country
counterpart, is also hale and hearty, and even older, having
been built in the fifteenth century; which makes it the most

Episcopal Manor House, Provan Hall, near Glasgow—*circa* 1450

ancient domestic structure still roofed in Scotland. It stands in ten acres of land, all that is left of a property of some 2000 acres, and is safe in the care of the National Trust for Scotland. The man who bought it, and Provand's Lordship, was William Baillie, who although not a cleric was styled Canon of Glasgow and Prebendary of Barlanark. He was an eminent lawyer and rose to become Lord President of the Court of Session, the Scottish supreme court, when he took the title of Lord Provand.

The old consistory tower and the former sacristy and chapter house are firmly in the Scottish building tradition, but the cathedral in general is an early pointed structure and not conspicuously different from other large medieval churches of the thirteenth and fourteenth centuries, though of course it has some features that set it apart and give it a local cachet. The choir, which is the most beautiful part and the best built, belongs to the thirteenth century, but the nave, not so expertly constructed, was added a century later. The tower, which was not finished until the fifteenth century, is quite Scottish, with its galleried parapet and slightly stunted stone spire with two encircling crowns dividing it; and the way in which the transepts do not extend beyond the line of the nave and choir aisles is a recognizable Scotticism. Robert Blackadder, who was the first Archbishop of Glasgow, had plans to extend the southern transept, and actually built the lower portion of his proposed extension. This is now known as the Blackadder Aisle, but it does not rise above ground floor level, that is, stops at the same level as the crypt which is built on falling ground at the east end of the cathedral. It is probable that there was a building here before Blackadder's day, and that this was the site of the tomb of the hermit Fergus, whom St Mungo found dying in his cell in the woods of Partick and placed on a cart attached to two wild bulls, letting the animals stop where they would. Allusion is made to this legend in the aisle, where a rough version of the cart bearing the body survives, with the inscription 'THIS.IS.YE.ILE.OF.CAR.FERGUS'. Robert Blackadder became Archbishop in 1483, when the Scottish Church, plagued for centuries by arguments with successive Archbishops of York, who claimed jurisdiction over it, decided to appoint two archbishops of its own and make one primate. Hitherto there had been only bishops, one of whom was Primus, that is, *primus inter pares*, or head amongst equals, as in the old Celtic Church. This is the system that pertains in the existing Scottish Episcopal Church, which has no arch-bishop, having gone back to the ancient system when dis-established for its loyalty to the Stuarts* at the end of the seventeenth century.

There is one particular feature about Glasgow Cathedral that sets it apart from its contemporaries in the arrangement at the east end, where, in order to facilitate the passage of pilgrims to the shrine of St Mungo, the ambulatory, or walk-round, is carried on beyond the high altar, as in France, but with a rectangular finish instead of the more usual chevet of radiating chapels. Thus large crowds could make the entire circuit of the cathedral without hindrance. There is also intact a stone screen, or pulpitum, shutting off the presbytery, or choir, from the rest of the building. Only one such other feature remains in Scotland, at Lincluden College, near Dumfries, a Douglas foundation which now lies in ruins beside the waters of the River Nith. St Mungo's has its quota of memorials, some of which are worthy of note. The most grandiose, and recently restored, is that of Archbishop Law, who died in 1632, and whose successor, Patrick Lindsay, had to bear the full brunt of the Covenanting revolt of 1637. The See then remained vacant until the Restoration, when Robert Leighton, the saintly man who tried unsuccessfully to unite Presbyterian and Episcopalian, was translated from Dunblane to Glasgow.

The Primacy of the Scottish Church corresponded to that of England, if one substitutes Glasgow for York and St Andrews for Canterbury. Unfortunately the Cathedral of St Andrews is amongst those almost totally destroyed and used as a common graveyard; the same fate befell Elgin, second in size to St Andrews and the finest church, architecturally speaking, in the land. It survived for a short while after the Reformation until the lead was removed from the roof to make bullets, and the later collapse of the central tower, destroying much of the rest of the building. Dunblane, on the other hand, Leighton's Dunblane, has been restored, the nave in the nineteenth and

---

* The family is known as Stewarts before 1603, Stuarts afterwards.

the choir in this century. It is largely in thirteenth-century 'pointed' style, very English and pure, and was much admired by Ruskin. The tower, as has been noted, is old at its base and younger higher up, and is, perhaps, the most Scottish part of the cathedral. Six original choir stalls survive from the pre-Reformation era and these, rather oddly, have been placed at the west end of the church as a sort of memorial or souvenir, and not used, the late Sir Robert Lorimer having designed entirely new, and somewhat elaborate late-Gothic furniture for the restored choir. The precincts of Dunblane Cathedral have survived rather better than those of Glasgow, though some of the seventeenth-century and older houses have only just escaped demolition through the efforts of local well-wishers and the Scottish Churches, who have recently established ecumenical headquarters here, in the little city of Robert Leighton.

When he died in 1684, the saintly bishop, then Archbishop of Glasgow, but living in the south, bequeathed his library to the clergy and town of Dunblane, when it became the first public library in Scotland. It is still there, and still available to those who pay the appropriate fee and annual subscription, for it was not the first 'free library'; that is a few miles away at Innerpeffray, near a bend of the River Earn formerly chosen by the Romans as a strong point. It is worth making the journey there, for attached to it is one of the few small medieval parish kirks in Scotland which has not been restored and is yet in use, not perhaps as a parish kirk, but certainly as the chapel and burial place of the Drummond family, who built it in the sixteenth century. Its windows retain the iron bars that were common to all such buildings once, and which were there not only to prevent body-snatching, but in earlier times the desecration of relics and other sacred objects. There were no seats in these kirks, and the people simply stood to hear the Mass on a rough straw-strewn floor. There is also a leper's window, or squint, through which the infected could witness the Elevation of the Host without contaminating the rest of the congregation. The site is charming, and the library, founded by David Drummond, Third Lord Madderty, Montrose's brother-in-law, includes amongst its treasures the Scottish paladin's pocket bible, in French. In Georgian times Robert

Hay Drummond, Archbishop of Canterbury, replaced the original building of 1691 with the present handsome pavilion; and nearby is roofless Madderty Castle, which can be visited freely.

Of the remaining Scottish Cathedrals only four others are still in use, and all have had to be restored, or rebuilt in part. The tiny former Cathedral of Argyll, on the Island of Lismore, is today represented by a latter-day kirk built on medieval foundations, while Brechin Cathedral has been almost totally rebuilt. It is famous more for its free-standing Round Tower than for itself, though there are older portions incorporated in the existing structure. It is unfortunate that the cathedral, which stood more or less intact until 1818, should have been so badly treated and so drastically rebuilt that more recent attempts to rectify the situation have only succeeded in mollifying some mistakes without restoring the original conception. One thing has survived, however, and that is the delightful *palatium nostrum* of pre-Reformation bishops, which is on Lord Southesk's estate at Kinnaird, and has just been restored with the help of a Ministry grant. Farnell Castle, as this country palace is called, is that rare thing in Scotland, a fortified manor; Provan Hall is a manor, but not in the least fortified, whereas Farnell still bears some of the crenellations of its first beginning, probably in the thirteenth century. It was damaged in the Wars of Independence and rebuilt, and its crow-steps on the east gable are suitably provided with individual gablets in true ecclesiastical style. Prior to the restoration of the last few years Lord Southesk removed many of the additions of Victorian and Georgian times, chimney-pieces and cupboards and so on, which were put in when tenants were housed here, laying bare the rude masonry where-ever possible. Interesting things were revealed, some of them now covered up again in internal plaster and external harling, or rough-cast, but not the supporting corbels of an erstwhile wooden balcony and outside stair, nor the crowned Virgin Mary device which appears on one of the skew-putts, or projecting end stones at the foot of the gable coping.

Dornoch Cathedral, much further north, and once the seat of the bishops of Caithness, who removed themselves here from Halkirk in the thirteenth century, has been treated even more drastically than Brechin, and like it is used as the local parish kirk. With the adjacent tower of the bishop's palace, however, now an hotel, the grouping is interesting, if not quite as it was originally intended by Gilbert of Moravia, Norman founder and forebear of the Murray family. The bishop, and later saint, was himself the architect for the cathedral, as indeed he was of Kildrummy Castle, in Aberdeenshire, 'the noblest of northern castles', to quote the Ancient Monuments Guide Book. Kildrummy has a fine chapel with delicate lancet windows much in the same style as those of Dornoch when new, and the castle, which became the seat of the Earls of Mar, was only dismantled after the Jacobite rebellion of 1715.

The last and most successfully adapted of the pre-Reformation Cathedrals is St Machar's, in the Altoun of Aberdeen. Only the nave is intact, the choir and transepts having been thrown down in Cromwellian times, when the foresquare bishop's palace alongside was also demolished, in order to provide building materials for one of the Lord Protector's Scottish forts. The cathedral survived the first wave of the Reformation and its bishops continued for a time to reside in their palace, Aberdeen being a stronghold of native episcopacy, which, in fact, it still is. Its Doctors, the University Professors, refused to sign the Covenant, declaring it illegal and contrary to Christian teaching, and for this the city was subjected to sack by Montrose, in the days before he changed sides and offered his sword to the King. At that time a local Presbyterian minister took the lead in destroying the fittings in the choir, himself hacking down anything he could reach or which yielded easily to his axe. Fortunately he was halted before everything had gone, and the residue, in the form of an unique collection of pre-Reformation stalls and a Jacobean pulpit and bishop's throne were re-assembled in the chapel of King's College, which is part of Aberdeen University. These fittings, taken with the chapel's own fifteenth-century woodwork, constitute the only sizable display of such objects in Scotland.

St Machar's, its nave and twin towers, looks very Scottish, not just because they are built of granite but because of their embattled, northern style. There is a fine crow-stepped porch, reminiscent of the softer, sandstone one at Linlithgow, which is equally domestic in appearance. The towers are buttressed and topped with octagonal stone spires rather like Glasgow but much shorter, and these rise in the manner of broach spires directly from the masonry of a secondary tower, itself having an Irish look with its stepped-up corner pieces. The lower parapet has heavy machicolations of decidedly military appearance, and the total effect is very impressive. Inside, as at Glasgow, the original timber roof remains, only in this case it is flat, not curved, and decorated with the armorial devices of the Pope, the Kings and Queens of Christendom, Queen Margaret and other Scottish saints and heroes, bishops and nobles. It is a remarkable sight and an even more remarkable survival from 1540, when it was completed on the orders of Bishop Gavin Dunbar by 'James Winter, an Angus man'. Curiously enough, the present cathedral is not on the same site as the first, Norman foundation, which stood someway to the west of St Machar's, at Tillydrone, overlooking the River Don. In a letter written shortly before his death, the late Douglas Simpson told me that his house, the old 'Wallace Tower', which he saved from oblivion by having it brought stone by stone from central Aberdeen to its new position, was within a few yards of where the original cathedral and bishop's palace, Tillydrone 'motte', once were. Both were involved in the burning of the city by Edward III in 1333, when the English took their revenge all over Scotland for the defeat of Bannockburn.

Another victim of southern vengeance at the time was the auld Brig o'Balgownie, which Dr Simpson describes in *The Ancient Stones of Scotland* as the oldest medieval bridge still surviving, and refers to a tablet on it recording a repair of 1605 which mentions that 'annals testify' to its erection by King Robert Bruce. The present bridge was rebuilt in the fifteenth century by Bishop Cheyne, and is contemporaneous with, and indeed very similar in construction and appearance with the beautiful bridge over the Till near Twizel, in the Borders. It was across this latter bridge that an apparently over-chivalrous King James IV allowed the English to pass before Flodden, thus endangering his own chances. The difference is that whereas Twizel bridge spans 90 feet in a single gracious arch, the Brig o'Balgownie only manages 65; but that is pretty good just the same. It is, perhaps, more famous on account of

(*above*) Rosslyn Chapel,
Midlothian, showing
buttresses and stone
barrel-vaulted roof, and
(*below*) detail of south door

its traditional association with Robert the Bruce than for its architecture, and also possibly for its being featured by Byron in *Don Juan*. The Hero of Missolunghi's mother was, of course, a Gordon of Gight, and he spent much of his boyhood in and around Aberdeen, when, in a singular dare-devil act he challenged the curse on the bridge which said that if ever the only son of man or animal crossed it, it would collapse!

The Brig o'Balgownie is an episcopal bridge, the Barony of the Altoun of Aberdeen being ecclesiastical not secular; and it is one of several others built at the behest of the fifteenth- and sixteenth-century Scottish bishops. The so-called Guard-bridge, really Gare, over the Eden, near St Andrews, is another, having been erected for Bishop Wardlaw, the founder of St Andrews University, in 1420—that is, almost at the same time as the bridge over the Don. The Guardbridge was repaired by Archbishop James Bethune, later of Glasgow, about 1530, which is the approximate date of the building of another Aberdeen bridge, the Brig o'Dee, to the south of the city. This was another of Bishop Dunbar's enterprises, he having called in Thomas Franche, a Scots mason of French descent whose father had worked for James III at Linlithgow and Stirling, to complete St Machar's and build a seven-arched bridge over the Dee. Franche also designed the tower of King's College Chapel, with its splendid crown-spire, made by leaning four flying buttresses inwards against each other, the centre being topped with a smaller stone crown. This resembles the better known spire of St Giles' High Kirk in Edinburgh, which, how-ever, has an Imperial crown, with smaller flying buttresses meeting between the larger ones, and finishing in an elaborate pinnacle and large gilded cock.

It is at this time, during the second half of the fifteenth and first part of the sixteenth centuries that we find the names of individual masons coming to the fore. Some of them were of Continental provenance, such as the Franches, and a number of Flemings. The latter helped to build fabulous Rosslyn Chapel, in Midlothian, which was intended by its founder, William St Clair, Prince of Orkney, to be a complete collegiate kirk, like St Giles', with provost, canons and singing boys; and to re-semble Glasgow Cathedral on plan. Only the choir was finished, and this is a marvel of rich and strange carving a discussion of which will come later. Flemings were, in fact, fairly numerous in Scotland then. When the English were driven out they had helped to man the towns and repopulate them, the Celtic people not being founders of permanent settlements and not building towns or even villages. Thus, when the Anglo-Normans governed the country they had to start from scratch in this respect, and many English and Flemish families came to live in Scotland in the Middle Ages. The names Inglis and Fleming are still quite common and bear witness to these historic associations and migrations.

Besides the Franches there were the Mylnes, most celebrated of all Scottish masonic families. When John Mylne, Principal Master Gunner and Captain of the Pioneers to Charles I and Charles II died in 1667, his nephew, Robert Mylne, who succeeded him as Royal Master Mason, carved on his tombstone a fulsome inscription part of which reads, 'Sixth Master Mason to a Royal House of seven successive Kings'. The first of these was Alexander Mylne, who was Bishop of Dunkeld and Abbot of Cambuskenneth, and later first Lord President of the Court of Session, which was formally set-up by James V in 1532. He died in 1548 after having been responsible in his masonic capacity for building the first stone bridge over the Tay at Dunkeld, replaced by Thomas Telford in 1809, and designing the tower of the Royal Abbey of Cambuskenneth, near Stirling, the burial place of James III and his Norwegian Queen—the non-arrival of whose dowry brought about the annexation of Orkney and Shetland by the Scottish Crown in 1469. Alexander Mylne's tower is the only part of the abbey still standing and roofed. Others of his family built the Palace of Holyroodhouse, as well as many bridges, including old Blackfriars Bridge, which was the work of Robert Mylne of London, in Georgian times. Then there were the Jacksons. Robert Jackson was engaged by James III on the Great Hall at Stirling Castle, while his grandson worked at Linlithgow, on the Palace and Collegiate Kirk of St Michael; and for James IV he designed the so-called 'Kirk o'Steil' in Berwickshire.

II

Religious Buildings:
Abbeys and Later Churches

As ALREADY noted not one of the more than a hundred monastic establishments existing in pre-Reformation Scotland has survived as originally conceived, though one, the thirteenth-century Priory at Pluscarden, near Elgin, in Moray, is in part being used by a group of latter day Benedictines. Their order superseded the earlier Valliscaulium foundation in 1460, but they died out after 1560. The Reformation in Scotland, thought rather erroneously to have been particularly violent and destructive, was only so in respect of property, there were few martyrs until the seventeenth century, when the Covenanters made a business of it. Patrick Hamilton, for instance, was burned at the stake in the reign of James V—a papist murder, while Cardinal Beaton, Archbishop of St Andrews, was killed in his own castle in the same reign—a Protestant murder. It was done in reply to the burning a few months earlier of George Wishart, who was not only dispatched for his religious beliefs but for treason, having become the dupe, willing or otherwise, of Henry VIII. There was no suppression of the monasteries after the English fashion in Scotland, no Pilgrimage of Grace, no ensuing 'Bloody Mary', but instead a remarkable show of tolerance of persons, matched with an extraordinary display of iconoclasm and vandalism of ecclesiastical buildings.

The ancient bishoprics were not made defunct but secularized, so that the bishops still sat in the Scottish Parliament, with their abbots, as Lords Spiritual; and as they died out were replaced by purely temporal figures, usually their own relatives who were now in full possession of former church properties. Under James VI and I a more legitimate form of episcopacy was re-established, and the Apostolic Succession restored; and this, except for a brief period during the Cromwellian era, subsisted until 1690, when the Protestant bishops were deprived of their livings and their churches were confiscated because of their devotion to the Jacobite cause. The abbots did not, of course, enjoy a new lease of life as the bishops had done, as there was no place in a Protestant country for monasteries, though for a time Commendators were appointed to take their place in the Jacobean Parliament. That is why amidst the ruins of our abbeys one often finds well-preserved domestic quarters, these having been adapted by the secular Commendators for their own purposes.

At Pluscarden the dwelling quarters were partly restored in the nineteenth century, and but for the death of the third Marquis of Bute, and then of his son Lord Ninian Crichton-Stewart, who was killed in action in the first World War, a great deal more would have been done. The Marquis had earlier employed the scholarly Scottish architect John Kinross to restore the old kirk of the Greyfriars, in Elgin, and there can be little doubt that had the same expert and lover of Scottish historic buildings been given the chance to continue the work at Pluscarden we might well have seen the complete resuscitation of an original Scottish monastic foundation. As things are the monks have temporarily roofed part of the abbey kirk, of which only the choir and transepts were ever built; they live in Lord Bute's incomplete wing and farm the lands, winning many prizes at local agricultural shows. Elsewhere, at Iona, the Community started by Lord MacLeod in the slums of Glasgow and now world wide in its associations, uses the restored buildings; but they are not monks and neither church nor its ancillaries could be termed monastic at any stretch of the imagination.

The monks, incidentally, did not eat in utter silence, for they were read to by one of their number, from a special reading pulpit in the Frater. Part of what must surely have been one of these has recently been discovered in the former Prior's Lodging at Pittenweem, where, between the dining room wall and a nineteenth-century addition the base of a Gothic pedestal of quite large proportions may be seen. At first it was thought to be one jamb, or side, of an old chimney-piece, but it has no twin and would, in any case, have belonged to a much bigger fireplace than this modest building would have supported. The fifteenth-century Prior's Lodging, despite later additions, and taken together with the adjacent Great House, now a home for retired clergy, constitutes the oldest and best-preserved parsonage in Scotland. Nothing of the church remains, its place having been taken by a Jacobean Tolbooth and eighteenth-century parish kirk, but at the Reformation the domestic quarters were already in the hands of a secular Commendator, a bastard of King James V; and they have continued in some sort of use ever since. After becoming the property of the burgh, who pulled down one bit and rebuilt it as the Town Hall, the remainder was bought by the Jacobite Bishop Low, who restored the Great House and the Prior's Lodging and attempted to re-introduce monastic life by founding a seminary in the Great House. He enlarged the Prior's Lodging putting crow-steps on the gable ends and pushing out dormer windows from the roof, but the lower floor, which is vaulted and certainly medieval, remains unaltered, with its hidden stair down from the dining room. This was the Prior's private way to his wine cellar, nothing more, and is not 'secret' except in the sense that it opens from inside a cupboard.

Sixteenth-century Great House of Pittenweem Priory, Fife

The Great House has two uniquely-preserved oriel windows of late Gothic inspiration reminiscent of the ruined one over the entrance to the ruined castle of Cardinal Beaton in St Andrews. They may well be contemporary, and since Pittenweem Priory, like the original Priory at St Andrews, was an Augustinian House, may have been erected by the same masons. The Commendator's House at 'fair Melrose' is the only roofed and used part of that famous abbey; and this home of former abbots now houses an interesting museum. At Paisley too, part of the monastic dwelling has survived, beside the heavily restored abbey. This was founded by the, as yet, non-royal ancestors of H.M. The Queen, in the twelfth century, and after being laid in ruins more than once and never properly restored, both Sir Rowand Anderson and Sir Robert Lorimer were employed bringing it back to life. The tower is quite new and the building has had to be re-roofed and refurnished. Inside is what purports to be a portion of the tomb of Marjery Bruce, daughter of Robert I and spouse of Walter the High Steward, whose son became the first Royal Stewart and ruled as Robert II on the death of David II, Bruce's childless heir, in 1371. Paisley Abbey is the only Presbyterian place of worship where the singing is led by a surpliced choir of boys. It is also the only one I know of where there is anything approaching a Sanctuary Light, in the Chapel of the eighth-century St Mirin, who is supposed to have had a cell hereabouts. Dr James Richardson, first H.M. Inspector of Ancient Monuments in Scotland, had considerable misgivings about this light, which became the subject of one of his numerous and inimitable stories.

The choir and tower of Culross Abbey, in western Fife, have survived and the choir is used as the parish kirk. This was a Cistercian foundation dating from the twelfth century, but only one wall belongs to that period and most of what remains had already been reconstructed in the reign of James IV. It was not a very thriving or important community in the sixteenth century and its demise, with that of the nine monks who lived there, occurred without incident. The tower still bears the Arms of Abbot Masoun who functioned between 1498 and 1513, the year of Flodden; while in the interior is the elaborate alabaster tomb of Sir George Bruce of Carnock and his family, a Jacobean tribute not unlike similar monuments in England. Sir George was knighted by King James VI and I on a visit to the town which the worthy burgher had made prosperous by his invention of machinery for draining the coal workings under the Forth. A century later the seams had run out and the sea back in, and Culross sank to become what it now is, the most perfect example extant of an auld Scotch burgh of the Jacobean era; a backwater, but a marvellous one, full of fine old turreted and crow-stepped houses, cobbled alleyways, called causeways, and replete with Sir George Bruce's own Flemish style 'palas' and neighbouring Town House with ogee-roofed Dutch tower. The National Trust for Scotland is mainly responsible for this happy state of affairs, and indeed, Culross represents their first large-scale exercise in the restoration and renovation of historic Scottish buildings.

Far away in the south, almost as far south as one can go in Scotland, in the delightful Royal Burgh of Kirkcudbright, is the much less well-known remnant of the kirk of the Greyfriars, which now serves the local Episcopalian congregation and contains the Early-Renaissance altar-tomb of Sir Thomas McClellan of Bombie, Provost of Kirkcudbright. In 1572 he built a large castellated mansion nearby out of stones taken from the old Franciscan convent; which rather unsatisfactory but typical ending might provide a suitable epitaph for Scottish religious houses as a whole, except, perhaps for the royal ones, two of which I must deal with briefly before passing on to collegiate and votive kirks and other more substantial things.

Dunfermline Abbey was the creation of Malcolm Canmore and his Saxon wife Queen Margaret, though their original foundation, the nine hundredth anniversary of which in 1972 was commemorated by a Royal Visit, is no longer visible, and the superb Norman nave, the work of stonemasons from Durham, no longer serves as a church; it is under the care of the Department of the Environment. At the Reformation the mob broke in and destroyed the marble tomb made in Paris for Robert I, but the much-venerated shrine of Saint Margaret escaped desecration since Mary of Guise, the mother of Mary Queen of Scots, sensing what might happen once the Knoxian flood-gates were opened, had her remains removed to France.

The church suffered greatly in this attack, but the monastic buildings fared better, belonging to the Crown and largely already converted into a Royal Palace; while the Abbot's House was the home of a secular commendator with the title of Lord Dunfermline. It still survives, and has recently been restored as a community centre by the Dunfermline Carnegie Trust. It is a characteristic sixteenth-century Scottish building with turrets and spiral stairs, high pitched roof and crow-steps, not at all religious looking. As for the palace, in which Charles I and his sister, Elizabeth of Bohemia, the 'Winter Queen' were born, it is a dramatic ruin in the manner of Heidelberg, its buttressed, but unroofed masonry falling cliff-like down the sides of a romantic glen.

Anne of Denmark, consort of James VI and I held Dunfermline as part of her dowry, and engaged William Schaw, her Chamberlain and Master of Works, to restore and improve both the domestic and ecclesiastical buildings, including the north-western tower of the abbey kirk which today remains as he finished it. At that time the shell of the abbey kirk had survived, and it was only in the reign of Charles II that the

The buttresses supporting the Norman nave of the Abbey Kirk, Dunfermline

D

famous central tower, very like that at Durham, fell and finally made services impossible in the church below. Apart from William Schaw's Jacobean tower, which is battlemented and topped with a stone spirelet, the enormous buttresses supporting the Norman nave are worth a mention, as they are built in a purely native manner, that is, instead of rising by a series of light arches, they rise in steps, with a single supporting arch springing directly from the ground, and massive upper portions. The present church, built on the site of the former choir, was the work of William Burn, who in the Victorian era similarly destroyed the original conception of St Giles' Kirk in Edinburgh, except for its tower; and here even the tower has been replaced with one in which the words 'KING.ROBERT.THE. BRUCE.' are carved in banal fashion around the top parapet!

The Royal Stewarts were particularly partial to living in or near 'religious houses, and apart from Edinburgh and Stirling Castles, in which they built themselves quarters in the fourteenth and fifteenth centuries they usually enlarged or adapted existing ecclesiastical property rather than built new royal palaces as such. Thus Holyroodhouse, the present official home of the Queen in Scotland, is an extension of the medieval abbey whose ruined nave still stands. The full story of the building of this beautiful Royal Residence, the most homogeneous in Britain, must come at a later stage in my narrative, but there is one aspect of it which belongs here. I refer to the fate of Holyrood Abbey and its transition from pre-Reformation monastery to seventeenth-century royal residence. The kirk, whose nave had survived the first blast of Calvinism, was restored by Charles I for his Scottish coronation which took place in it in 1633. Inigo Jones is said to have assisted in the work when the West Front was tidied up and a new traceried east window inserted where the junction of transepts and choir had been, but this is unproven.

The smaller restored abbey kirk remained hale until James VII and II turned out the resident congregation and made it the Chapel of the Most Ancient and Noble Order of the Thistle, which he reconstituted and gave the rules it still observes. When King James fled the country the mob came and destroyed the knights' stalls and all the contents of the building, going so far as to break open the tombs of their kings and queens and scatter their bones on the ground; but the walls stood firm and the roof remained intact for a while until it too was toppled, and the kirk has not been used for anything since. Like so much else in Scotland it is an 'Ancient Monument' around which tourists walk with their hats on, talking and behaving as if they were anywhere but in a church, the veritable Westminster of Scotland. More extraordinary even than this, and the main reason for my mentioning Holyrood Abbey here instead of saving it up for my chapter on palaces, is the story of the Commendator's House, which was actually built right in front of the restored Carolean kirk, where it remained, an obstruction both to view and passage, until removed in the eighteenth century. All old prints show this structure, a completely domestic building with gable-ended chimney stacks, tall roof and dormer windows, spoiling Sir William Bruce's new Palladian palace which he designed for Charles II, and in which James, Duke of York resided as Lord High Commissioner to the General Assembly of the Church of Scotland.

In 1906, when the tenth Earl of Melville and eleventh of Leven died, the sum of £40,000 was left to be spent, at King Edward's discretion, on the restoration of the old abbey kirk, which was once more to become the Chapel of the Order of the Thistle. It was a noble gesture from a man who was himself a Knight of that Order and had more than once been Lord High Commissioner. Under his Will the then Lord Crawford and Sir John Stirling Maxwell were appointed to survey the possibilities of carrying out the scheme. The advice they were given was that unless something in the nature of a complete reconstruction was carried out, to make the walls safe and prevent the roof collapsing as it had done some two centuries earlier, the project would fail; and that if a reconstruction was attempted it might remove the abbey's authenticity as a medieval building. Despite a division of opinion on this latter point, however, the scheme was abandoned after failing to get the approval of the First Commissioner of Works, which was necessary, and thus, to quote Sir John, 'the broken arches of the old abbey remain undisturbed, while a new building of exceptional beauty has come into existence'. The last is a reference to the existing Thistle Chapel which Sir Robert

Lorimer designed as an addition to the High Kirk of St Giles, after a family re-adjustment of the original bequest.

We now come to consideration of the remainder of Scotland's forty former collegiate kirks, of which St Giles' was the largest and most famous. Having no bishop, it was not, therefore, a cathedral, and indeed did not become one before the Reformation. Nevertheless it is of Scottish cathedral proportions, and supported everyone but a bishop—that is, a provost, canons and choir. Its size and curiously square shape resulted from the numerous private and guild benefactions that came to it in the fourteenth and fifteenth centuries, when chantry chapels and other additions were made around the inner, cruciform plan. It did become a cathedral temporarily in the seventeenth century, when King Charles I carved a new diocese of Edenburgen out of the unwieldly archiepiscopal See of St Andrews, and it remained a cathedral, except for the interregnum of the Commonwealth, until 1690, when the Scottish Lords Spiritual were thrust out of Parliament House and rabbled by the triumphant Covenanters, an episode invoked

St Giles' Collegiate Kirk, Edinburgh: plan

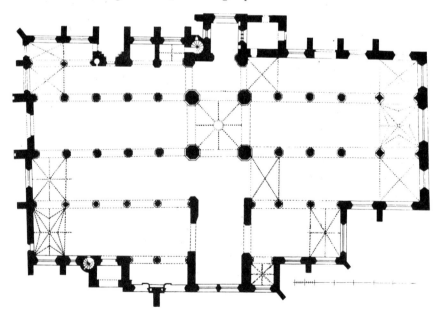

by Robert Louis Stevenson in his *Picturesque Notes on Edinburgh*. It was the scene in 1637 of a somewhat apocryphal riot, apocryphal at least in its most important particular, namely the part played, or not played by a certain Jenny Geddes. The legend first saw the light of day some fifty years after the event, and the only Jenny Geddes known to history was a royalist stall holder of one of the so-called luckenbooths attached to the outer walls of St Giles', who burnt her booth with joy on hearing of the Restoration of Charles II. Unfortunately fame in Scotland very often depends on mythology, rarely on unwelcome facts, far less on beauty or cultural rarity. Yet Edinburgh's historic High Kirk, not withstanding its nasty outer coating of Victorian masonry, deserves attention as a piece of architecture; and it undoubtedly has a significant place in the history of Scotland's historic buildings. Its crown spire we have described, other details I will turn to in the chapter on Edinburgh.

Apart from the very fine medieval example on the tower of St Nicholas' Cathedral in Newcastle-upon-Tyne, which Charles I sent John Mylne to study before he restored those of St Giles' in Edinburgh and King's College Chapel in Aberdeen, crown-spires seem to have been a Scottish peculiarity, probably deriving from French or Flemish sources. They date from the end of the fifteenth century when flamboyant-Gothic was the vogue and which Scottish masons preferred to English 'perpendicular'. Other churches once boasting crowns but now lacking them are the present parish kirk in Haddington, Scott's 'Lamp of the Lothians', and the Collegiate Kirk of St Michael in Linlithgow; while Dundee parish church has a sturdy tower which was specially built so to receive a crown which it never actually acquired. St Mary's church in Haddington is only a church in so far as the nave is concerned, though restoration of the choir has been underway for sometime. It has been one of Scotland's finest fifteenth-century kirks; and its reddish sandstone silhouette rising near an old bridge over the Tyne gives it a romantically attractive appearance. More complete and wholly in service as a place of worship is St Michael's Linlithgow. Its crown steeple was only removed in the nineteenth century, when it became unsafe; and old prints show it looking most impressive beside the decayed but massive royal palace alongside, both reflected in Linlithgow loch. A new motorway to the north of that loch will open an entirely new view of kirk and ruined palace which will, at a distance, invest the group with an evocative charm not experienced before.

St Michael's now has a light-weight and not, in my opinion, very satisfactory crown tacked onto the top of its tower. It is not much like what was there earlier, and the tower itself has been finished with battlements and corner turrets it did not have until the old crown was removed, when it needed finishing in some other way. Perhaps we shall get used to this gilded bow of spikes that presently replaces the old crown, though it might have been better to try and recreate the original design. Closer to the church one is not distracted by the new crowning feature. It stands at the very entrance to the former palace, rendered roofless after a fire in the mid-eighteenth century, and is an integral part of the architecture of that palace, which is largely fifteenth-century except for improvements undertaken by James IV and James V in the sixteenth when they married foreign princesses of standing, Margaret Tudor

St Michael's Kirk, Linlithgow: plan

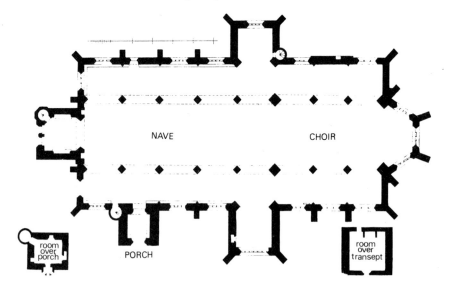

Fifteenth-century
'Beauvais' apse to the
Kirk of the Holy Rude,
Stirling

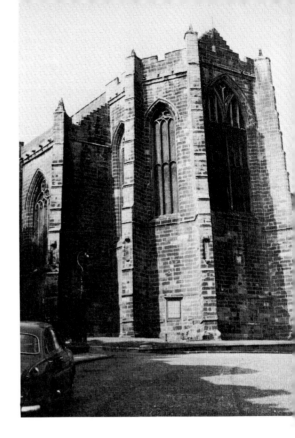

and Mary of Guise respectively. A handsome port, or gate, leads from the west end of the church into the palace precincts. It resembles very closely the West Port at St Andrews, but is earlier, as witness the Coat of Arms and other devices dating from the reign of James V. A statue of St Michael himself, a rare pre-Reformation survival, stands guard in his niche near the porch, reminding one of another effigy of the same protecting archangel that tops an old well in the High Street, above the inscription; 'St Michael is kind to strangers'. Instead of the usual transepts the church has two chapels attached where transepts would be, and curiously these, with the porch, have separate crow-stepped gables at both ends, instead of neatly joining the main roof. The little polygonal apse too, seems rather stuck on, like an after thought or as Sir John Stirling Maxwell suggests, a 'bow-window', and this feeling is again apparent, only on a much smaller scale, in the unusual oriel window over the porch entrance. Burn's strictures about a 'poor, pimping place poked in the corner of Popish grandeur', seem to have been taken to heart by a modern generation of Presbyterians, for the whole effect inside now is open and clean and meaningful. The roof is a fake, being a plaster reproduction, but not wholly objectionable, and an interesting side feature is the stone seat running round most of the nave and parts of the chapels.

The Church of the Holy Rude at Stirling has links with St Michael's Linlithgow, historical as well as architectural, and its dates are fairly similar. It is larger but by no means so attractive, being built in a series of bursts of activity, so that looking at it longways it resembles a series of buildings, almost unconnected in the way the roof lines differ; and the tower seems too far away from the east end, and so unlike it in style one is reminded of the relationship between the head and tail of some prehistoric monster. This may detract from the appearance of the building but it does not affect its individual parts which are particularly interesting. The tower is double in so far as it rises to half-way, gains a parapet, then doubles its length and does the same thing again, adding a turret for good measure. The nave, which is the oldest part, and dates from the beginning of the fifteenth century, has retained its open timber roof, which was discovered intact when later plaster-work was removed. For three hundred years until 1936 this was divided from the choir by a wall, also now happily removed. The traceried windows are 'decorated', and this period is continued in the later, lofty choir, with its splendid polygonal apse in the manner of Beauvais. This is supposed to have been added by Cardinal Beaton, which would make it very late indeed, while the handsome choir itself dates from 1510. The church was intimately associated with the Royal Stewarts and their comings and goings at the Castle, where James VI built a Chapel Royal, recently restored by the Department of the Environment. Mary Queen of Scots was crowned in the Kirk of the Holy Rude at the age of nine months, and her son at the age of one year, when the preacher was John Knox.

Stirling parish kirk is not, strictly speaking, collegiate; the Chapel Royal, in the castle is, though not used as a place of worship, having been adapted first as stables and then as a regimental dance hall. St Michael's Linlithgow is, as were St Giles' in Edinburgh and the Chapel of King's College Aberdeen. St Nicholas Church in the same city was also a collegiate foundation, but like Stirling was divided into an east and a west kirk, and more unfortunately rebuilt in different styles at each end. Even the present tower is a Victorian replacement of the lovely one that fell nearly a century ago and which inspired the young Ninian Comper to suggest its recreation in the new episcopal cathedral which American money was to have built this century but for the Wall Street crash of the thirties. Only the crypt under the east end and the remnants of the transepts, really chapels as at Linlithgow, survive of original medieval work, and they are no longer part of the two churches but used as vestibules between them. The most interesting of the alterations to the church are those designed by James Gibb, a native of the 'Granite City' and architect for St Martin-in-the-Fields and other London churches. Here the furnishings are plain but dignified, and their design was a gift from the architect to his home town.

St Nicholas' is one of the largest parish churches in Scotland, but amongst our sixteen or so surviving collegiate kirks some of the smaller ones are more complete and more interesting. At Arbuthnott, in Angus, the chapel or aisle of the Arbuthnott family is another miniature Beauvais, with tall polygonal apse supported by handsome buttresses, plus rounded angle turret taking a spiral stair up at the north-western corner. Inside is the figure of a knight in armour and although the altar has gone, a Holy Water stoop and piscina remain. Above the vaulted roof is the priest's room, with a wall cupboard or aumbry for the safe-keeping of the sacred vessels. These were common in north-east Scotland where some of them were quite elaborately decorated at the sides and top with angels and representations of the Host or Chalice. They began to resemble Continental tabernacles in the end, though their purpose was different. Even under the guise of Sacrament Houses, the consecrated elements were only reserved for the sick, not to be taken out and carried about in procession.

Perhaps the most perfectly apsed Scottish kirk of the late Gothic period is the so-called Kirk o'Steil, at Ladykirk on Tweed, which James IV built in 1590 as a thank-offering after being saved from drowning in the swollen waters of the border river. It is quite intact, except for the top of the tower, whose cupola designed by William Adam, seems, however, to fit quite nicely. The name, Kirk o'Steil, is yet another Scots sentimentalization of perfectly ordinary circumstances, for although the church is built entirely of stone, floors, walls and roof, and, therefore, indestructable by fire or water, most important kirks of the time were so constructed. The internal barrel and groined roof is topped by an outer casing of thick stone slabs, which were also a common feature. Particularly interesting though is the repetition of the polygonal apse of the east end at the transepts, making the whole cruciform building a most splendid example of French flamboyant Gothic. It is almost matched, but not quite, by the Collegiate Kirk at Seton, nearer Edinburgh, which again has a polygonal, buttressed east end, but with square-ended transepts and no

Former votive Kirk of Our Lady, the 'Kirk o' Steil', Ladykirk on Tweed, Berwickshire

Crichton Collegiate Kirk, Midlothian, with its fortified tower.
(*below*) Crichton Kirk: plan

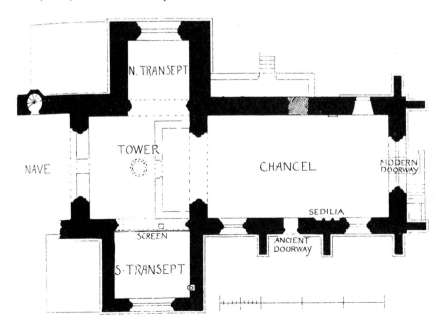

nave, the widow of the third Lord Seton, whose Renaissance tomb illumines the interior, having stopped work after her husband's death at Flodden. Seton Collegiate Kirk, which is now in the care of the Department of the Environment, has a broach spire reminiscent of English church towers in, say, Rutland, and not so satisfying as Adam's completion of Ladykirk. It also supported a provost, six prebendaries, one clerk and two singing boys, which suggests a good endowment.

South-east Scotland is especially rich in collegiate kirks, as is only to be expected with functionaries of the court and others living in the vicinity. They mostly date from the mid-fifteenth century, and include Crichton, which was built by Sir William Crichton, Chancellor to James II and the man mainly responsible for the 'Black Dinner' when the members of the Douglas family were murdered in front of the young king at Edinburgh Castle. The church, like Seton, is incomplete, having no nave, and is, therefore, a typical 'T' kirk, a form that was particularly suited to protestant worship after the Reformation, when the pulpit was placed against the blocked-off west end, and the seating re-orientated towards that instead of the altar. There is a fine aumbry with carved surround, and the tower is simply battlemented and finished with a delightful bell-cot. Within sight of it, but not as near as Seton, is the lord's castle, a favourite with Sir Walter Scott who used to come and sit and gaze at it when he lived at Lasswade. It is a ruin and does not concern us here, though one might mention its most unusual feature, the diamond-cut masonry of the courtyard which has a definite Italian provenance having been built by Francis Stewart, Lord Bothwell, a 'natural' cousin of James VI and I and a wizard who dabbled in necromency.

At Dalkeith the former collegiate kirk is in a very poor state, the nave having been rebuilt and the choir roofless; the latter does, however, contain a fine tomb of the founder, and is also the burial aisle of the Dukes of Buccleuch and notably of Anne, Duchess of Monmouth and Buccleuch, whose husband, Charles II's son by Lucy Walter, was beheaded for high treason in 1685. The church at Borthwick, just round the corner from Crichton, is new, but still boasts a fine family aisle with the original undamaged recumbent figures of the founder and his spouse, with some of the original colour surviving. The aisle is a splendid specimen of the fifteenth-century Scottish Gothic with a typical stone slab roof of the period. However, all these examples pale before Rosslyn Chapel, which is not only unique in Scotland but in Britain. Like most of the others it belonged to the reign of James II of Scots, of the 'Fiery Face', and was the creation of William St Clair, Prince of Orkney, 'the recitation of whose titles would weary a Spanish Grandee', according to Scott; and it is to the Bard of Abbotsford that we owe Rosslyn's most celebrated legend, the story of the Prentice's Pillar. This is the most beautiful and ornate object in the most remarkable and ornate flamboyant Gothic building in Britain. The story goes that while the master mason was away one of the apprentices carved the column in question, and when his master returned he was so jealous of the former's skill that he killed him. The facts, as usual, are less dramatic, though not without interest, for until Scott perpetrated this one the column was known as 'The Prince's Pillar', and is so referred to by Defoe in his *Tour*; and records suggest that William St Clair may have had a hand in it himself, or at least have designed it. He was a great traveller and the extravagances here assembled have prompted commentators to equate Rosslyn Chapel with Manueline churches in Portugal. Yet the building predates any Manueline specimen, and although certain parts of it are related to Iberian work it is quite likely that the whole extraordinary display of the Scottish medieval stone carver's skill results from a resident mason's interpretation of the founder's intentions.

The chapel, which was intended as a complete collegiate kirk of large proportions, indeed, whose plan closely follows that of Glasgow Cathedral, with open aisle running round behind the high altar, consists of chancel and Lady Chapel alone, and the barrel-vaulted roof, rich with carved inset panels, is covered outside with a plain skin which one feels sure was not intended, the more common sturdy stone slabs being more likely. Everywhere, inside and out, hardly a space is left undecorated. Pinnacles, buttresses, windows, doors and niches, all are so rich and strange one wonders where next to turn for relief from the exotic plants, animals, religious symbolism, bag-pipers, sailors and saints that cover every available

Corstorphine
Collegiate Kirk,
Edinburgh, with its
stocky tower and
stone spire. (*below*)
Corstorphine Kirk:
plan

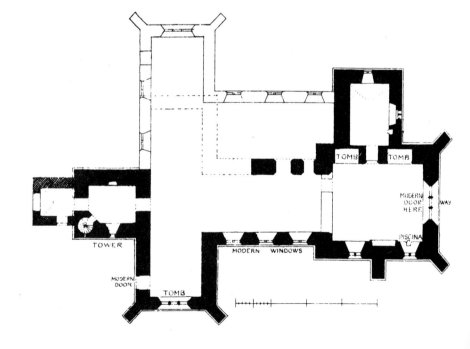

TOMB

TOMB

MODERN
DOOR
HERE

WAY

PISCINA

TOWER

MODERN WINDOWS

MODERN
DOOR

TOMB

inch. The building was saved from destruction at the Reformation by being private property and not, therefore, required as a parish kirk. It was renovated partly through the efforts of Sir John Clerk, second baronet of Penicuik and often called the Scottish Lord Burlington. Poets and royalty have visited the place and all marvelled at it, though not all with the same pleasure; and one rather feels that had the original scheme been carried out in full Rosslyn's principal rival for profuseness of decoration and elaborate contour might have been Milan Cathedral! The interior is floodlit during the Edinburgh Festival, when the effect is nothing short of magical, resembling some underwater scene on a coral reef.

Corstorphine Kirk, now within the boundaries of the City of Edinburgh, is an interesting collegiate foundation dating in its older parts from 1429 and endowed by the king's hereditary forrester, whose arched and recessed family tombs are in the chancel. Like St Giles', it has an oddly irregular appearance, the original plan being almost indistinguishable behind all the bumps and bulges of side chapels and laird's aisles that break out in separate shed-like structures all round. Each has its own, stone-slabbed roof and gables, and to make confusion greater, the choir, as at Stirling, is higher than the nave. The stocky tower, with squat stone spire, is Scotch to a degree, with its own masonic circlets and tiny lucarnes, or stone dormers, and has many counterparts throughout the country. Fife is especially rich in such towers, which had a vogue that lasted from the fourteenth to the seventeenth century when Jacobean versions, notably those at Pittenweem and Anstruther Easter, are almost childlike in their playful use of amusing decorative features.

Of the early Fife churches of note that of St Monans is perhaps the best known and most dramatically sited, being built on a rocky headland by the seashore and cut off from its congregation at exceptionally high tides. It has a fine stunted tower rising plainly from a foursquare base the foundations of which go back to the fourteenth century, when King David II is said to have founded it as a votive kirk following the miraculous removal from his eye of an arrow which he received at the Battle of Neville's Cross. In fact he was a prisoner of war in England at the time, though no doubt he did come to St Monans at a later date and did found a church there, possibly replacing an older chapel dedicated to St Ninian. This is perhaps borne out by the way the present day fisherfolk still pronounce the name of the burgh as St Minnans. There were other shrines the king could have gone to, to St Ninian's own tomb at Whithorn, or even nearer home to the Whitekirk, in East Lothian, where a Holy Well was drawing crowds, making the place a veritable Scottish Lourdes. Indeed, a century later, when Aeneas Sylvius Piccolomini, the future Pope Pius II, came to Scotland as emissary of the Congress of Arras in 1435, it was to the Whitekirk that he walked barefoot to give thanks for his safe arrival on our shores. The cruciform red sandstone building, crow-stepped and with square central tower, may or may not have been precisely the same then as it is now, possibly not, though it was expertly restored by Sir Robert Lorimer after suffragettes had set fire to it in 1914; and part of the Hospitium where pilgrims were received survives in a field nearby.

Probably David II did go to St Monans, however, to visit the small Oratory of St Ninian, and part of the present 'T'-shaped church resulted. In many respects it is the twin of Crichton, with no nave, only choir and transepts, though the spire, which is newer, is different. The kirk was one of Ian Lindsay's later restorations, when the pews were turned to face the pulpit against the west wall. One curious effect of this is that since one enters from the south transept, itself at a lower level than the rest of the building, one finds oneself having to do quite a lengthy promenade to get to one's seat. The walls have been whitewashed all over, as they must have been in the Middle Ages, when our religious buildings were gay with colour, frescoes and 'Sunday-school' murals. There is a beautiful model of a fully rigged ship hanging from the ceiling near the door, which gives an appropriate touch in this coastal community, but why oh why were the old fisherman's benches done away with, and replaced with spidery sorry things better suited to a public utility centre?

Further along the coast the tower of the church at Crail is perhaps the oldest in Fife, its lower portions dating from the twelfth century. This is one of the first Royal Burghs created in Scotland, by Queen Margaret's son David I, when Crail was already a walled town of consequence, an important market; and it now acquired a collegiate kirk of some importance. The main building has been greatly altered, though it is good of its kind, a whitewashed, post-Reformation church of character, and again with hanging model ship. It has definite links with two similar but later churches in neighbouring St Andrews, where the University kirk of St Salvator's College still serves it original purpose and possesses a tower finished very much in the style of Crail. The actual chapel has been altered somewhat, but it does contain the tomb, made in Tournai, of Bishop Kennedy, who founded the college in

(*left*) The 'L'-shaped tower of Holy Trinity Kirk, St Andrews, from the north-east. (*right*) 'L'-shaped tower of Crail Kirk, Fife, the lower portions dating from the twelfth century

E

1455, as well as the pulpit from which John Knox thundered in the Town Kirk of Holy Trinity in 1547. This is another restored building, indeed, it is virtually a new edifice; but again the tower is original and particularly interesting, for although not completed until the fifteenth century it is clearly constructed of much more ancient masonry. An old Consecration Cross may be seen near the west door of the church, while on the north side is a round-arched Romanesque window head.

The overall appearance of this tower is especially intriguing because, although looking square, from the south, it actually is 'L'-shaped, with a long side facing west and return on the north, the addition containing a stair with separate turret, extra to the larger one covering the tower proper. It really is a defensive structure, very much like a laird's tower such as Scotstarvit, near Cupar, which is one of the best-preserved small towers surviving in Scotland. A visit to it after examining St Andrews is most instructive. Inside the church the restoration has been almost as thorough as outside, though the grandiose marble monument to Archbishop Sharp, in the manner of van Nost, remains intact and *in situ*, a reminder of the Archbishop's cruel murder on Magus Muir one May evening in 1679. He was on his way home with his daughter after supping with the Minister at Ceres, when the coach was stopped by a group of Covenanters who killed him in front of his daughter, each murderer in turn taking personal vengeance on the ill-fated prelate. Sharp was not a good man in the sense that his contemporary Robert Leighton was, but he was not a particularly bad man either, certainly not when one considers the conditions prevailing in Restoration Scotland, where bigotry and the cult of violence were rife.

The Sunday following the Archbishop's killing the sermon was preached in Holy Trinity with the dead man's blood-stained rochet slung over the pulpit, the same one Knox used and is now in St Salvator's College Chapel. It was the Reformer's first big public appearance, his next important address coming in St John's Kirk, Perth, which resulted in the almost immediate attack by the 'rascally mob' of local kirks and some clergy. St John's is another of the larger churches in Scotland that have suffered something approaching a sea-change at the restorer's hand. For long divided into separated parts it was opened up again and tidied by Sir Robert Lorimer to become the Perthshire War Memorial, and that is about all one can usefully say about this celebrated kirk, except that, as is often the case, the tower fared rather better than the rest. The north porch, formerly known as Halkerston's Tower, has been restored with its second storey. It was the work of John Halkerston, Master of Works to Queen Mary of Gueldres, Flemish consort of James II of 'The Fiery Face' and mother of James III.

Perthshire and Angus never became really enthusiastic about Calvinism and accordingly there exist a number of comparatively unspoilt kirks there, the most interesting being the tiny but genuine collegiate church at Foulis Easter, near Dundee. It is still used as a parish kirk and retains its original rood screen timber doors, plus a number of unique painted panels some of which were once part of the screen and others which may have lined the wall behind the altar, which has no window. The subjects dealt with are Our Lord's Crucifixion, His Entombment, and His association with The Apostles. The first is thought to date from the second half of the fifteenth century and to be of Continental provenance. The Sacrament House is also particularly fine, with the head and shoulders of Christ at the top, supported by angels, and set in an ogee-shaped opening. Several Holy Water stoops survive, also a medieval font and a bell from 1508. The arrangement of the windows is most unusual, for the few that matter are placed one above the other in the middle of the church so as to light the rood screen.

On the western side of Perth, at Tullibardine, is the most complete Collegiate Kirk in Scotland which was wholly finished before the Reformation and unaltered since. It was built and endowed by Sir David Murray of Dumbarton, an ancestor of the Murrays of Tullibardine, in 1446 and has survived the vicissitudes of time and religious contention through becoming the burial place of the Drummonds of Strathallan. It is cruciform in plan, has a low square tower at the west end with uncrenellated parapet, and is entered by a door whose rounded archway could easily be taken for Romanesque if one did not know its date. There are some rather English looking square-headed windows, but not many, and the building is dark inside, especially since again there is no east window, the space here having hooks for cloth hangings. An oddly defensive slant is given by the presence of deep narrow slits in the west wall, and a shot-hole—though the latter may only be a shut-hole, common in domestic buildings of the period. The Strathallan estate marches with that of Gleneagles, not the hotel but the 'Glen of the Church', in Gaelic, which has been the possession of the Haldanes of that ilk ever since they arrived here in Norman times. Between their seventeenth-century whitewashed mansion and the ruins of their medieval castle is the Chapel of St Mungo, now a family shrine but once a public place of worship. The present modest crow-stepped building, restored recently, probably dates from about the same time as Tullibardine, but undoubtedly stands on the site of a much older one, while to the south of the house, in the glen itself, is St Mungo's well, clear evidence of early missionary penetration in the district.

Another family chapel, and another Drummond one, is at Stobhall, a rare example of a sixteenth-century manor as opposed to a tower or castle. It is sited on an attractive bend of the River Tay between Perth and Dunkeld, and consists more of a group of buildings rather than a single hall or chapel, the two being linked by an outer wall and courtyard entered via a gatehouse. Stobhall was the dowry of the Drummond ladies who, in Jacobite times, were allowed to stay on here while their husbands were away fighting or in prison; and their chapel has retained its beautiful painted ceiling and essential fittings in excellent condition. On the north wall, as was the custom in old Scotch kirks, is the aumbry, but this one has kept its oak door with fretwork air vent and original iron hinges and handle. The altar slab, or mensa, has also survived, and what may or may not be a Holy Water stoop. The ceiling, which is amongst the finest of many contemporary ones in Scotland, dates from the reign of Charles I, who is depicted on it, together with other royal brethren and the legendary Prester John. At the west end of this lovely chapel is a two-storeyed turreted annexe containing the priest's room and a suite in which Ruskin and Millais resided during the period when they were wife swapping and fishing.

At Grantully, in Strathtay, in the hills behind the ancient castle of the Stewarts, survives the extraordinary little church of St Mary. Extraordinary because unless it was signposted right to the door one would scarcely know it was a church, for it looks exactly like a country cottage, a 'but and ben' to be precise. It is long and low and whitewashed, and has no distinguishing features of an ecclesiastical nature. Its date is late sixteenth-century, restored in Carolean times, when the fine painted ceiling was installed. This covers a barrel-vaulted timber roof and consists of religious and secular subjects, Renaissance motifs and the heraldic devices of various branches of the Stewart and Lennox families. There is also an upper loft at the west end which must have been the priest's room but is now used by the grasscutter and the Department of the Environment who look after the church. A notice down by the main road, near Grantully Castle, states that there is a service in the church on Sunday evenings. In a way one wishes there was not, at least, that if there was the fittings were a bit more sympathetic. Simplicity is no barrier to worship, but rows of tubular chairs in such a place, and office furniture where the altar used to be are hardly conducive to religious contemplation. Nor is the presence in the aumbry of an old electric light bulb quite what was originally intended. Viewed in the light of the gaily painted ceiling and the true purpose of this building one feels a state of silent emptiness might better allow the visitor to pay homage to the beauty of the setting and the spirit that imbued the founders.

From Perthshire to Ayrshire is a longish distance even as the crow flies, and in some respects more so in atmosphere and cultural expression, for the division of Scotland is more on an east to west line than a north to south one. This is the land of Burns, of the Brig o'Doon, Tam o'Shanter and the kenspeckle thatched cottage in which the 'poet of the plough' was born. There are other things too in this green and pleasant land, one of the best and least-known being in the old kirkyard at Largs, beside the Firth of Clyde. This is the family aisle of the Montgomeries of Skelmorlie. It dates from the reign of Charles I and again the roof is barrel-vaulted in pine and painted, this time with *trompe l'oeil* ribs to simulate real vaulting. The subject matter includes local scenery, such as Skelmorlie

Castle and the now defunct kirk at Largs, plus what is perhaps the most sophisticated and elaborately conceived mixture of Italianate patterns and heraldic devices in the country. The founder, whose tomb this building was erected to contain, had both the means and the knowledge to create a place which would not disgrace a genuine Italian palazzo or baroque church. His large tomb rises almost to the ceiling from a sunken well, and is in the same rich, pillared and canopied style as the tombs of the greater aristocracy in England, but outstripping anything of the kind in Scotland. The chapel containing all this magnificence is also worth a glance, being nicely proportioned and simple but well built and finished. It is entered through a central oak, studded door under an ogee arch, with an iron-barred window on either side set within particularly handsome mouldings. Above the door are the Arms of Sir Robert Montgomerie, whose monument and memorial this is.

Still in the west, at Douglas, in Lanarkshire, is the small kirk of St Bride's, burial place of the ancestors of Sir Alec Douglas Home. A much older edifice stood on the same site,

Montgomerie of Skelmorlie Aisle, Largs, Ayrshire

and the present building only represents the choir of a later church. It is full, one might almost say crammed, with memorials, the most interesting being the three arched altar tombs of 'Archibald the Grim', 'James the Gross' and the 'Good Sir James'. The latter was Robert the Bruce's paladin, the knight charged with taking his heart to the Holy Land in expiation of the king's murder of the 'Red Comyn' in the kirk of the Greyfriars, in Dumfriesshire, for which crime he had been excommunicated by the Pope. Sir James fell fighting the moors in Spain, but managed to pass the locket containing Bruce's heart onto another knight, who brought it back to Scotland and had it buried near the High Altar in Melrose Abbey. The tiny, evocative interior of St Bride's kirk must contain more mementos of Scottish history than almost any other comparable space, and is still the repository of the remains of a family which in its heyday rivalled the Stewart kings in power. When Douglas Castle was demolished a number of stained glass replicas of the Arms of the Douglas family were taken and placed in the chancel of Sancta Sophia, the small episcopal church in the village which was made out of the former dower house.

As we have already seen, Scottish cathedrals, even where they were not destroyed or used as quarries were generally too large for Protestant worship, and with abbeys the situation was the same. On the other hand, moderate-sized town kirks were more readily converted, as were a number of smaller parish churches, some indeed continuing to do service right up to the present time. Amongst the most remarkable of these, and the remotest, is the Church of St Clement at Rodil, on the southern tip of Harris. It was built by Alasdair Crotach MacLeod, who was buried in it in 1547—only three years before the pre-Reformation Roman Church was abolished altogether in Scotland, and this makes St Clement's particularly interesting since its architecture belongs to a previous age. It is the only cruciform church in the Hebrides and in many of its decorative details it reflects older work at Iona. It is roofed and boasts a fine square tower at the west end, while inside are several tombs at least one of which looks more Irish than Scots. Yet another remnant of ancient Hebridean religious architecture is the Teampull of St Moluag at Eorrapaidh, at the Butt of Lewis. It actually dates, so far as its walls are concerned, from the twelfth century, it was re-roofed in 1912, and services are held there in the summer. In its windswept setting, within sight and sound of the Atlantic breakers, St Moluag's makes one think of Sir Ninian Comper's description of a church as a tent to cover an altar. This tiny church, or temple, is actually more of a shed, a stone shed, yet in its austere adequacy it does seem to fulfill the great ecclesiologist's dictum.

The Reformation brought surprisingly few experimental kirks, though there were a few such as St Columba's Burntisland, in Fife, which was rebuilt in Jacobean times as a square edifice with central tower over a central pulpit, and galleries all round. Considerable ingenuity was shown in supporting the tower by means of large corner buttresses and a number of sturdy internal columns linked with stone arches springing from all four corners and meeting in a smaller central square. The galleries are reached by means of outside stairs, and each section of society, laird, tradespeople and fisherfolk were catered for in separate compartments, their respective occupations being indicated by painted panels such as one that shows a ropemaker winding his rope, or a mariner using his astrolabe and staff; while another panel depicts a ship on fire and probably recalls the burning of Burntisland when Cromwell bombarded it from the sea.

In contrast to the very presbyterian St Columba's, which left no space for an altar, is the kirk at Dairsie, again in Fife, which Archbishop Spottiswood, Chancellor of Scotland and Primate, the man who crowned Charles I at Holyrood, built in 1621. This was an attempt to recreate the Gothic spirit in post-Reformation church architecture and set a standard that others might follow. The attempt is interesting in so far as the octagonal turret at the west end is corbelled out in medieval fashion and the buttresses at the east end are bunched together to suggest a chancel on this otherwise plainly rectangular kirk. The traceried windows are, however, somewhat odd, and show as ill-digested a knowledge of Gothic as early Renaissance attempts to recreate original Roman details had done. The church follows normal Scottish practice in having a level floor throughout and forming the division between

(*left*) Jacobean Kirk tower, Dairsie, Fife. (*right*) Fenwick Kirk, Ayrshire: detail of stair to gallery

chancel and nave merely by a screen, as was done in most small kirks here in the Middle Ages. A good example of this exists in the roofless but otherwise hale church of the Templars at Temple in Midlothian, which dates from the thirteenth century and is nothing more than a simple oblong, with windows back and side and bellcot at one end.

The complete transition from pre- to post-Reformation practice can actually be seen in the Perthshire kirk of Kilmaveonaig. It stands on the spot where St Adamnan, biographer of St Columba, preached to the heathen Picts in the seventh century, and there was a stone parish church here before 1275. The present building was rebuilt in the sixteenth century by the local laird, Robertson of Lude, and continued in use after the change in religious policy in Scotland in 1690. It is contemporaneous with the nearby kirk at Old Blair, which although ruined contains the body of 'Bonnie Dundee' who was killed at the Battle of Killiecrankie in 1689. The lairds of

Lude are still associated with the kirk, whose old plate has survived, a bell of 1629 and a minute book which reveals many secrets about the non-jurors and their congregations; it came here after one of them, Reverend Robert Lyon, was executed for actively supporting the Stuart Cause. The church, despite later improvements, remains a single-roofed rectangle, with bellcot on the west gable, and must be virtually unique in Scotland both in respect of its architecture and the liturgy used in it. In the nineteenth century when the celebrated engineer and bridge builder Thomas Telford provided forty 'Parliamentary' kirks and manses for the Highlands he repeated the same plain, barnlike form as earlier church builders in Scotland, which is so much more satisfactory than the elaborate and largely unfunctional mock-Gothic that proliferated later in the same century; and which even shows through Archbishop Spottiswood's abortive effort at ecclesiastical decency at Dairsie.

In 1643 the kirk at Fenwick, in Ayrshire, was built. This shows a merging of old and new which surpasses the efforts of the builders of Burntisland and Dairsie in that it combines a cruciform plan with galleries and outside stair. The original fittings have mostly survived, including the pulpit, with its somewhat inhibiting hour-glass. The building is whitewashed but with its stone margins left exposed, has crow-stepped gables and a charming bellcot supported by square classical columns. The outside stair still functions and there is a good ogee finial to the dormer window. One wonders why its type did not become the model for many others, there are, I think, only two similar churches, one at Golspie, in Sutherland. It is curious too how well the cruciform plan, medieval and Catholic in ethos, suits a galleried kirk, a new one that is, not an adapted pre-Reformation one. Fenwick consists of a Low Town, which was peopled by weavers in thatched cottages, now alas slated, and a High Town or Kirkton, where the church is, and where, according to the weavers, it was most needed. The people in Kirkton were shoemakers, and also, apparently, not very law abiding, for the jougs, or metal neckpieces by which ill-doers were held to the pillory, were in frequent use in the second half of the seventeenth century, for brawling and wenching and for fraternizing with the forces of

Lauder Kirk, Berwickshire, with Town House in background

law and order. Fenwick was a hotbed of covenanting dissidents and militants. They sought martyrdom with every breath, and got it, the barbarity of the age being amply exemplified in the inscriptions on their gravestones in the kirkyard, the last lines of one of which reads;

> Thus was the head which was to wear a Crown
> A football made by a profane Dragoon.

The gravestones actually have little metal martyr's crowns attached to them, and this 'martyr' had his head cut off by a dragoon who kicked it 'over the green'.

The principal instrument of government policy in Scotland at the time was the Duke of Lauderdale, who promised to make Scotland safe for the king at any cost. It was he who caused the Palace of Holyroodhouse to be rebuilt and employed Sir William Bruce there, and at his own castle at Thirlestane. Bruce was the first professional Scottish architect, and at Lauder, at the gates of Thirlestane Castle, he designed the parish kirk for his powerful patron and cousin by marriage, the Duchess of Lauderdale being partly a Bruce. This is his only complete ecclesiastical building, and like the kirk at

Fenwick, is cruciform. The tower, however, is at the crossing and is Lauder's *pièce de résistance*, being octagonal and probably derived, as indeed the shape of the church itself may be, from Mansart's Chapel at the gates to the Château de Balleroy, in Normandy. In 1820 the kirk was filled with galleries and not particularly sympathetic seating, but perhaps the restoration to commemorate its third centenary in 1973 will include a lightening of some of this rather heavy-handed furniture. There may have been a laird's loft, or gallery for the Lauderdale family in Bruce's day, though there do not seem to have been any retiring rooms such as he provided for the Earl of Hopetoun at Abercorn. There the Earl and his family spent most of Sunday, the morning in their gaily-decorated gallery in the kirk, taking cold collation in their adjoining suite of panelled rooms that included a privy and squint through which to see when the afternoon session had begun; and then they went back into the gallery.

The laird's loft is almost a Scottish speciality, not really to be compared with the average Squire's pew in England; and in some cases it was a very grand affair indeed. The Hopetoun loft has precedents in the Royal Box in Turin Cathedral, and is just as baroque and secular looking as that. Many are imitations of Bruce's design at Abercorn, but not all have complementary retiring rooms. At Polwarth, in Berwickshire, is an interesting church of the same period which actually retains its 'Laudian' altar rails, though lacking any altar. It is a 'T' kirk, with the laird's room in the short arm of the 'T', on the north, and has a solid looking square tower with a broach spire at the west end. An orange does service for a cross at the east end, symbolic no doubt of the leanings of its lordly begetter, the first Earl of Marchmont. At Newbattle, in Midlothian, the Marquis of Lothian commissioned Alexander McGill, architect to the City of Edinburgh, to build a new parish kirk near his mansion, and here a classically inspired laird's loft again fills the short 'T', with a tower to balance it to the south. Beside the church is the old manse, now a private house, but interesting because it was once the home of Robert Leighton before he became a bishop.

Other well known laird's lofts include the very fine one at Durisdeer designed by James Smith, Bruce's disciple and

(left) Late seventeenth-century Kirk of Polwarth-on-the-Green, Berwickshire. *(right)* Carnbee, Fife: eighteenth-century kirk with bellcot made from old table-gravestone legs

senior partner to McGill. This is also the family kirk and burial place of the Dukes of Queensberry and Buccleuch, whose ogee-roofed mausoleum, with marbles by van Nost, within Smith also designed. At Kilbirnie is what must surely be the most demonstrably anti-social of all laird's galleries, literally a sort of grand circle with canopied central box at the back of the church reserved for the gentry. It dates from a little later than the others and is really much too ostentatious, even profane in its effect. Here the first Viscount Garnock, who built it, went one further than the Hopes of Hopetoun by actually cooking his lunch on the premises. A doucer specimen exists in the tasteful laird's loft in the parish kirk at Cromarty, on the Black Isle, put in by the Ross family when they developed the burgh and their estate on model landlord lines. We are now in the Georgian era when Scottish church architecture reflected more and more sophisticated styles in vogue in the

Abercorn Kirk, West Lothian, showing Hopetoun Suite added by Sir William Bruce in 1708

south, and was not conspicuously vernacular in form except in minor buildings. This is not to say it died out altogether. At Dunnett, for instance, in Caithness, the eighteenth-century parish kirk has a saddle-back tower, while in many later kirks close inspection of the bellcot will show that it is made up of bulbous supports from old table-graves, an example of Scots thrift at its most characteristic.

Perhaps one might end this chapter with a cautionary tale about a church tower, or the lack of one. In 1770 Sir James Clerk of Penicuik, son of the antiquarian who helped to have Rosslyn Chapel renovated, designed a new parish kirk for the local congregation. It is a dignified Palladian edifice, facing longways onto the street and entered through a handsome columned portico, but it has no tower. The story goes that Sir James's father specially designed one but that the Kirk Session turned it down on the grounds that it smacked of episcopalianism. Thus, the good people of Penicuik are still called to the kirk of a Sabbath morn by a bell rung in an old tower at the back of Sir James's Palladian building, all that remains of an earlier church.

III
Castles and Towers

SCOTLAND is renowned for her castles, the number and variety of them, largely as a result of the writings of Sir Walter Scott and the efforts of romantic architects and builders, such as the Prince Consort, who designed Balmoral himself. There are indeed a great number of Scottish castles, the majority in ruins, others much restored and a few more or less as they were left when their owners, usually Jacobite in sympathy, fell from favour and were unable or unwilling to bring them up-to-date according to Georgian or Victorian standards. As we have seen Scotland's buildings, secular as well as ecclesiastical, differed only slightly from those of her neighbours, except possibly in scale, until after the English invasions and the defeat of Edward II at Bannockburn. Then France became the main source of inspiration and a native style based more on Continental ideas than English evolved, surviving in some shape or form until the end of the seventeenth century. The Pictish brochs I mentioned at the beginning of my narrative were, it is true, completely indigenous, and to some extent the Celtic fragments that appeared before the arrival in the north of the Saxon Margaret and her Norman-trained sons could also be described as native, though having many Irish associations; but it was not until the second half of the fourteenth century that features introduced by Continental craftsmen in place of English became widespread and part of the local architectural heritage. These features were more noticeable in secular buildings, for fairly obvious reasons, the defensive alliance made by successive Kings of Scots with French Kings naturally led to cultural as well as political exchanges. The reversal of these did not come until after the Union of the Crowns in 1603, and more so after the union of Parliaments in 1707.

Thus, the style of Scottish building, unique and inimitable as it is, is inextricably bound up with that country's history

as a separate entity, indeed, spread beyond the actual period
of separateness to extend to some of those Scotch Baronial
piles that arose in Victorian times and which, though one may
laugh at them, do have a legitimate place in our cultural annals.
They belong, late in time but in time just the same, to the saga
of the ill-fated Royal House of Stuart, to the misunderstood
story of the Scottish clans; and they are certainly outward
and visible reminders of those causes, lost and otherwise, that
characterize Scotland's turbulant history and which were
taken up and romanticized in the late eighteenth and early
nineteenth centuries.

Bearing all this in mind it is, perhaps, not surprising that
not many of our numerous castles pre-date the middle of the
fourteenth century and that none of these are inhabited. The
oldest inhabited castle in Scotland is said to be Duntroon in
Argyll, which, however, although built on medieval foundations is a seventeenth-century house, the only original portion
remaining being part of a former enceinte, or defensive outer
wall, and this crenellated in wholly un-native fashion in the
nineteenth century. Probably the oldest continuously inhabited house in Scotland is Traquair, in Peeblesshire, which
is not really a castle in the accepted sense of the word but a
series of buildings that began as a single 'pele' tower, and was
added to bit by bit until it became the attractive and intriguing old Scotch building it now is; resembling nothing so
much as some ancient *manoir* in Normandy, or the Valley of
the Loire. Traquair is decayed in a pleasant, grandmotherly
sort of way, not ruined, nor as Ruskin remarked, 'put on a
velvet carpet to be shown'. Samuel Butler in his description
of the Castle of Angera, in *Alps and Sanctuaries*, was particularly
stern about ruins, declaring; 'all ruins are frauds, it [Angera]
is only decayed. It is a kind of Stokesay or Ightham Moat,
better preserved than the first and less furnished than the
second.' He might almost have been writing about Traquair,
which is actually furnished but being probably the longest
lived-in dwelling in Scotland, possibly in Britain, has evolved
and grown in a natural manner, like a person, each age being
represented by some change. It is also the perfect example in
the Scots vernacular in the present context, since it has not
been tampered with for nearly three centuries.

Traquair enters history as early as the twelfth century, when it took the form of a royal hunting lodge. Architecturally this would resemble a border pele, and was not, therefore, initially built of stone but of timber, and probably, as in other cases, was surrounded by a wooden palisade. The traditional pele tower most people think of nowadays, a tallish free-standing rectangle of masonry with few windows and gable-ended roof, possibly with a turret at one corner and a run of parapet by way of battlements, simply did not exist before the mid-fourteenth century, and most were built much later. They grew from the old Norman 'motte and bailey' plan, the motte being the central mound, often artificial, which was crowned by a wooden 'keep' and the bailey, the outer palisade and gatehouse. Abroad, and in England, such structures were usually replaced in stone as time went on, as at Newcastle, Dover and Windsor, where the motte still supports a round keep.

In Scotland this stage was rarely reached, and because of the Scottish 'scorched earth' policy such stone keeps as were built were thrown down in order to prevent them falling into English hands. So we have no comparable buildings left, all our motte and bailey castles being either demolished or burned down. On the other hand the typical Border pele did develop from these sources, though not until the fifteenth century, and not as a defence against a powerful foreign enemy but against close neighbours.

The age of the first stone pele erected at Traquair is un-known, but being a royal property the change from timber came at an early date, probably by the time King William the Lion granted Glasgow her royal charter in the thirteenth century from here. Ancient vaultings survive at the foot of the oldest corner of the building, together with a decidedly primitive corkscrew staircase, enormously thick walls and the suggestion of a look-out turret and cap-house, or stair exit onto the battlements, which have since been converted and incorporated within a pitched slate roof of the seventeenth century. This 'french' style of roof links the various parts to make a cohesive whole; but one can still see where the different periods begin and end by looking at the house from north to south, left to right on the main elevation, and this despite the

F

Traquair House, Peeblesshire: (*above*) from the east, and (*below*) with its courtyard, from the west

half-completed scheme undertaken by James Smith, in the reigns of Charles II and James VII and II, when a plan for regimenting the house and producing the kind of symmetry Sir William Bruce had brought to Holyroodhouse was prepared. First we see the tall stone pele with its altered turret, plus a line of windows each diminishing in size towards the dormers at roof level. This older portion is 'L'-shaped on plan, a common arrangement whereby the small arm, or projecting nib, contained the stairs and also provided cover against unwanted visitors, who could be spied from shut-holes and fired at from a shot-hole, both being placed low down near the door. Such features, together with other embellishments once thought necessary, like corbelling, bartisans, or sentry walks and look-outs, gargoyles in the form of false cannon, conically capped turrets and garde-robes, or roof lavatories, eventually became the stock-in-trade of Scots masons and the status symbols of the gentry, and their peculiar use in Jacobean times by the nouveau-riche and newly ennobled mark Scotland's unique contribution to the castellated and domestic architecture of Britain and Europe.

The Frenchness of Scottish castellated architecture has frequently been noted, but very often this is more a case of resemblance than of actual imitation, and Scots masons seem to have arrived at the same point in some instances as their Continental opposite numbers without copying. Traquair, for instance, is as French as anything I have ever seen, though not a copy, that is the secret. One could cite many other examples both large and small, from castles to quite modest laird's towers. After all, Montaigne himself lived in a tower in the country, and any Scots visitor to the Departments of Auvergne or Dordogne will find numerous reminders of home in the form of small *châteaux* and *manoirs*, each with its *colombier*, or doocot, as in Fife, Angus and the Lothians; but except in the Royal palaces of Falkland, Stirling and Linlithgow, and a few buildings whose owners had close Continental connections, direct French influence was more something remembered in tranquility by their builders than a precise exercise in imitation. It just so happens that intellectually speaking, as in some other fields, French and Scots have minds in common, hence the enduring strength of that famous 'Auld Alliance' which was already 800 years old when Mary, Queen of Scots married the Dauphin François in 1558, and which survives to this day in spirit.

One has to say this otherwise no proper understanding of the peculiar properties of the Scottish vernacular can seriously be contemplated. Indeed, it was the almost complete misunderstanding of its ethos that caused the erection on so prodigious a scale of Scotch Baronial edifices in the nineteenth century, only a moiety of which were authentically native in form. Balmoral was one of the best, while Abbotsford, despised by many art historians and architectural pursits, seems positively plain beside many larger effusions in the same manner. I think I have said enough to make the point that however French-looking the true Scots vernacular sometimes is, few buildings of the fifteenth, sixteenth and seventeenth centuries, which is what matters, are actually other than purely Scottish, even when reflecting certain Continental features.

So far as Traquair is concerned I have mentioned how the first stone pele remains the core of the old house, and how, if one runs one's eye along the main elevations one can see how it was added to and gradually enveloped into a bigger whole. I have mentioned the 'L' shape of this early tower, and its twin purpose of providing defence around the door and a stair turret. Here the projection is quite small, just enough for the stairs, but in bigger examples, Glamis for instance, the arms of the 'L' are larger, with the stairs contained within a handsome semi-circular tower in the middle of the building. The first extension at Traquair returns the 'L' in a new and larger stair turret which was made in the sixteenth century, and this in turn was enlarged by a matching turret and new central front door by the first Earl of Traquair in 1642. The Earl was Lord High Treasurer of Scotland under Charles I and usually considered a bit of a trimmer, but in this he was no worse than most of his contemporaries, only less adept at the game, changing sides too often and at the wrong times, thus ending up a beggar in the streets of Edinburgh during the Cromwellian dictatorship. It is due to him, however, that we owe the present face of Traquair, for it was he who first linked up the separate portions to make a single cohesive whole, re-roofing the entire building and giving the façades a degree of symmetry. Not the

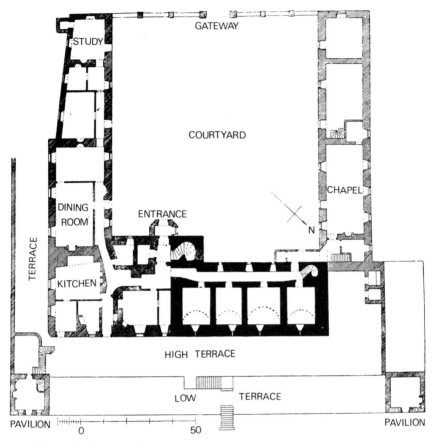

Traquair House: plan

symmetry that his successor desired when James Smith was employed to complete the task, but almost. This latter work, the last undertaken at Traquair if we discount a recent slight re-organization of its comforts undertaken for the present laird, consisted of throwing out side pavilions on either side of the main front and enclosing the courtyard so created with what are the most sumptuous and beautiful wrought iron gates and railings in Scotland.

The wrought iron at Traquair was the work of Scottish craftsmen trained in the native tradition, using constructional methods, notably mortice and tenon joints, that are hardly ever found in England and which originated in Flanders. Two similar sets of gates once regaled the entrances to Gogar House, in Midlothian, and Caroline Park, in Edinburgh, but in the first case the gates have been replaced with copies and in the second they have disappeared altogether. The Earl's Coat of Arms appears at the centre, tinctured in heraldic hues and supported by the most graceful and elaborate floral side pieces, which with the fleur de lis finials to the railings and the curvacious baroque urns atop the stone pillars creates an aura of sophisticated charm and finesse rare in Scotland in the mid-seventeenth century. These gates, incidentally, should not be mistaken for the better known ones called the 'steekit yetts', or shut-gates, with which the long avenue leading from the house to the main road ends. A yett in Scots, although merely describing a gate, as such, more often, and certainly historically refers to a specific kind of gate, not what we are talking about here but a rather cunningly devised defensive gate which was placed immediately behind the main door to most Scottish laird's towers and castles. It was composed of a network of strong iron bars which penetrated each other; the intersection of horizontal and vertical bars was reversed at opposite corners and repeated in diagonally opposite sections of the yett, creating a strong defensive feature unknown elsewhere (see illustration, page 93).

The so-called steekit yetts at Traquair are actually Georgian in date, and not at all like the traditional castle yett I have described, though they do resemble both in construction and to some extent in decorative detail the older Charles II gate and railings enclosing the forecourt to the house. They are, perhaps, the most popular feature of Traquair so far as the general public is concerned and mainly on account of a quaint legend that attaches to them. According to this they were closed when Prince Charles Edward passed through them in 1745 and may not be re-opened until a Stewart again sits on the throne. The snag is that no record exists of the Prince ever visiting Traquair, and a more plausible theory is that the gates were closed after the funeral of the last Countess some years later, the only flaw in this being that the lady died abroad. More probably they have never been opened and were never intended to be. They have no locking furniture and are almost certainly a Georgian conceit, one of the most ingenious Follies in the country. Old prints confirm this, showing no drive through the gates to the house, only a grassy avenue where animals feed, the existing drive running parallel being just another clever blind.

Besides tidying up the main front and giving symmetry to the view with his side pavilions and new gates, James Smith began to try and make something of the garden front at Traquair, building two tiers of terraces on the north-eastern side and ending these with identical ogee-roofed gazebos. The latter have survived and one is still decorated inside with interesting paintings which, with some contemporary panelling, awaited the restorer's attention, in 1972. The present laird, a descendant of the first Earl, has done much to bring Traquair back to life without spoiling it and has revealed a number of features hidden by the Victorians and Georgians, who prob-ably thought them of little importance. Amongst the most interesting are some very fine and unusual wall paintings which were discovered in the attic of the original pele tower. These are of animals and birds not unlike those in French tapestries of the late-medieval period and are probably con-temporary with somewhat similar paintings found at Hunting-tower, near Perth, which the official guide book dates as early sixteenth-century and describes as amongst the oldest in the country. Huntingtower has other interesting links with Traquair in that apart from its resulting from two or more extensions it is not a castle but a 'palas', that is to say, a hori-zontal manor as opposed to a vertical one. It is known in history as the seat of that Earl of Gowrie who kidnapped the youthful James VI and tried to rule Scotland thereby. The King escaped by pretending to go hunting, and in due course retribution followed; the Place of Ruthven, as it was called, was confiscated and changed in name, its owners becoming the victims of a counterplot in Perth in which the King himself had a part and in which the sons and other members of the Earl's family were killed. The Earl himself was a wizard and well-known on the Continent; his waistcoat containing a little book of charms and a quantity of pins when examined after his death.

There is a story that Shakespeare wrote *Macbeth* partly as a result of hearing about the Gowrie Conspiracy and its outcome in order to flatter the new King of Great Britain. Be this as it may, one of those who took part in the kidnapping of the sixteen-year-old sovereign was the Master of Glamis, and Glamis, of course, does feature in *Macbeth*. Glamis too is the next building we must consider. It is the most ancient Scottish house which is actually a castle and not a tower or manor, and is still inhabited and by the same family who built most of it. It is also I suppose the most celebrated of our *châteaux*, both as regards its architecture and its connections with Her Majesty the Queen Mother, who was brought up there, and H.R.H. Princess Margaret, who was born at Glamis and has a special place in the hearts of Scottish people. The existing castle dates in part from the mid-fifteenth century, was altered in the sixteenth and restored and enlarged in the seventeenth, and again in the eighteenth and nineteenth centuries, when 'Capability' Brown laid out the park, much to the annoyance of Sir Walter Scott who abominated such things; and come overlarge, over-baronialized additions were made to the original 'L' plan. This, however, can still clearly be seen, being emphasized by a clever contrivance on the roof whereby the two arms are provided with flat walkways instead of a pointed ridge, and these end in amusing circular pavilions. The wrought iron work edging these roof walks dates from about the same time as the gates to the courtyard at Traquair but is more robust in execution and largely composed of simple thistle and rose motives. At the centre is the great semi-circular staircase and entrance, the latter protected by a strong, nail-studded oak door with iron yett behind, while stretching out from here in two horizontal bands and two vertical ones is an exhibition of royal and noble heraldry sculptured in that distinctive bold relief that was typical of Scottish masonwork of the sixteenth and seventeenth centuries.

Inside Glamis there are some splendid plaster ceilings the largest and most beautiful of which covers the barrel vaulting of the Great Hall. This was made in strap-work designs and ornate hanging pendants such as one sees in Jacobean and late-Tudor mansions in the south; and there is a fine display of armorial pomp over the chimneypiece commemorating the

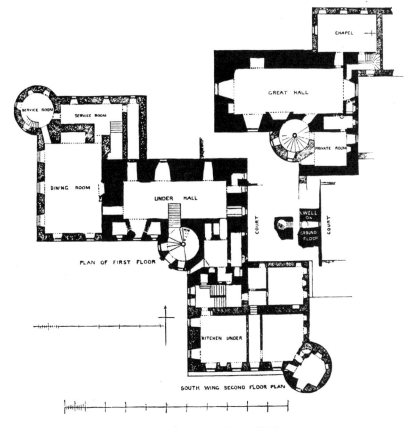

Glamis Castle: plan of first floor and Great Hall

Union of the Crowns in 1603, with supporting double caryatids on either side. The plasterers seem to have begun here, for similar moulds were employed but less professionally at two other castles in the north east, Craigievar, near Aberdeen, and Muchalls, near Stonehaven. The first was the home of a successful timber merchant, William Forbes, who wishing to emulate the gentry and to be upsides with his brother the Bishop of Aberdeen, created what is generally accepted as the climactic expression of Scottish castellated architecture. Muchalls was a subsidiary seat of the more ancient family of Burnett, of whom Bishop Burnett was a member, their principal residence

being at Crathes, on Deeside. The plaster caryatids and other features perceptibly weaken in style and execution as one passes first from Glamis to Muchalls and then to Craigievar, suggesting that perhaps Scottish apprentices were responsible for these other decorations or that the original plasterers got tired or had lost some of the moulds. In any event, the double caryatids are reduced to single male and female figures at Craigievar, while at Muchalls they are still represented in pairs, though cruder than at Glamis. Curiously there is no plaster work of this kind at Crathes, but one rather suspects it was intended and never carried out, for surely the great cavernous barrel vaulted ceiling in the drawing room was not meant to be left as it is today, in rough-hewn, coarse stonework with only one small portion clothed in any way whatsoever?

Traquair, which was in origin a tall, vertical tower house became, as we have seen, a horizontal manor, while Glamis, though spreading out its arms continued to go up and up. Its roofline has no equal for evocative grandeur anywhere; and besides its magnificent wrought-iron railings, and pavilions and expressively placed chimney stalks, it bristles with 'extinguisher-roof' turrets, corbelled out at the corners from the main line of the red sandstone masonry, and in one case rising from the finial of a dormer window, making one think of middle-aged wimpled ladies and prying witches. For Glamis is a strange place, haunted by a real ghost, with a curse on its family and full of that sense of gloomy fey which has caused the untimely deaths of several of its lords and ladies. The iron bars over some of the windows are another sinister but authentic feature, as too is the laigh, or lower hall, vaulted and almost certainly comprising stonework from the first castle built on this site. What date that could be is conjectural but history tells us that Malcolm II died here in 1033.

The scene of the murder of Duncan is shared with Cawdor, though is more likely to have been Glamis, and the story of *Macbeth*, as has already been suggested, has a possible base in the story of the Gowrie Conspiracy. The vaults of the laigh hall, were probably in existence when the first Stewart king, Robert II, gave the barony of Glamis to his daughter on her marriage to Sir John Lyon in the second half of the fourteenth

Glamis Castle, Angus, from the south-west

century, and the first laird's tower on the 'L' plan was itself
built about 1445. This is almost exactly contemporaneous with
Cawdor in Nairnshire. The chapel at Glamis was decorated
by Jacob de Wet, who was also responsible for the series of a
hundred or more royal portraits that hang in the Long Gallery
at Holyroodhouse, these being painted in less than a year and
modelled, except for Charles II and James VII and II, on
earlier likenesses made by George Jamesone, the 'Scottish
Van Dyck', for Charles I's coronation. Amongst the most
intriguing of the Glamis paintings is one showing Mary
Magdalene greeting Christ in the garden on Easter Morning,
with Our Lord wearing a hat. Legend has taken hold of this
representation to inform us that the artist, failing to be paid
by the Earl of Strathmore and Kinghorne, painted the hat in
to annoy his patron. In practice it was de Wet who broke his
contract, sending inferior artists from Dundee to complete the
work instead of coming himself, and, of course, it was perfectly
normal for Christ to wear a hat in this particular context,
when Mary Magdalene mistook him for the gardener. The
chapel is most interesting just the same and is the only place

Cawdor Castle: plan of ground floor

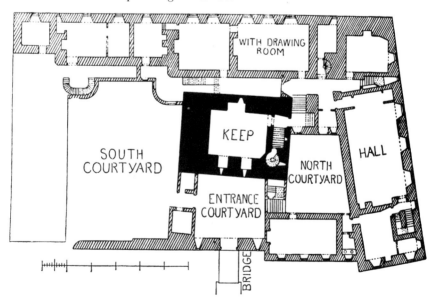

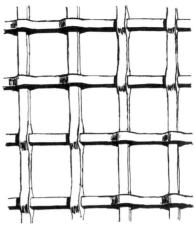

(*left*) Entrance to Drummond Castle, Perthshire, showing yett. (*right*) Diagram to show construction of a yett

where the old, Jacobite liturgy of the disestablished episcopal Church of Scotland is still regularly used as printed.

Cawdor is much less grand than Glamis and not nearly so consciously 'baronial' in appearance. It is also different in that its core is a simple central tower, not on the 'L' plan but rectangular and capped at each corner with a pepperpot turret. It might almost be called a keep, though dating from the fifteenth century and owing its turrets, sentry walks and garde-robes to the sixteenth. Around are the walls of what might in a previous age have been called the enceinte, with gatehouse and drawbridge, the latter being the only one extant in Scotland. The present laird's house is attached to this enceinte and was built for the most part in the reign of Charles I. Later the usual nineteenth-century additions and improvements came, but fortunately these were not too extensive and Cawdor Castle today retains an old world look not wholly un-evocative of its history and legends. Like Glamis it has its muckle iron yett, though James VI and I, always anxious to curb the power of the gentry and also in a genuine dislike of violence and bloodshed, ordered all such provocative objects to be destroyed. There are many surviving despite the royal edict, notable examples being at Drummond Castle, Perth-

shire Seat of the Earl of Ancaster, Lennoxlove, which is the
East Lothian home of the Duke of Hamilton, and Coxton, in
Moray, a 'toy' tower of defence dating from as late as 1644.

None of the buildings discussed so far are castles in the
medieval sense; they are inhabited houses with turrets and
certain baronial features, but except in the case of Huntingtower and Cawdor, scarcely defensive, or at any rate military,
in feeling or direct purpose. There are not many of these left;
they were too uncomfortable for one thing and for another
they were abandoned or radically altered in more peaceful
days. However, there is one, and that the supreme example
of its kind and still inhabited. This is Borthwick, which, however, dates from the same period as Traquair, Glamis and the
rest, making its martial appearance and remarkable state of
preservation all the more extraordinary. It is also a much
enlarged version of the 'L'-shaped tower, only in duplicate,
which is peculiar to Scotland and which forms the basis of
almost every Scottish house of defence. Borthwick is formed

Laird's burial aisle, Borthwick, Midlothian, with stone slab roof

of two 'Ls' joined in the middle making a massive building, tall, with the minimum of penetration and culminating in a heavily machicolated, uncrenellated battlement and heavy stone slab roof. Crenellations on the English and to some extent Continental models were very rare in Scotland, where the plain balustrading of the battlements was only occasionally pierced with an indentation near the corner, providing a bartisan, or small round-edged sentry's lookout. The entire building is faced in finely wrought and coursed stone, or ashlar, which is as good today as when new. In a structure as large as Borthwick the projecting short arms are much too big merely to contain wheelstairs, they are part of the defence, and the stairs are carried up within the thickness of the walls themselves. Everything is constructed of stone, even the ceilings, some of which are barrel vaulted and semi-circular, while the Great Hall is contained within a huge pointed Gothic vault. It is warmed by an enormous open fireplace, with conical hood supported by pillasters with handsomely carved capitals, and still possesses such refinements as a buffet recess and pantry with washhand basin, plus separate entrance to the kitchen quarters, the comings and goings to and from which were originally masked by a screen. There is also a chapel, replete with piscina and slab credence. The figure of 30,000 tons has been estimated as the weight of the masonry in this inspiring pile, which has no equal in Britain. To it came Mary, Queen of Scots and Bothwell shortly after their marriage in 1567, but they soon departed, and this is the secret of the castle's preservation; it was never seriously besieged and had, until Cromwell knocked a short run of its battlements off, a continuously peaceful history.

Borthwick stands on what was once a motte and keep, part of its enceinte, or outer defence wall, today represented by a restored gatehouse. It is, however, neither a motte and bailey castle, nor a 'castle of enceinte', as the medieval successor to the first came to be called, but a Scottish tower of defence like all the others except for its size, unusual strength and immaculate condition. Castles of enceinte, or castles in which the idea of the central redoubt was given up for one in which an enlarged gatehouse became in effect the main point of defence, and the outer walls comprehended the ancillary

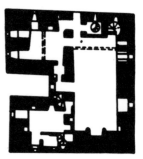

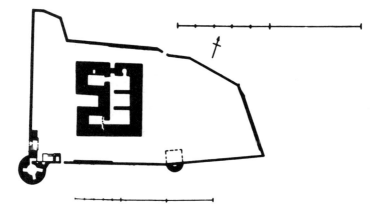

Borthwick Castle: (*above*) plan of first floor; (*below*) basement and enceinte

buildings, with the central area an open courtyard, were built throughout northern Europe in the second half of the Middle Ages, and some were erected in Scotland, notably at Kildrummy, in Aberdeenshire, which has already been mentioned, Bothwell, in Lanarkshire, which has a circular keeptower and Doune, in Perthshire, which is the completest of the three and has been partially restored in recent times. Such castles are not specifically Scottish and belong neither to the period nor the style of building under discussion, but they have a place in the evolution of what was to become in the sixteenth and seventeenth centuries the courtyard or palace plan, being distant ancestors of Falkland, Holyroodhouse and Linlithgow. I shall have to deal with these in a later chapter, meantime it may be worth saying something about two interesting intermediary structures, Rowallan Castle, in Ayrshire, and Stobhall, or Stobschaw as it used to be called, in Perthshire. These are neither quite castles of enceinte nor palaces, but show in embryo form how the latter derived from the former; they are also very Scottish and therefore within our present context.

Rowallan is conspicuous for its twin round towers capped with conical stone roofs that mark its gatehouse entrance, and which are attached, not separated from the rest of the building. This runs, like a castle of enceinte, along the outer walls, with an enclosed courtyard behind. The date is early

Rowallan Castle: plan at courtyard level

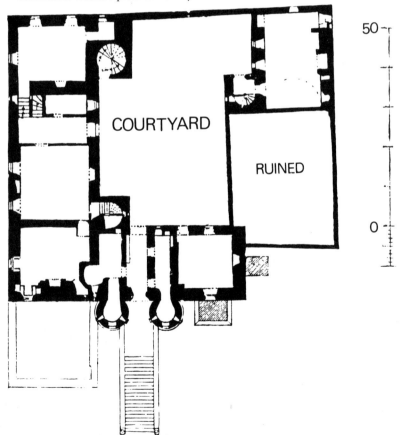

sixteenth-century, and the effect is not unlike the more
sophisticated essay in the style James V undertook at Falkland,
when he employed French and Flemish masons to construct
a hunting lodge for him on the model of Chambord. One
must not exaggerate, and Rowallan is a much simpler, almost
gauche affair by comparison, but the form is there, the semi-
circular gatehouse turrets with entrance beneath, and palas
against the barmkin wall. Oliver Hill in his *Scottish Castles of
the Sixteenth and Seventeenth Centuries*, comments on the lack of
corbelling, a feature most unusual in Scotland, where corbelling
was a most popular device both in defensive buildings and as a
decorative form in Jacobean times. This lack is, perhaps, a
sign of the trend towards palas architecture, and in place of
it are binding cable courses, a favourite feature in Manueline
Convents in Portugal, *châteaux* of the Loire and in the greater
Scottish castles of the James V era. Rowallan was the birthplace of Elizabeth Muir, first wife of Robert II, and the
present attractive castle, roofed but not inhabited, was largely
the creation of John Muir, whose grandfather fell at Flodden
and whose father fell at Pinkie in 1547. The Royal Coat of

Stobhall, dower house of the Drummonds, near Perth

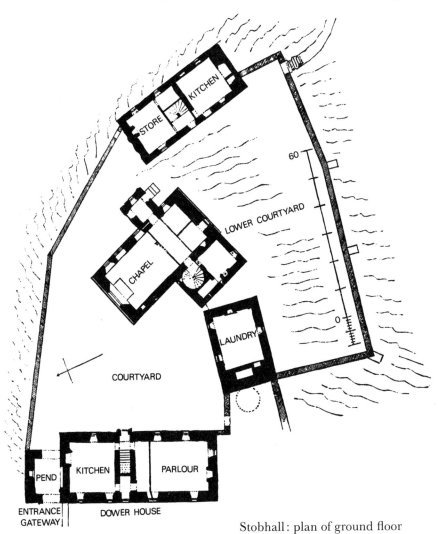

STORE

KITCHEN

60

LOWER COURTYARD

CHAPEL

LAUNDRY

0

COURTYARD

PEND   KITCHEN   PARLOUR

ENTRANCE
GATEWAY   DOWER HOUSE

Stobhall: plan of ground floor

Arms appears with those of the Muir family above the gateway
which is approached by a steep, straight stairway, the building
crowning a slight knowe above a burn.

Stobhall was begun about the same time and became in
the early seventeenth century the Dower House of the family

of Drummond. It is today the Scottish Seat of the Earl of
Perth, chief of the Drummond clan. The chapel, which is the
most important part historically, has already been described;
it stands roughly in the middle of the site almost where one
might expect a keep, while the rest of the buildings are ranged
around the outer walls as with a castle of enceinte, the whole
being entered via an arched pend under one end of the Dower
House. This arrangement combines ancient and modern
ideas in a remarkable and delightful way, and is enhanced by a
lovely Jacobean rose garden with contemporary sundial,
formal paths and clipped hedges.

There is no garden worth the name at Borthwick, which
even now remains a gaunt reminder of sterner times and hardly
inviting as a place of residence in any age, though it is lived in
occasionally. One would think such a solid mass of masonry
was meant to put the fear of death into a greater foe than some
poor lowland neighbour, yet this is not so. It was a private
fortress, the mighty tower of a strong man armed. It may, of
course, be argued that it stood near enough the Border to deter
the English, but we are now a hundred years or more after
Bannockburn, and so far as the Borderers were concerned
nationality was of secondary importance, they were English
or Scots last and Borderers first. What mattered was the
family, the clan, its place and possessions and what it could
get of other people's. Hence it is that here as nowhere else in
Britain a fairly similar style of military architecture crosses
the boundary between Carlisle and Berwick to produce the
so-called 'pele tower', which is known as such in Northumberland as in the Scottish Border Counties. The wooden redoubts
and timber palisades were of course replaced in the fifteenth
and sixteenth centuries by free standing stone piles, such as
the tower incorporated in Traquair House and the bigger,
double one that is Borthwick, both 'L'-shaped with their main
defences around the door. A smaller version and possibly
better appreciated one on account of its smaller size is the
Castle of Affleck, just north of Dundee, which, like Borthwick,
has survived intact, and although no longer inhabited, but
standing in the grounds of a newer property like some medieval
plaything, is untouched and completely authentic.

Affleck is a fifteenth-century structure whose interest lies as much in its interior as its exterior, which is a simple 'L' on plan with the usual stair rising in the short nib. The hall, or Solar, remains unaltered except for its lack of furnishings. There is a large open fireplace at one end, deeply recessed windows with bench seats and a private stair to the laird's lavatory, with window both to the outside and back into the hall so as an eye could be kept on things whilst en route to obey calls of nature. Above is a withdrawing room and chapel, or oratory, which again is intact in all its particulars, with piscina, aumbry and Holy Water stoop; in which respect it is almost unique in Scotland. This miniature Borthwick, if one can call it such, was built by a branch of the same family as James Boswell of Auchinleck, the pronounciation of which has always been nearer to Auchleck, hence Affleck. The entrance to the castle is at ground level, which is not usual, it being commoner for lairds to provide themselves with a movable ladder, as the Celtic monks did at Brechin and Abernethy at the entrances to their round towers, and to have the door on the first floor. The lower spaces were reserved for stables and stores. Curiously too only one floor at Affleck is vaulted—the bottom—while the walls are built of random rubble and not of that marvellous ashlar like Borthwick. Some of the windows retain their original iron bars, there is a parapet at roof level projected on a

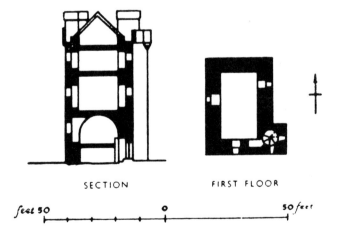

SECTION   FIRST FLOOR

feet 50   o   50 feet

Affleck Castle: section and plan of first floor

simple two-course run of corbelling, and two cap-houses, or ways out onto the roof, one above the chapel and another at the top of the main stair. These open onto sentry walks with four rounded bartisans, and the gable ends are finished with domestic crow-steps in the normal Scots manner.

There is a big jump between the dates of Borthwick and Affleck, and succeeding peles and towers of defence in the same state of wholeness, the first because contentious history largely passed it by, the second because it remained inhabited until the mid-eighteenth century when its comforts, apparently adequate for a Scottish laird and his lady in the time of the later Stuarts, were scarcely so in that of the Georges. Peles of course were not built for comfort at all and that may explain why so many of them were allowed to fall down or decay when James VI moved to London and the Border ceased to have any major political or economic importance. It would also explain their extension into larger houses, as at Traquair, while others were kept as masonic heirlooms in the grounds of brand new buildings. At Amisfield, near Dumfries, the Johnstone owners of the property actually undertook the erection of their pele after the ending of Border strife; and it remains to this day, the most perfect specimen of its kind in the country, never having seen a raid or suffered any scaith since it was completed in the early seventeenth century. Almost every feature of this remarkable specimen of the Jacobean Border vernacular is little more than an architectural affectation, from plainish, oblong base to roof-line, which bursts upon the eye with a veritable fistful of turrets and corbels, dormers, martial pretences and a double cap-house. All of which makes it more like a wizard's eyrie than a gentleman's residence, a place for human rooks, with four rooms one above the other instead of ranged on one or two floors, which would not only have been more convenient but perfectly safe and appropriate at the time.

Not far from Amisfield is Elshieshields, which is not a Jacobean Folly standing in the garden of a more modern mansionhouse but a genuine Border tower, replete with authentic outlook turrets, necessary cap-house and an enormous chimney at its highest point which was used as a fire-bucket to give the alarm when a raid was imminent. Elshieshields is attached to a later house, but is roofed and in part inhabited.

The most bloodthirsty and lawless borderers were probably the 'fierce Fenwicks', of whom one of their own number wrote in 1597; 'If Jesus Christ were amongst them, they woulde deceave him, if he woulde heere, trust and followe theire wicked councels'. They lived on either side of the Border and fought each other as well as everyone else. The remains of one of their keeps survives in a farmhouse called Fenwick that stands on the eastern banks of the Teviot Water as it flows towards Hawick, within sight of Branxholm, where, according to Sir Walter Scott, in *The Lay of the Last Minstrel*, twenty-nine knights of the Scott clan once hung up their shields. Nearby is Harden, another Scott hideout, and so carefully sited as to be invisible until one is right upon it. Stolen English cattle used to be driven up into a fold in the hills hereabouts and could be kept there for quite a time in perfect safety; but not only cattle suffered at the hands of the reivers, for murder was prevalent too, the common people living in terror of their lives whenever a raid took place. Witness of this communal aspect of Border lawlessness are the bastel houses, bastles in Northumberland, such as the one at Jedburgh, where folk fled to safety when the alarm was given. This particular bastel is now a museum and known as 'Mary, Queen of Scots' House'; but it was built as a shelter for the populace and closely resembles a private pele except that it used to be roofed with thatch not tiles. Dotted about the hillsides were other, smaller bastels, but none have survived except where incorporated in modern farmsteads. The name is obviously related to the French Bastille, and also, perhaps, to the Bastides, French and English, that existed and still exist in south-western France; fortified towns and hamlets built by the opposing sides in the Hundred Years War. There is a good English bastle at Melkridge, near Haltwhistle, which has retained its fire-bucket like the one at Elshieshields.

Further north the term pele loses its meaning and the more correct term for a not dissimilarly conceived building is a tower of defence. These were erected under Royal Licence, but apart from their having no fire-bucket were much the same as peles in shape and size and were equally menacing to their neighbours. A splendid example is Hallbar Tower, in the

Clyde Valley near Lanark. This was the property of the Lock-harts of Lee, who owned, indeed still do, the 'Lee Penny', or Talisman, which inspired Sir Walter Scott's novel. Curiously enough it was a Lockhart of Lee who, although a lowlander, was chosen as the model for the kilted figure that stands atop the 1745 Monument at Glenfinnan, the sculptor having mis-taken his portrait for one of Prince Charles Edward, who was only wearing trews.

Hallbar is lived in periodically as a weekend retreat, and rises rather interestingly from an orchard on a green hillside, as one imagines these small laird's towers did originally, for old records mention how in their vicinity the otherwise barren countryside was cultivated with fruit trees, plantations of flax, oak, willow, alder, aspen, plane and elm; and each laird had his kailyaird, or cabbage-patch, bee-boles, stables and doocot. The tower comprises a single oblong, without nib or other projection, and has its entrance at ground level, possibly because it also boasted a decent barmkin which kept out enemies and precluded the necessity of immediate retreat to the first floor at the sight of an adversary. The stair, with no separate turret, rises wholly within the thickness of the walls, winding round each storey like a dog-legged serpent, if one can imagine such a thing. The roof is a simple gable-ended affair with crow-steps, and on either side are small battlements, reached via a cap-house cum sentry-box, which, however, is rectangular and not rounded, and capped with a pointed stone roof, like a pinnacle. The roof proper is made of heavy stone slabs as at Borthwick, and there is a projecting garde-robe supported on corbels at second floor level. From the southern gable-end are other supports, probably for a missing wooden doocot and possibly also used as a defence platform when required. Doocots, attached to buildings or free-standing, rectangular and circular, played an important part in winter feeding in Scotland and their size, shape and number were strictly controlled by law. They were part of the accepted appurtenances of bonnet lairds, or small gentry, in Jacobean times when they became as much the symbol of social position as a source of food. I shall have more to say about them in a later chapter.

MacGibbon and Ross in their *Castellated and Domestic*

Architecture of Scotland, written in the second half of the nine-teenth century but still the *vade mecum* of many Scottish art historians, compare Hallbar tower with Coxton, near Elgin, though the first dates from the sixteenth century, at the latest, while the second was not built until 1644; when Inigo Jones was already established in the south; and even in Scotland several fine Renaissance buildings had already been erected, including Innes House, in the same locality as Coxton and for a member of the same family. Yet here we have in miniature practically every accepted feature of the traditional pele-cum-keep that appeared in our country from the fifteenth century onwards, all, that is, except the 'L'-plan with stair in the small arm, for at Coxton, as at Hallbar, the stair rises within the thickness of the walls. Otherwise, this square laird's tower of defence is approached via a single door at first floor level, is roofed in stone slabs, gable-ended with crow-steps, boasts stone-capped pepperpot turrets at two corners and a miniature sentry walk and crenellated bartisan at another. The rich, double-coursed corbelling supporting this tells of the late date, as does the elaborate and finely carved heraldry displaying the Innes Coat of Arms. The iron bars around the small and very few windows remain *in situ,* also the sturdy iron yett, lurking mischievously behind a studded oak door as at Glamis. Coxton tower is harled, with only the ashlar masonry being visible around the bartisan, turrets and chimneys. Harling is a term which needs some explanation since it is used indiscriminately nowadays to describe a number of external renderings, and especially roughcast. The latter is modern without any significance in original Scottish building, for harling is properly composed of river balast, lime and sand and was applied to exterior wall faces with a circular movement, often by hand, sometimes with a wooden float, thus giving the surface a particularly interesting and varied appearance. This surface should normally not be rough at all, but smooth, the rounded pebbles not cutting the knuckles as the finer chippings used today do, and any colour required was provided in the lime itself or by pigments added to it, not by oil-bound paints which seal the walls and prevent them from breathing and generally kill any aesthetic quality there might be. What one would really like to know is when harling was first used in

Scotland, and its origin. One quite expects it at Coxton, for it was introduced before the reign of Charles I, but when? Amisfield is not harled, though dating from the early seventeenth century, and indeed is notable for its coarse masonry, nor is Affleck, which is a century older, but Elshiesheilds is. Hallbar and Borthwick do not come into the discussion since they are faced in good ashlar. Glamis is not harled, neither is Cawdor, but Traquair is. My own theory is that nothing was harled until the mid-sixteenth century at the earliest, and that this method of hiding rough masonry behind an outer coating was brought to Scotland from the Low Countries as part of the great trade and cultural exchange that took place in the Jacobean period; and that such buildings as Elshiesheilds and Traquair were probably harled when they were enlarged or improved in the seventeenth century. Coxton, as has been suggested, would probably have been harled originally.

One extraordinary feature about Coxton, and particularly for its late date, is that every floor is vaulted and each in the opposite direction, alternating between semi-circular barrels and pointed. The entire building, therefore, is constructed of stone, and must have been extremely uncomfortable, inconvenient, damp and chilly, which makes it all the more surprising that it was considered at the time of its completion as an ideal home for a Scottish cavalier and remained inhabited, in part, until the nineteenth century, when a gardener lived there. It is difficult to say exactly why it was built except on account of the continuance of religious feuds in the north-east, where Protestant and Roman Catholic families contended with each other for power, even survival, long after 1603, and it remained necessary, therefore, to go on building for defence. On the other hand, no such explanation exists in the case of Scotstarvit Tower, in central Fife, which rivals Coxton in wholeness and interest, and which was built a short while earlier, in 1627. It was the home of Sir John Scot of Scotstarvit, a famous man of letters whose eyrie in one of the most prosperous and peaceful airts in Scotland became the resort of the learned and gifted of his generation. His wife was sister to the poet Drummond of Hawthornden, the first Scotsman to write in literary English and the man for whom Ben Jonson trudged all the way to Midlothian to compliment on his *Teares on the*

Scotstarvit Tower, Fife

death of Meliades, composed on the death of Henry, Prince of Wales, and a work, incidentally, that inspired Milton's *Lycidas*. How curious then that such exalted and artistic company should have found themselves gathered in what was, to all intents and purposes, a medieval tower, newly built, whose only concession to current modernity was a handsome Renaissance chimneypiece, since removed, in an upper chamber.

Scotstarvit is well constructed of regularly-coursed ashlar and is an 'L'-shaped tower, with studded oak door but no yett. The stair, as usual, mounts in the short covering projection. The place lacks shot or shut-holes and clearly was not primarily intended for defence, though there are no more or larger windows than one would expect in a medieval keep and the tower rises dramatically from nothing to dominate the countryside for miles around. The battlements are heavily corbelled and the cap-house is formed by an amusing and very nicely-finished circular turret, with stone roof and tiny decorative lucarnes, like a Fife Church tower. Beside it, between the eaves and the foot of the parapet, is a minute doocot, for a pair of doves? A peculiar feature of the roofline is the free-standing chimney stalk that rises like some pillar or obelisk at the west gable directly from the parapet, and which is attached to its gable by stone stays. The sight of this gives Scotstarvit an unusual but unforgettable appearance when seen from afar, especially as each fireplace has a separate chimney, the other two coming up more naturally at the gable-ends. The roof is covered with Angus slates, really split stones and two of the floors are barrel vaulted. The small windows are deeply recessed with stone window seats and probably once had wooden shutters. Other missing items are the tapestries, plasterwork and panelling that almost certainly gave some sense of being lived-in in the days of Sir John and his friends. There may also have been paintings on the undersides of the beams on the two non-vaulted floors, but there were only four rooms, one above the other, and although they did not have, as at Coxton, so primitive an arrangement that a mere hole in the floor was sufficient for food and other provisions to be brought up and down, it is difficult to imagine how Scotstarvit's house-parties were adequately provided for, both as regards nourishment and bedding. The laird might, I suppose, be thought of as a species of Scottish Montaigne, with his tower in the country. Certainly he had a poor opinion of many of his contemporaries, politicians and clerics, whom he ridiculed and lambasted in *Scot of Scotstarvit's Staggering State of Scots Statesmen*. He was also associated with the Reverend Timothy Pont's pioneer map-making, the first attempt to chart the whole of Scotland county by county, which was completed and appeared under the imprint of Blaeu of Amsterdam in 1654. The tower is in excellent condition, though no longer inhabited, and is open to the public. It is within sight of Hill of Tarvit, a mansion enlarged and partly rebuilt by Sir Robert Lorimer earlier this century, and which was originally designed by Sir William Bruce of Kinross and named Wemysshall. It then conformed to the Palladian mode as introduced into Scotland by Bruce in the reign of Charles II, less than fifty years after the building of Sir John Scot's medieval tower.

Despite its out-of-dateness vis-à-vis architecture in the south, and the suddenness with which its species was about to become extinct, Scotstarvit was by no means alone, for it was still important in the first half of the seventeenth century for *nouveau riche* lairds and other recipients of Royal Stewart favour to express their new found gentility or wealth by going baronial. Scotland has scores of towers and smaller castles from this period, many of them brand new, others made more impressive by the addition of extra turrets and towers, fake cannon and boastful sculpture. A good example of this is Tulliebole, on the borders of Kinross and Perthshire, which until acquired by a successful Edinburgh Lawyer at the beginning of the seventeenth century was a perfectly adequate, if plain, tower house, with no aggressive architectural features, merely well proportioned windows diminishing as they rose upwards and a series of roofs that told of modest extensions in the past. All at once the new laird celebrated his 'arrival' by throwing out a small but excessively ornate wing near the door, which he crowned with conical turrets, linking one to a 'toy' sentry walk, or crenellated gallery along which no sentry would or could ever walk. In the corner of his new projection, where it joined the old house, he ran up a semi-circular tower supported on heavy corbelling, and near this he made a shut, not shot, hole and placed the date, and his and his wife's monograms and Arms. Inside Tulliebole there is what might be termed a great hall, with minstrel's gallery,

Houston, West Lothian, a seventeenth-century laird's house

very similar to one at nearby Aldie, and with a big open chimneypiece supported by a lintel some eleven feet wide. This resembles one in The Study at Culross, a contemporary private house associated with Bishop Leighton and now National Trust for Scotland Headquarters for West Fife.

Aldie is a genuine castle and was built as such; it was a seat of the Mercers of Meiklour one of whom served with Joan of Arc against the English in the Hundred Years War. Ian Lindsay restored both it and Tulliebole, the latter representing, without its Jacobean status symbols, the same sort of tall tower house he himself inhabited at Houstoun, in West Lothian. This is a non-martial, non-baronial manor house such as were fairly common in more settled lowlands, not over-turreted, but with crow-stepped gables, prominent chimney stalks and surrounded by a typical Scots garden in which, as in France, the different sections were divided by hedges and paths into *potager*, orchard and formal garden. Other examples worth mentioning are at Fountainhall, near Haddington, in East Lothian, which was the home of the Law Lord of the same name whose *dicta* are often quoted and who judged minor cases in an upper room of his country house. It is a straggling but charming place which some have compared to a Cotswold manor, though it has its corner turret over the entrance, very Scottish crow-steps and other features. There is a handsome sundial on the west gable and two doocots, one real and the other added for symmetry. The garden is particularly attractive and like the one at Houstoun arranged in a series of separate sections according to use. Not far away is Pilmuir, which in its present form dates from 1642, which makes it particularly interesting compared to Coxton, for it has not a single baronial or defensive feature and is wholly a country house, two storeys in height with an attic, and showing on its garden front a regular façade with steps and door at the centre and equally spaced windows. The entrance is on the north side in a little porch, which makes the building 'T'-shaped, and this small crow-stepped extension has at one side a curious squinch, or arch across a corner supporting a spiral stair turret. There are some original bee-boles in the garden and a pretty large rectangular doocot, which rather suggests the house may have been bigger once, though there are no signs of this in the actual structure, nor the enlargement of windows, some of which are amongst the earliest sashes erected in Scotland before the use of weights.

With Pilmuir and to some extent Fountainhall we are getting into the realms of small mansions rather than towers or castles, though both are in the Scottish vernacular tradition despite their Caroline dates and internal comforts. Ford House, near Dalkeith, is in similar vein, smaller than the others yet convenient enough to be the country residence of the Frasers of Lovat when they came south. It is today the home of the County Architect and Planner for East Lothian who has restored it and maintains it in excellent condition, even to the inimitable orange colour of its harled walls. This effect was achieved in the past by adding copper wires to the lime in the mixture, but copperas is now used instead. The high pitched roof is covered with sepia-hued slates which go well with the orange walls and grey stonework, and the 'L'-shaped house has at the re-entrant angle an octagonal stair turret capped with an ogee cupola and gilded cock. In the old walled garden are bee-boles and there is a doocot against the house. Both the present dining room and drawing room are panelled in the late-seventeenth century manner, and there can be little doubt that in these interiors the influence of Sir William Bruce's work at Holyrood for the King can be traced.

A castle which is also a laird's country house more on the lines of Houstoun and Tulliebole is Kellie Castle, in Fife, which although attached to an earlier tower is wholly domestic in character. It is not harled, however, as others are, the warm, iron-streaked local stone being allowed to be seen and not covered up with a layer of 'porridge', which makes one wonder if there is any special reason for the difference. Ian Lindsay was most keen on harling, Sir Robert Lorimer, who was brought up at Kellie, clearly was not. The castle used to belong to the Oliphants, then the Erskines, who became Earls of both Mar and Kellie. One of them added a Jacobean manor house to the original keep, so that in some respects Kellie has affinities with Traquair, certainly in size and also in its being completed in the seventeenth century, when newer windows were inserted, possibly by Bruce, whose own estate of Balcaskie adjoins and who probably also added the existing handsome chimney stalks. Charles II's plasterers, who worked at both Holyrood and Balcaskie, may not actually have made the splendid baroque ceiling in the Vine Room at Kellie, but if not they certainly guided the hands that did; and here again are shades of Holyrood in the central painted panel, which was the work of the ubiquitous de Wet. What makes this house even more interesting and significant is the way in which the varying periods, unlike at Traquair, where they were systematized, so to speak, by James Smith, are exposed to view like so much archaeology, especially on the north elevation, facing the garden. One runs one's eye along the building from west to east to be regaled with the most remarkable array of gablets, turrets, dormers, chimneys, crow-steps, squinches and oversailings, or turrets in which the conical roofs have been sliced off and replaced with a lean-to. The total effect is more like one side of a street in an old Scotch burgh than of the façade of a castle. The reason for much of this apparently romantic diversity is of course functional—it represents the architectural answers arrived at by Scottish masons when overcoming some odd structural difficulty; but why does the squinch have to be there when the turret it supports could just as easily reach to the ground instead of having to be corbelled out a few feet above it? To me this suggests a certain amount of obstinacy on the part of the masons, but whether they were so by nature or merely caught out by their own waywardness one cannot say. Certainly such il-logicalities are not uncommon in Scottish masonwork of the period, and at Burleigh Castle, in neighbouring Kinross-shire, a flat-arched squinch supports even more extraordinary convulsions in which semi-circles, rectangles and 'S'-shapes combine in a truly fantastical display of architectural ingenuity. It is as if no shape was impossible and the builders simply overcame their self-created problems as they arrived, giving some buildings a fluidity of form that almost presages the use of re-inforced concrete.

Thus the freedom of outline apparent on the garden façade at Kellie was not intentional as in some other castles, such as Claypotts, on the outskirts of Dundee, where the traditional 'L'-plan has become a 'Z', with two semi-circular towers linked by a rectangular centrepiece; and these towers burst

(*above*) Claypotts Castle, Dundee. (*below*) Claypotts Castle: plan of the four floors

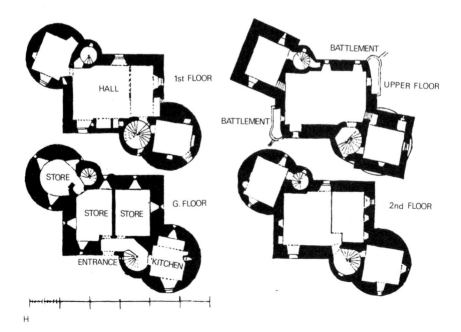

1st FLOOR

HALL

BATTLEMENT

UPPER FLOOR

BATTLEMENT

STORE

STORE STORE

G. FLOOR

2nd FLOOR

ENTRANCE KITCHEN

H

forth at their tops with little oblong single-storeyed houses crow-stepped and corbelled out from their bases like cottages on stilts. Here the inhabitants lived safe from all the skirmishing at ground level, protected from glancing cannon balls by their round towers and from being intruded upon by neighbours by an elaborate system of spy-holes and shot-holes around the door; but Claypotts was built all at once, quaint as it is, as a piece of self-defensive architecture. Its date is *circa* 1560, which shows how late internecine strife went on in Scotland. It is roofed and complete though no longer lived in.

Kellie, which is mostly later and certainly more inconsequential in appearance, was tenanted and restored in the nineteenth century by Professor James Lorimer, father of the architect who, when a youth, was given his head to lay out the garden. I have already said something about the difference between the traditional Scottish garden and the better known English kind, the main one being its retention of Renaissance and other older-fashioned features well into the twentieth century, when herbaceous borders and flowers near the house spread north and transformed things. Robert Lorimer tried to compromise, and although not directly influenced by Gertrude Jekyll and Sir Edwin Lutyens seems to have arrived at much the same conclusions and to have become, like them, imbued with the spirit which sought to merge architectural formalism with a more natural approach. At Earlshall, a neighbouring estate in Fife, the youthful architect got his first important commission, and *carte blanche*, to restore an ancient Scottish house and to re-lay from a ploughed field its garden. The building was not ruinous, merely decayed and empty, but roofed, so that a great deal of the work was concerned with rehabilitation of the interior; and here Lorimer showed his genius for the native style in furnishing and furniture and in his recreation where necessary of existing painted decorations such as those in the Long Gallery. This runs the length of the building on the attic floor and consists of a barrel-vaulted ceiling composed of boards painted in *grisaille*, displaying the armorial devices of the principal Scottish gentry together with a series of improving mottos which were a fad of the day. These were in a poor state when Lorimer came to deal with them but not entirely irredeemable and their resuscitation and partial repainting must be counted amongst the minor miracles of the age. Another ceiling of the kind, but less inhibited in subject and painted in full colour, survives at Pinkie House, near Musselburgh, and this may have served as a guide.

Earlshall, possibly on account of its proximity to Dundee, is 'Z'-shaped and clearly related to Claypotts, though only one tower is completely round and there are a number of sophisticated features that may have derived from work done at Falkland Palace by French and French-trained masons for James V. Indeed, the laird's family were connected by marriage with the family of the King's Master of Works, who had his home at Myres Castle, which sports similar Renaissance details, as does Monimail Tower, central Fife retreat of the Archbishops of St Andrews. Elsewhere, in the former Great Hall at Earlshall, Lorimer set up a magnificent oak screen copied from the one at Falkland, which is virtually indistinguishable from Continental models in France and in Spain. More pertinently still he was able to create both a new formal garden and one in the then-becoming-fashionable mode

Renaissance Garden, Edzell Castle, Angus

sponsored by Lutyens, in which the clipped hedges and topiary work of one are linked to the other by pergolas and paths and divided by changing levels and walls all arranged in the most beguiling manner.

In recreating the historical part of Earlshall's garden the architect may have had in mind the few remaining old gardens in Scotland such as that at Edzell, in Angus, which was made in the early seventeenth century by the Lord Edzell of the day, a much-travelled and erudite man who brought Continental work people and craftsmen over to assist him to develop his estate economically and artistically. German miners were amongst these and some of the sculptural panels decorating the walls of his Renaissance garden were copied directly from Nuremberg prints. The central space is occupied by geometrically-disposed rose beds lined by box hedges and rising to a small 'knot' in the middle in the Italian way. It has been reconstituted by the Department of the Environment and is beautifully kept by them. The protecting walls are punctuated in an intriguing and clever pattern to display horticulturally and masonically the arms and crest of the laird, a series of chequered holes being filled with blue and white lobelia which, set against the red sandstone voids of the masonry, form the Lindsay Coat, whose crest, three mullets, or stars, appear at appropriate intervals above. The 'dished' holes were formerly painted blue and white for winter, and the flowers they contain in summer are brought every year from Holyrood. A bath house and gazebo, both in the Scots vernacular, with crow-steps and Angus slate roof, complete this fine Scottish garden.

Further north, at Pitmedden, in Aberdeenshire, the National Trust for Scotland have recreated, with the help of Dr James Richardson of the old Ancient Monuments Office, a classical Scottish garden of the late seventeenth century. This belongs to the age of Sir William Bruce and is again bordering on the next chapter, but as the general layout really devolves from earlier precepts one might say something about it here. It was conceived as a whole, with fountain centrepiece, sundials and statuary as a part, but principally as a series of intricately laid out patterns of paths and low hedges interspersed with flowering features delineating thistles and roses, armorial devices and other formal designs. In drawing up his scheme Dr Richardson was inspired by a print of the gardens at Holyroodhouse as they appeared in the Charles I period. Pitmeddan, like Edzell, has its gazebos and bath house, the latter capped with a typical late seventeenth-century ogee-shaped roof such as Bruce used at Kinross and James Smith at Traquair. Not far away, at Crathes, is another seventeenth-century Scottish garden recently recreated but keeping the original pattern of clipped yews some of which are nearly 300 years old and exceed twelve feet in height. They seem as much part of the architecture of the place as the castle itself, which consists of a sixteenth-century tower and a Queen Anne wing. The latter has had to be rebuilt rather more plainly after a recent fire, while the former probably stands on older foundations, for it was Robert the Bruce who first granted the lands and right to build on them to the ancestor of the last laird, Sir James Burnett of Leys, at the same time as to the Irvines of Drum, who still live in a neighbouring seventeenth-century mansion attached to a squat unadorned keep of the fourteenth century.

The Jacobean tower at Crathes is one of the masterpieces of Scottish castellated architecture and features in all the books on that style. Its upper floors sprout with corner turrets, gables and jolly chimney stalks, dormer windows, gargoyles and engaging details of one sort or another. It is harled except for the stone finishes of the highly decorative corbelling and heraldic outcrops that break the surface so interestingly; but curiously enough Crathes scarcely resembles Craigievar, its most serious rival for attention and with which it is often associated. It is, of course, earlier in date and was the property of an ancient family, Norman in origin, and not the ready-made creation of a wealthy merchant. The interior is remarkable for a number of things, not least its painted ceilings, which are largely devoted to the heroes of antiquity and the Bible. Thus the Chamber of the Nine Nobles commemorates the exploits of three pagan heroes, Hector, Alexander the Great and Julius Caesar; three Jewish heroes, Joshua, David and Judas Maccabeus; and three Christians, King Arthur, Charlemagne and Godfrey de Bouillon, first King of Jerusalem. The date of these is 1602, but it could just as well have been

Jacobean doocot at Craigston, Banff

any time from the middle of the sixteenth, to the middle of the seventeenth, when the subject matter could have been seen anywhere in France, Italy or Spain, woven into tapestries, carved in stone or wood or painted as here. Hector, David and two other carved figures survive at Craigston Castle, in Banffshire, home of the Urquharts of that ilk, one of whom was the celebrated cavalier and wit Sir Thomas Urquhart of Cromarty, the Scot who first translated Rabelais into English and is reputed to have died in a fit of laughter on hearing of the Restoration of Charles II in 1660. No tapestries of the period have survived, but they were ordered for and certainly once hung in Stirling Castle and at Falkland, while stone heroes regale both these Royal residences to this day. There are painted ceilings all over Scotland, and others at Crathes itself, also a Long Gallery ceiled with oak, which is rare in Scotland, and a small chapel at one end, which was customary.

Aberdeenshire is well known for the number and variety of its castles, so much so that it is no accident that when Queen Victoria and the Prince Consort came to live on Deeside

they built Balmoral in what the Prince thought was true
Scotch Baronial. He copied features from Craigievar, the ogee
cupolas on the cap-houses, and from Castle Fraser the elegant
balustrading at the top of the round tower; though the rest is
a little too ordered and German, too methodically studied to
be quite vernacular through and through. Still it was a
genuine attempt to be so, and that is something. Apart from
Drum Castle and Crathes, both on the way from Aberdeen to
Balmoral, there is Midmar, a 'Z'-shaped pile of great charm,
and Braemar itself, an oddity now but once an excellent example
of an 'L'-type tower, with turrets at the corners and semi-
circular stair at the re-entrant angle. It was burned down by
the Farquharsons of Invercauld, neighbours of the Royal
Family, in 1689, but they have since made amends by restoring
it as a modern house. They have not removed the crenellations
that replaced the original extinguisher-roofs in the mid-
eighteenth century, when Braemar was taken over by the
British Army and made into a fort, with gun-turrets and star-
shaped outer defences. It still has its iron yett however, and
the pit prison made by the Earls of Mar long ago.

Most famous of all Aberdeenshire Castles, Craigievar
belongs to Donside, to the north, where one will also find
Castle Fraser; which is another 'Z'-shaped edifice with round
and square towers linked as at Earlshall and Midmar, only
here there is a decidedly French look perhaps due to the
origins of its builders, plus refinements commensurate with its
late date, about 1620. The very highly pitched roof broken
with stone-finialed dormers showing the Fraser *fraises*, Renaissance balustrading in place of battlements and nicely proportioned cap-house turret all speak of travelled owners and
professional building, though in one particular, the use of the
wounds of Christ in armorial form in the chapel may seem out
of place in an ostensibly Protestant country and century, out
of place, that is, unless one recalls that Aberdeenshire was the
main refuge of native episcopacy, its worthies refusing to subscribe to Covenanting invaders even at the point of the sword.
Above the entrance to Castle Fraser hangs, one can only use
that term though it is literally not correct, a stone 'tapestry'
entirely composed of heraldic features the principal part of
which displays the Coat of Arms of James VI of Scots and I

Craigievar Castle, Aberdeenshire, from the south

of England. No such chivalric splendour informs the exterior
of Craigievar, though the Royal Jacobean Achievement does
appear in plaster over the chimneypiece in the Great Hall.

If Craigievar was not actually a structure of stone and
mortar, slate, iron and timber one would be tempted to call it
a toy, a child's plaything not to be used except to provide
amusement and pleasure. Under the National Trust this is
more or less what it has recently become, but since 1620 it
has been the home of the descendants of William Forbes, an
Aberdeen timber merchant, who entered it by the one and
only door and left it by an upstairs window, the stair, which
begins as a straight one from the door before becoming a
serpent within its own special tower, being so narrow and
contortious that coffins had to be lowered down from the
windows of the rooms in which the lairds and their dames
expired. Indeed, the bonnet of the last laird, which I have seen,
was too wide to be worn on the upper stair. The castle is all
of a piece and shaped somewhere between a 'Z' and an 'L'

Craigievar Castle: plan of ground floor and enlarged plan of Hall

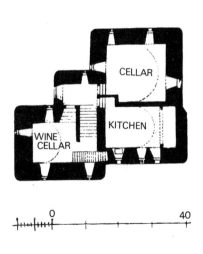

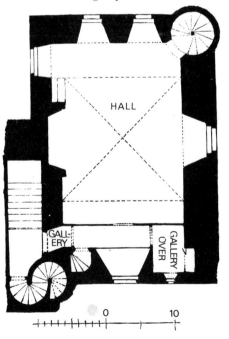

with the square re-entrant tower becoming curved near the top by the corbelling out of a large half-turret. This is crowned by a handsome Renaissance balustrade contemporary with work at Castle Fraser and possibly by the same hand. There are two ogee roofed cap-houses, numerous outbursts of double storyed turrets with conical roofs, crow-steps and dormers, none of which, it is said, has been added to or altered since the castle was built. One wonders about the sash windows in this context. This form was not introduced into Scotland until the second half of the seventeenth century, while the form that would have been prevalent at the time of Craigievar's building was the latticed casement. This was sometimes fixed and glazed at the top but open and unglazed below, where wooden shutters were provided, hence the term shutter-board window. I know of no castle or large house that has retained these in original condition though they have been re-instated in several, and notably by The National Trust in 'The Study', at Culross.

In the Great Hall a so-called secret stair enters via a cupboard at one end, while another leads to the kitchen at the other. The secret stair was, of course, the laird's private way down to dinner, and is only secret if one ignores the tell-tale bulge in the wall at the north-west corner of the castle, which runs the whole way from the upper floors nearly to the ground, is lit by tiny windows and supported near its foot by heavy corbelling. The kitchen entry is behind what is now called the Minstrel's Gallery, but which is probably a quaint survival of what was at Borthwick and other older castles known as 'The Screens', hiding the culinary activities from those of the Hall. One has to remember that although there are tartan covers to the chairs at Craigievar and that latter-day lairds, with titles, sported large blue bonnets, that Aberdeen and its immediate environs is not in the Highlands, and that Willie Forbes when he had made his 'bonny penny' and built his castle would probably have thought of Highlanders as uncouth. One must be careful therefore not to subscribe to Victorian and other romantic notions when considering such places. The name was, of course, pronounced as two syllables like Fettes and Foulis, and Burns too, when his people lived in Aberdeenshire. Their forbears were Jacobites and staunch ones, so that that brought the wearing of tartan into the scheme of things, many lowland or marginally Highland clans adopting it in defiance of their Edinburgh-based enemies. Baltic timber, which the first owner of Craigievar imported for a living, is well represented in the castle as might be expected, and apart from the transforming of a box-bed into a bath there used to be no electric light or other modern touches in the place at all. The box-bed, by the way, was a special Scottish device for keeping warm, and was often built into a recess in the main living room in the seventeenth and eighteenth centuries, so that the laird and his family slept where the fire was. The servants had theirs in the kitchen, for the same reason. Craigievar is harled in pinkish hues, not exactly the colour of an old fashioned tennis court as John Fleming suggests but near enough, and at one side is a run of barmkin wall, ending in the most bewitching of hooded-round towers, replete with minute swept-dormer.

The Scottish vernacular covers most of lowland Scotland and spills over into the Highlands. It shows an extraordinary homogeneity of style that no one could mistake for anything else anywhere else, except possibly in parts of central France and the Low Countries, but even then it is only a reflection not a repetition. North of Aberdeenshire, in Banff and Moray, there are many more castles of the Jacobean period, or older piles adapted, the largest and most interesting of which is Fyvie, whose size and symmetry and general air of perfection belies the fact that it is not a Victorian exercise in recreated Scotch Baronial but that rare thing in the native manner, a genuine castle which has become ordered and tidy by design not by mistake. Thus, two separate but equal towers, each turreted with pepperpots and gay with rich, variegated corbelling and highly decorative dormers, are linked by a larger, twin-towered feature guarding the entrance and displaying family heraldry. These are cunningly joined above by an arched device and topped by a central gable, cupola, two dormers and two conically capped corner turrets, stone figures of retainers adorning the latter. This clever arrangement is worth comparing with one or two similar attempts to achieve the same daring effect, and especially since Sir William Bruce copied it when he joined two separate portions of Thirlestane

Castle together to produce symmetry and please the Duke of Lauderdale; and this in turn inspired Sir David Bryce, in the nineteenth century, to repeat the exercise when he re-castellated Blair which had become a Georgian mansion when the Stanleys inherited the Dukedom of Atholl.

The first example is probably Huntingtower, which we have already looked at. The two separate portions here were for a long time left divided except for a narrow gangway at roof level, along which, legend says, a daughter of the house made her difficult way, at night, to see her lover, but finding the way barred on one occasion actually leapt some ten feet over the gap below to get back into her own bed before being found out. After that, it seems, a central linking portion was built, but no serious attempt made to create either symmetry or a neat finish. At Craigston, on the other hand, only a few miles from Fyvie, and obviously inspired by the latter, the double 'L'-shaped castle is joined over the main entrance by a triumphal arch topped with a highly decorated balcony in the early Renaissance manner, with amusing figures of a piper and jousting knights, grotesque heads and gargoyles and supported by deep and ornately carved corbelling. Behind, a subsidiary central tower rises, in almost identical manner as Bruce contrived at Thirlestane, some sixty years later.

The windows at Fyvie are Georgian, and many improvements have been made inside and out to this big but mainly authentic building, which retains its yett and also a wide and splendid wheel-staircase constructed with the proper right hand ascent for defence in retreat, and on a scale and in a style reminiscent of French châteaux built at the time of François Premier. The lairds who created this were the Setons, closely related to the Stewarts, whose fortunes rose and fell with those of our native kings. This probably accounts for the obvious Continental affinities and greater size of Fyvie compared to other castles in the neighbourhood, for the valley where it is situated is almost as famous for its towers and keeps as the Dee or the Don. The majority of these have now fallen into ruin. Craigston and Fyvie have survived hale and free from scaith, but both are more mansions than castles, even with their turrets and other Jacobean features. They are almost the last of their species but not quite, that epitaph must go to

Drumlanrig, Dumfriesshire seat of the Duke of Buccleuch, which was begun in the reign of Charles I and not completed until that of James VII and II. It is both palace and castle, the grandest and largest in Scotland; and if the *Dictionary of National Biography* appears a little unfair in describing it as 'a poor mixture of the classic and the grotesque' there is some truth in the comment, as we shall see when we deal with Drumlanrig and its palatial antecedents in the next chapter.

IV

Palaces and Mansions

THE ROYAL STEWARTS, Stuarts after the sixteenth century, pious almost to the point of being superstitious, generally lived near or in some religious establishment. Scone, a few miles to the north-west of Perth, was the first of these, the original palace now being represented by a nineteenth-century Tudor-style mansion of no great pretensions and scarcely Scottish in any way. The capital was where the Court was, and Edinburgh did not formally acquire its existing status until the reign of Charles I, which may explain why the Palace of Holyrood-house was so long a-building and was only completed in 1679; and never became a fixed royal residence until this century. It did, on the other hand, rise beside a former ecclesiastical foundation and in this respect is as typical as other palaces belonging to the Royal Stewarts. Stirling shared with Linlith-gow in their affections, Linlithgow's splendid group being reduced to a roofless ruin during the 1745 rebellion. It was the favourite retreat of James IV and the birthplace of Mary, Queen of Scots. Had it survived intact its place in the story of Scotland's Historic Buildings would have been second to none; and in common with other palaces of the period it stood beside a handsome kirk, described in an earlier chapter.

Stirling Castle and Palace owes its wholeness to the presence of the Army, as indeed Edinburgh Castle does, a presence which has not been entirely beneficial in that the celebrated 'Palace Block', built by James V to receive his French Consort, Mary of Lorraine, and the slightly earlier Great Hall erected by James III, have suffered considerably in the process. The Army, of course, is concerned with defence, not aesthetics and thus the ceiling of the King's Presence Chamber, which was once composed of Renaissance roundel portraits of kings and queens and heroes of Bible and Roman lore has disappeared. It bore comparison with others in the Valley of the Loire and came to grief, and to some extent to the notice of well-wishers

Stirling Castle: (*above*) palace block, and (*below*) the Great Hall

anxious to preserve it, in the eighteenth century, when one of the carved wooden roundels fell and hit a soldier. The rest might have been torn down and consigned to the fire had not a former governor of Stirling Prison rescued as many as he could. The bulk are safe in the Smith Institute in Stirling with three especially good examples in the Museum of Antiquities in Edinburgh; two of these are thought to represent James V and Mary of Lorraine respectively, the third is of a gay *putto*. When the full restoration of Stirling Castle is undertaken it is planned to replace them as near *in situ* as possible.

Stirling vies with Hampton Court as the first important building in Britain in which Renaissance details appear to any marked degree. In Cardinal Wolsey's Palace these consist of a set of roundels in *terra cotta* which were actually made in Florence and placed at salient points as decoration. They are not dissimilar from the wooden specimens at Stirling except for their subject matter, the Hampton Court portraits being almost wholly of Roman Emperors. In fact, the Renaissance made a more pronounced appearance in Stirling in the design of the 'Palace Block', with its regularly-spaced, pleasantly-proportioned windows and characteristically rich sculpture, much of which was done by French stone-masons brought over for the purpose, though engaged by a Scotsman, Sir James Hamilton of Fynnart, the King's Master of Works. Formed in true Renaissance mould Sir James combined in his person the attributes of a much-travelled connoisseur and patron of the arts with those of lecher, traitor and murderer. Eventually he went too far and was hanged for his pains; but it is to him we owe the best parts of Stirling, ruined Linlithgow, and Falkland, the Royal Hunting Lodge James V built in Fife in imitation of François Premier at Chambord.

Sir David Lyndsay, tutor to the infant James V and later first Lyon King at Arms, described the King's Master of Works as 'that bluddie bouchour ever thirstand for blude', and in his *Satyr of the Three Estatis* he warned king, church and nobles of impending trouble if corruption and license was not reduced. Of James V's buildings Lyndsay commented that they 'micht be ane patern in Portugal and France', which is praise indeed, for the writer knew the Continent well. French influence is no mystery, Scotland had a French Queen and was allied to France by an ancient treaty; but looking again at Stirling one cannot help being struck by the affinities between a great deal of the curvacious and strangely grotesque sculpture on the façade of the Palace Block and that decorating the Manueline Convent at Tomar, in central Portugal. This was the headquarters of the Society of the Cross founded by King Manuel I, under whose banner the caravels sailed the unknown seas to discover a new world in Africa, India, the Far East and America. At Rosslyn we saw how seemingly Portuguese influences there actually predated the invention of the Manueline style, which, developing in the wake of the voyages of Magellan and Vasco da Gama, often found masonic expression in such devices as 'cable courses', sailors' ropes and knots; and it was more probably to Spain that the founder of Rosslyn turned for inspiration. Here in Stirling, however, Portuguese influence is both obvious and logical in the twisted pilasters rising between the window openings, in the gargoyles, niched statuary and wealth of exotic carving throughout.

Amongst the most notable sculptures at Stirling are assumed portraits of James V and his courtiers, amusing themselves firing off cross-bows and early shot-guns, not to mention a series of youthful athletes and some of the first nudes to appear in Scotland, including the so-called 'Venus of Stirling', who holds an orb and an arrow. That particular lady may be more French than Portuguese, but the links are there, some direct, others secondary. Scots craftsmen, with their love of ornate carving and especially of rounded curves and heavy relief, recreated under Continental masters something akin to their brethren in another small but virulent nation whose influence abroad was considerably in excess of its material resources or political power. Other evocative carving adorns the capitals of the supports to big open fireplaces in the King's and Queen's Presence Chambers, the sculptor, according to Dr James Richardson, being the same who made the famous fountain in the courtyard at Linlithgow, which Queen Victoria had copied for the forecourt at Holyroodhouse. Stylized lions feature here, perhaps in recognition of the fact that the Stewart kings kept a captive lion at Stirling, in the courtyard of the Palace which is still known as 'The Lyon's Den'. Part of the building has already been restored, but the upper floor still houses a Regimental Museum and ceremonial mess. These are full of memories for the men of the Argyll and Sutherland Highlanders whose colours are now hung up in the nearby Jacobean Chapel Royal, also restored.

James VI, not yet the first of Great Britain, built this delightful royal chapel largely for the christening of his firstborn, Henry, future Prince of Wales, in 1594. As much as £10,000 was spent on the building and the festivities associated with the infant's baptism, at which the Earl of Sussex represented Queen Elizabeth, and which was followed by a magnificent banquet in the Great Hall of the Castle. James III built this latter structure, the architect being Robert Cochrane, his Master of Works and 'favourite' whom he made Earl of Mar; a commoner and, therefore, unacceptable to the Barons, who expected the king to surround himself with warriors not artists. Cochrane was one of several such attendants, which included Dr Roger, the royal Master of Music, as well as poets and painters and a tailor; which so enraged the 'guns before culture' faction that they murdered six of the king's friends in an episode known as 'Belling the Cat'. This took place at Lauder Brig in Berwickshire in 1482, when the Earl of Angus wrenched the gold chain from Cochrane's neck and hanged him with a hempen rope, hence the bell and cat allusion. Dr Roger was also done to death, though he had taken no part in the political side of things only playing to the king, leading the boys of the Chapel Royal in the services and organizing performances in the Minstrel or Trumpet Gallery of the Great Hall.

It is unfortunate that some of the worst damage done at Stirling occurred in this building, and particularly in the interior, which was gutted when new floors and partitions were built for the comfort of the troops. All that remains are the bare walls, and not all of them as they were in the heyday of their royal use. What has survived is enough to indicate how sumptuous and finished a work of architecture this Great Hall was, and how well versed in his craft Robert Cochrane was too. He went abroad to study buildings in France and Italy and his oriel windows and delicately traceried niches containing small statues rival anything at Hampton Court, though antedating Wolsey's work by a generation. One can only wait with impatience for the resuscitation of the hall to begin, its external features were not unlike those of the Great Hall at Falkland Palace, which was begun by James III and is still entire; but whether or not the hammer-beam oak roof of the same period can ever be re-instated is doubtful. Happily there is a near counterpart in the Great Hall at Edinburgh Castle, which was for centuries hidden behind Georgian plasterwork and thereby saved from destruction.

Below the battlements at Stirling visitors look down on the north side to the 'King's Knot', a big grassy patch arranged in rising and diminishing terraces to form an artificial *monte* or mount, and one of the first of its kind in Scotland. It was laid out by order of James IV who at the same time added a new park in which not only wild boar and deer roamed but also wild white cattle, the only remaining specimens of which in modern Britain are the Chillingham herd, in Northumberland. In the 'Great Garden' itself, cranes and peacocks strutted, so that the sight of wimpled ladies of the court and their escorts in tights and fur-edged jerkins strolling amidst the formalized Renaissance beds of box hedge and gravel must have been picturesque in the extreme, and not at all commensurate with the supposed barbarity of life in the north. In fact at this period Scotland acquired through the efforts of this forward-looking and gifted king an international reputation as a resort of culture and progress sufficiently important to entice Father John Damien, himself seeking to emulate the fantastic Leonardo da Vinci, to Stirling. There he entertained, astonished and finally horrified the court by attaching a pair of home-made wings to himself and jumping from the battlements. He was not killed and repeated the performance more than once, though with no more success than in the first instance. The event, however, places Scotland and James IV in particular right in the mainstream of European thought and culture. Today the King's Knot is part of a large field, only its rising terraces are visible and these not easily discernible until the grass is cut in summer; but it has its place in Scottish history and is a remarkable survival from the fifteenth century.

Another remarkable survival near the castle is the fragment known as 'Mar's Wark', which stands at the top of the road leading up from the town to the castle. The Earls of Mar were Hereditary Keepers, a fact that annoyed several Kings when they were denied immediate access to their own property. Indeed, in the reign of Charles II, the Duke of Lauderdale tried to buy out the Earl of that time, who was hard up and therefore considered a suitable subject for persuasion. As it turned out he resisted and his descendant still holds the post. In the fifteenth and sixteenth centuries the Earls also had their own residence at the Castle Gates, of which Mar's Wark was one. It is an extraordinary attempt on the part of a royal servant to emulate his master's cultural effusions, and is decidedly barbaric and odd by comparison. It dates from half a century after the completion of the Palace Block by French and French-trained masons and shows how taste had deteriorated since then. Almost immediately opposite is 'Argyll's Lodging', which many authorities think the finest town mansion in Scotland. It belongs to the reign of Charles I and was the property of Sir William Alexander, later Earl of Stirling and Viscount Canada, the latter title deriving from his part in the institution of the Baronets of Nova Scotia, whereby it was hoped to colonize North America. Sir William hailed from Argyll, where his name had been rendered as MacAlister; he was a poet and cavalier and his house here in Stirling is really a late-Jacobean castle in the style of, say, Fyvie, but with the interesting addition, suitable to a town, of a high wall facing the street. The front courtyard is entered via a handsome Renaissance gateway, rusticated in the manner of the Pitti Palace or its Paris imitation, the Luxembourg. Indeed, Argyll's Lodging reminds one very much in its site and plan of a Paris *hôtel* of the seventeenth century. It has lost many of its internal features and is now a Youth Hostel, but externally its fine gateway and entrance have survived, plus a number of corbelled turrets, heraldic finials and pediments. Its creator had a dower-house at Menstrie, to the north of the River Forth, which having fallen into disrepair was restored largely through the efforts of the National Trust for Scotland and contains a room devoted to Sir William Alexander and the Baronets of Nova Scotia, whose Coats of Arms are displayed on a wall surrounding a portrait of Charles I.

Apart from the Palace of Holyroodhouse, which is Her Majesty the Queen's official home in Scotland, Falkland is the only Royal Stuart residence still occupied as a house, and in fact by a Royal Keeper, who represents the Queen and with the help of the National Trust maintains the structure. Falkland is small as palaces go, half of it has either disappeared or been reduced to ruins, but in any case it is not really a palace at all, being the hunting lodge and country retreat of our kings, a place remembered with pleasure even by poor Mary Queen of Scots and her father, who died there. James V went to Falkland after his nobles betrayed him and his soldiers ran away at the Battle of Solway Moss, and died of melancholy on hearing of Mary's birth at Linlithgow 1542, declaring as he did so, 'It cam wi' a lass, and will gang wi' a lass', or words to that effect. He meant that the crown had come to his family through an heiress, Margery Bruce and would go with another, his own daughter. The main building stands in the high street of the little Royal Burgh in the midst of red-pantiled, crow-stepped houses, one actually thatched. These were the homes of grooms and gardeners, gentlemen ushers, chamberlains, foresters, falconers and averimen, or stablers, the post of

Falkland Palace, Fife: the Gatehouse and Chapel

Averiman being held at one time by Nicol Moncreif who built the two-storeyed thatched house fronting the Palace in 1610. His family was typical in that various members of it had served the Stewarts here since 1464, when the seventh laird of Moncreiff was Chamberlain to James III, then a mere boy. Later, in the early nineteenth century, General George Moncreiff succeeded to the office of Hereditary Keeper of the Palace; he commanded the Third or Scots Guards, which body had been raised in the reign of Charles II, who presented them with colours at Falkland in 1650.

The whole scale of the palace is intimate and inviting, the twin-turreted gatehouse, with its cable-coursed corbels and conically capped turrets closely resembling those of the northern wing of Holyroodhouse. They acquired their existing appearance in 1541 and comprised the Captain's Chambers within which the present Royal Keeper lives. Alongside is the original Banqueting Hall, or one of them, for there was another Great Hall to the north built by James III and now marked only by a few scattered remnants and foundations. The second hall is now a Roman Catholic Chapel and referred to as the Chapel Royal, though for how long it actually served that purpose in earlier times is doubtful. It is interesting on account of its fittings some of which were installed for the Coronation visit to Falkland of Charles I in 1633, at which time the place was used as a gallery. The handsome panelled timber ceiling dates from then, the panels having been repainted recently to resemble as much as possible their seventeenth-century appearance, with the Royal Caroline badges and cyphers picked out in heraldic tints. A small portion of what purports to be a Royal Pew has been preserved and heavily restored. It may have housed James VI and I when Andrew Melville, French-trained introducer of Presbyterianism into Scotland, addressed him from the Jacobean pulpit in the chapel as 'God's silly vassal'. More authentic and certainly entire is the lovely open-pillared oak screen at the west end of the hall. It looks very Castilian, and was made in the reign of James V and, as already intimated, gave Sir Robert Lorimer the idea for a similar screen at Earlshall.

Until fire destroyed the north range and damaged the east in the Cromwellian era Falkland was a courtyard structure like most late-Gothic and early Renaissance palaces. Today only the south range remains in its entirety, its exterior to the street in sharp contrast with that on the courtyard side. The former is massive and buttressed, with niches containing weather-worn statues carved by Peter the Flemishman for James IV. The latter displays the refined work of French craftsmen employed by James V and constitutes the most consummate exhibition of Valley of the Loire architecture in Britain for its date, which is before 1540. Nicholas Roy, French Master Mason to the king, was engaged here in 1538 and carved the series of roundels that decorate the spaces between the windows and on either side of a row of purely classical pilasters. These are fully developed in the Italian manner and formerly ran on round to the east range, a few of them surviving there still. Other craftsmen employed at the time include a French plasterer, Hector Beate, John Drummond, a Scottish wright trained in France and Jean Merlioun. Opinions differ as to the precise figures represented in the roundels but apart from the usual supposed royal portraits we certainly have here the stock Renaissance heroes and heroines, Paris and Helen, Achilles, Jason and Medea, but more sophisticated and finished than at Stirling and by a single master mason. Grotesques are noticeable by their absence, as are native aberrations and quaint imitations of Continental designs, so that the inner face of the south range at Falkland stands on its own, a never to be repeated design dating from the last years of the formal Auld Alliance between France and Scotland.

The great oak forest around Falkland where the Royal Stewarts loved to hunt has gone, part of it cut down by Cromwell and part by James IV to build *The Great Michael*; a ship meant to intimidate Henry VIII, or at any rate make him think twice before invading Scotland. It never saw a battle, though it got as far as Berwick, and was thought so wonderful in its day that a replica in cut hedges was made by its French builder at Tullibardine, in Perthshire. The Royal garden, on the other hand, has been recreated to an old plan and is regularly open to the public even when the Palace is closed. As early as 1484 records speak of the king's interest in horticulture and of how he refused to pay the gardener unless he worked well and provided plenty of fruit and vegetables. Eight barrels of onions were produced one year, but later reduced to an average of four, which eventually became the *reddendo*, or duty due to the sovereign from the gardener for holding his property. At the bottom of the garden is the Royal Tennis Court, unique in Scotland and dating from 1539. It is still in use and one can join the club for a modest fee. Modern lawn-tennis is not played but catchspeil, which was at first a hand game without racquets and with only a tasseled rope instead of a net. Only at Hampton Court is there a similar and contemporary example of a real tennis court remaining in play. This was a favourite resort of Charles I and Charles II both of whom seem to have inherited their ancestor's zest for this very difficult ball-game. Both visited Falkland, the 'Merry Monarch' being the last of his race to do so; and in 1950 the tercentenary of his coming was celebrated by the laying up of the old Scots Guard colours in the Palace and a parade. Charles I made Sir Henry Cary, Viscount Falkland. He was a celebrated cavalier and died valiantly in battle little realizing that one day an outpost of Empire would be named after him and become the bone of contention between a latter day British Government and a South American Republic. More appositely perhaps the historic links between this beautiful old palace and the Royal Stewarts are commemorated in the office of arms of Falkland Pursuivant-Extraordinary.

There is, of course, a distinct difference between the term palace as applied to the *palatium regium* of a king, or *palatium nostrum* of a bishop, both of which have Roman antecedents deriving from the famous buildings which once crowned the Palatinate Hill, and modern usages. The important thing was who inhabited the buildings rather than their size or shape, at least until comparatively recent times. A Scottish 'palas' which was neither royal nor episcopal was built by the Jacobean worthy Sir George Bruce of Carnock in Culross, in Fife, the term in this case being analogous to the English 'place' as applied to a number of Tudor and later country mansions and a few large town houses. This describes the form of building not the occupants' standing. It is, therefore, the ancestor of our country mansions, being a wholly domestic structure, without defensive towers or turrets, two or three storeys only in height and set around a courtyard or garden. The 'palas' at Culross may be considered the first of its kind north of the Border and although actually in the middle of the burgh and not in open country conforms to the more progressive, peaceful attitudes of its day. It is ranged around a courtyard, is built of local stone and roofed with bright red pantiles. With its jaunty dormer windows, topped with finials displaying either family crests or national symbols, and crow-stepped gables, it looks very Flemish; and indeed this is no mere impression, for amongst the proprietor's activities was the exporting of coal and salt to Flanders with red Flemish bricks and tiles coming back as ballast in his ships. The windows are of the shutter-board kind, with fixed leaded lights at the top and wooden shutters below, which is exactly the same as at Falkland and Stirling, and even at Holyroodhouse until Sir William Bruce's day, only on a less grand scale. Inside the little 'palace' other sources of the owner's wealth, the importing of Baltic timber, are apparent in the boarded rooms, some of which retain their original painted decorations. These are in advance of those found in many contemporary Aberdeenshire castles and the subject matter less heroic, revealing more concern with good living according to Old Testament and protestant precepts.

Sir George Bruce was an uncle of William Bruce, the architect who did not, as is often asserted, design Culross Abbey House, which stands above the burgh and is a somewhat larger and more advanced specimen of a purely domestic mansion than is the 'palas'. The latter was built between 1597 and 1611 and the Abbey House almost at the same time, but by Sir George's elder brother Edward, who was Commendator of the defunct Abbey and father of the first Earl of Kincardine. Sir William Bruce's supposed association with the Abbey House arose on account of its superior architectural qualities, it being regularly faced with symmetrically-disposed windows and influenced by classical or Palladian principles, its only obvious concession to more picturesque styles reflected in two ogee-roofed pavilions at either end of the building. Edward Bruce was close to James VI and I after that monarch went south to London, and no doubt the design of his house in Culross was influenced by things seen there. It certainly could not have been the work of his gifted nephew, the future Architect

Royal to Charles II, for William Bruce was not born until one year after it was finished. Culross Abbey House is the first mansion of its kind built in Scotland and makes a strong contrast with its near neighbour down in the burgh. A whole generation was to elapse before it had any comparable rivals north of the Border, the Civil War came, and not until Sir William Bruce began his architectural career was there any significant progress in the introduction of the Palladian style. It represents, therefore, an isolated example, outwith the general development of architecture in Scotland in the early seventeenth century, which was still vernacular except in the case of Royal residences.

With the ending of the Cromwellian regime and the restoration of the monarchy in 1660 a new chapter opens in the story of Scotland's historic buildings. William Bruce had played a prominent part in ending the king's exile. He befriended General Monk, Puritan Governor in the north, and acted as emissary between that key personage and Charles II in Holland His passport survives as witness to this; and when the king did come into his own again Monk and Bruce were suitably rewarded, the former with a dukedom, the latter with the post of Clerk to the Bills, an office whereby he received duty payment on every act that passed through the Scottish Parliament. This was followed by Bruce being appointed Surveyor to the King and given the commission to rebuild the palace of Holyroodhouse, and to complete the schemes of the last two centuries initiated by successive Stewart monarchs and never concluded. We cannot go into any great detail here on the subject of Holyrood; suffice to say that in his rebuilding of the Royal Palace in Edinburgh Bruce used the Three Orders of Architecture: Doric, the plainest; Ionic, the one with the volutes on the capitals, and Corinthian, the most ornate, for the first time in Scotland. He used them in the courtyard, where he may have got his inspiration from the Gaston d'Orleans' wing of the Château de Blois which François Mansart, the foremost architect in France at the time, designed before 1640.

Bruce was on the Continent on several occasions in his capacity as agent for the Restoration and both then and later, when he was sent abroad by the Duke of Lauderdale, Charles

II's 'Viceroy' in Scotland, he obtained *objets d'art*, materials and ideas for buildings at home. His patron was a member of the notorious 'cabal' which ruled Britain throughout the first half of the reign of the 'Merry Monarch', and he was married to one of the cleverest and most rapacious women of the age, Elizabeth Murray, formerly Countess of Dysart and a cousin through her mother of the Architect Royal. Bruce was familiar with her house at Ham, near Richmond, in Surrey, and an early commission of his was to design some gates for her there. Having done this satisfactorily he was given the much more important job of bringing Thirlestane Castle, Berwickshire seat of the Lauderdales, up-to-date. This marks his first major achievement; in it he not only brought together the divergent parts of a rambling, overgrown Border tower but applied classical principles wherever possible. The result is a remarkable merging of old and new in a building which for scale and proportion is without equal in its period or place. Bruce's method here, as indeed in others where he was confronted with an existing building of merit but wayward, was to repeat rather than demolish the older portions, join them in the middle with a new feature and thus create overall symmetry. At Holyroodhouse he did this, and at Balcaskie, his own country home which he worked on for nearly twenty years before moving to Kinross, he added side pavilions and curved wing walls in the manner of Palladio at the Villa Trissino, near Venice: and this prescription seems to have worked well almost everywhere he tried it. It is one of the things that make him different from almost all other Palladian architects, this respect for the past and for the native tradition too, which lasted his whole life and can be seen in some form in every one of his buildings. Indeed this attachment to historical precedent went so far at Kinross as to remove a carved medieval stone from the ruins of Loch Leven Castle, the one from which Mary, Queen of Scots escaped in 1565, and having it re-instated as the keystone to one of his garden pavilions near the house, thus demonstrating for posterity the continuity of ownership on the estate.

Thirlestane Castle has been described as the first Scotch Baronial edifice in the modern manner, and the precursor of many of those that were built in the nineteenth century.

Certainly David Bryce, who with William Burn recreated the style in Victorian times, learned much from Thirlestane, which he restored and enlarged. His work included the additon of pepper-pot corner turrets, oriel windows and other false medievalisms. Bruce on the other hand relied on linking the disjointed parts of the castle by means of a new classical entrance and high level balcony above, bringing the whole design together under a large ogee-roofed central feature. Bryce repeated this idea on a smaller scale at Blair for the Duke of Atholl, which ancient Perthshire castle had been completely transformed in the eighteenth century into a quite ordinary Georgian mansion; and Bryce's task had been to re-baronialize it. It was a chance to emulate Sir William Bruce, and he took it, removing the Georgian façades and linking the remaining older portions with his newer, baronialized additions under an arched central feature. We have seen how this simple but ingenious arrangement was also applied at Fyvie, so it had respectable native antecedents.

Thirlestane Castle, Berwickshire: front elevation

The actual front door at Thirlestane, approached via a grand staircase, is reminiscent of Ham, and inside John Halbert and George Dunsterfield, Charles II's favourite baroque plasterers, who had previously worked at Ham, and in the State Apartments at Windsor, were employed. Afterwards they went to Holyroodhouse and to Balcaskie, and their apprentices to Kinross and Prestonfield, Caroline Park and other Bruce or quasi-Bruce mansions. They were known as 'gentlemen modellers', and were allowed to wear their swords at work, though presumably they did not do so whilst lying on their backs *à la* Michelangelo on platforms near the ceiling, which they had to do when applying the wet plaster leaves, fruit and flowers. They used pieces of wood or metal, whatever they could lay their hands on, to achieve the truly splendid results we see today at Holyrood and elsewhere, the work having to be done in considerable haste before the plaster hardened. Attendants handed them up thistles, roses, lions, laurel leaves, or Lauderdale eagles at Thirlestane, in buckets, and these they fixed whilst still damp onto a set pattern already drawn on the ceiling. In moments of great inspiration they actually made new leaves and symbolic devices with their pieces of wood or iron, twisting them into shape and mixing them in with the rest, making the finished product a genuine work of art not a mere pastiche.

In *Architect Royal* I dealt with the life and work of Sir William Bruce in depth, so I do not intend to list everything he did here, but there are some buildings he did which must be included and one of these is Brunstane House, near Edinburgh. This is a modest mansion, or 'villa' which Bruce adapted for the Duke of Lauderdale whilst still engaged at Thirlestane. Again he was confronted with an older building, an 'L'-shaped Laird's tower in which the Duke, still an Earl and not yet married to Bessie Dysart, lived with his first wife until the winter of 1672. Almost as soon as he became a widower he married again and was made a Duke, when Brunstane, like his other Scottish properties, had to be enlarged and improved in accordance with his increased power and influence. Bruce gave it the usual treatment, repeating existing features and linking them with a central entrance; more significant, however, is what he did inside, for in the panelled octagon room at

Brunstane are the oldest sash windows in Scotland, some still with the slightly clouded glass fitted in them in 1673. The idea came from Holland, where such windows abound, and possibly also from Portugal, where again they have sash windows and not the more common casements; and, of course, the Queen, Catherine of Braganza, was Portuguese and brought with her to Britain several new fashions. Dutch craftsmen were known to have worked at Brunstane both as wrights and decorators, the latter painted the inset panels over the chimneypieces and doorways there and also in other Scottish houses of the period. Lauderdale speaks highly of their workmanship, especially the joiners, and this is borne out by the fact that sash windows, installed by them three hundred years ago and never restored or re-adjusted, open and close at the touch of a finger, unlike many modern versions.

At Balcaskie the King's Architect laid out the first large-scale Italian garden in Scotland, not a small formal garden of box hedges and parterres, nor yet a knot, but a real Italian garden with terraces and statues and vistas. It is one of the marvels of North Britain and served as the model for the more ambitious and extensive one he created later at Kinross:

Balcaskie, Fife

Kinross House from the garden

visitors to Scotland at the end of the seventeenth century described this as making Lady Lauderdale's garden at Ham 'but a wilderness', and Evelyn thought that the finest in England. The vistas at Balcaskie are threefold, so that standing in the middle of the terrace in front of the house one looks straight ahead, right across the Firth of Forth, to the Bass Rock, some twenty miles away. Turning to the left one was meant to catch a side glimpse of the May Isle, and to the right of North Berwick Law, but these two views have since been obscured by Georgian and Victorian plantings. At Kinross the principal vista extends right down the main avenue, though the front door and out at the other side, across the formal garden through the gate to Loch Leven Castle, romantically sited amidst a few trees on a low island. In the background are the Lomond Hills, and in fine weather the scene is as 'Italian' as one could wish, reminiscent of the unspoilt south eastern reaches of Lago Maggiore.

Francis Bacon in his *Essay on Gardens* makes the point that 'a man shall ever see that when ages grow to civility and elegancy, men come to build stately sooner than to garden finely', and he refers to gardens as 'the purest of human pleasures, without which buildings and palaces are but gross handiworks'. Sir William Bruce clearly shared these views for he began laying out his park and gardens at Kinross many years before any part of the masonry rose above the ground, so that when at last the house was completed and he went to live in his new Scottish *palazzo* the trees and plants were well established and handsomely grown. He is said to have had a hand in the planning of the 'Great Garden' at Pitmedden, in Aberdeenshire, which was founded by Sir Alexander Seton in 1675, and this may well be so though these were early days for Bruce, the Kinross estate had yet to be purchased, and if his influence was present at Pitmedden it must have derived from his 'Italian' terraces at Balcaskie, which association Dr James Richardson emphasized when in the recent reconstitution of the Pitmedden garden buttress hedges were planned against the main terrace to resemble the stone buttresses of Bruce's east Fife seat.

Much more in the Balcaskie tradition was the splendid garden at Hatton House which Sir John Stirling Maxwell describes in detail in his *Shrines and Homes*. This was written before the war, when Hatton was still lived in and its policies properly cared-for, the formal garden within its high terraces bounded by ogee-roofed gazebos and looking almost the same as they did when Captain John Slezer drew them in late Stewart times. They survived thus for a while longer, but soon after the war disaster came. The house and grounds were sold, the house burned down and the terraced garden turned into a farmyard. A modern bungalow sits where once a round pond and fountain were and of the old house itself only one turreted corner remains. The gazebos still mark the extremes of the buttressed walls, and there is a ruined bath house, but that is about all. Not a finger was raised to try and save this marvellous place which, until its firing, degradation and subsequent demolition retained its Caroline panelling, ceilings and furnishings, and stood in one of the finest formal gardens in the country. It was the creation of Lord Hatton, brother and heir to the childless Duke of Lauderdale and Treasurer-Depute of the Kingdom. He it was who paid Bruce his fees at Holyroodhouse and having picked the architect's brains and diverted funds, men and materials to his own purpose, built for himself this small replica of the royal palace, converting an older laird's tower in the process. The Bruce technique was applied, repetition of existing features to produce symmetry and the laying out of a fine park and 'Italian' garden.

The loss of Hatton House and surrounding garden would have been irreparable had not Kinross House remained undamaged and indeed been fully restored to its original state earlier this century, when the garden and park were resuscitated with skill and loving care by the late Sir Basil Montgomery. Daniel Defoe called the house 'The most beautiful and regular piece of Architecture in Scotland', and it still is; it had no comparable contemporaries and has had no successful imitators. It was built all of a piece in the most serene and patrician manner imaginable, and may be related in some ways to Vaux-le-Vicomte, near Paris, which was completed about twenty years before and which Bruce must have seen; the park and vistas and formal statuary also have their smaller counterparts here, and especially the axial vista from the town of Kinross towards the house, down the tree lined avenue some quarter of a mile long, with equidistant counterpart on the other side of the house in the direction of Loch Leven Castle. Cuttings in the trees suggest a Watteauesque setting of French elegance and formalized rusticity, while the alternate concave and convex wing walls epitomize the architect's love of symmetry and architectural cohesion. One ought also to add, his Scotch sense of purpose, for these curtains are no mere blanks, they provide shelter for servants to scurry behind on their way to stables and laundries as well as fulfilling Palladian concepts. This mixture of practicality and architectural awareness is also to be seen in his Stable Block, with its ogee-roofed pavilions and dormer windows, and circular doocot rising resplendently from the centre of the yard. He was good with chimneys too. He never put them on end walls but towards the centre of the building, which kept the house warm while improving the appearance outside.

Sir William Bruce has been likened to Sir Christopher Wren; the 'Kit Wren of Scotland' he has been called, and not without justice. He did actually hold the same post north of the Border that Wren did south of it and both worked in the classical idiom without weakening native traditions. Wren's chimneys were also notable, they did not smoke and like Bruce's needed no cans. Carlisle made an interesting comment about Wren and one of his better known buildings, Chelsea Hospital: 'I looked at it . . . and saw that it was quiet and dignified and the work of a *gentleman*.' Bruce was a gentleman and like Wren was able in his own way and country to adapt an international style of architecture, one with a strictly codified set of rules, to his own and his countrymen's particular needs and tastes. He did not produce a Scottish version of St Paul's but he did rebuild the Palace of Holyroodhouse quite as successfully as Wren did Hampton Court and his own house at Kinross has no equal north or south of the border in its completeness and faultlessness. That is why it has had no imitators of similar standing. James Smith is usually accounted Bruce's principal disciple and successor. He was certainly his successor as Surveyor to the King and he was also a devoted adherent of Palladianism. Indeed, modern research suggests that many of the drawings formerly attributed to Colen Campbell, keen reviver of the Palladian mode in early Georgian England and friend of Lord Burlington, were made by Smith. Be this as it may, his existing works do not point to any great ingenuity. He followed Bruce in the good placing of chimneys, in creating symmetry; and his buildings are well proportioned and not displeasing, but they tend to copy English examples where Bruce managed on his own, and he seems quite incapable of marshalling ornate architectural detail in the same masterly fashion as either Bruce or Wren.

The best of James Smith's works is probably Melville House, in Fife, which is really an English country mansion set down in one of the greener and pleasanter spots in Scotland and but for a certain gauntness caused by its height and lack of decorative relief would not disgrace the Home Counties. Bruce provided plans and was consulted on this project but it is easy to see how Smith when he was put in charge watered everything down, not only to please a parsimonious client but on account of his own inability to use architectural enrichment wisely if at all. The interior was brought entire from the south, having been purchased more or less by the yard by the first Earl of Melville, a prominent supporter of William of Orange and the man who first attracted the painter Sir John de Medina, the 'Scottish

Kneller', north. Melville House, the shell of it and much of the interior, has survived and is inhabited, but its avenues and garden have been cut down and altered to such an extent that any charm they once possessed has evaporated. There it stands, foursquare and bald, a not especially encouraging memorial to James Smith except in its douceness and strength, and regular proportions. Much more interesting to my way of thinking, and quite different in appearance, is the grandiose jumble of Drumlanrig Castle, richly decorated on its show front, too richly and somewhat clumsily by Dutch craftsmen lent by Bruce, and lacking his restraining control. Smith was called in to finish this enormous white, or rather pink elephant, which its owner disliked so much that he only spent one night in it before returning to his ancestral tower at Sanquhar. It was the last Scottish castle in the old castellated tradition and took more than fifty years to build.

I have already said a little about Drumlanrig. Its model was Heriot's Hospital, in Edinburgh, founded by 'Jingling Geordie', that is George Heriot, who had the foresight to lend James VI money and provide Anne of Denmark with jewellery when they were still in Scotland, and to follow them south in 1603. The reward came then, and he died a very wealthy man.

Drumlanrig Castle, from Colen Campbell's *Vitruvius Britannicus*

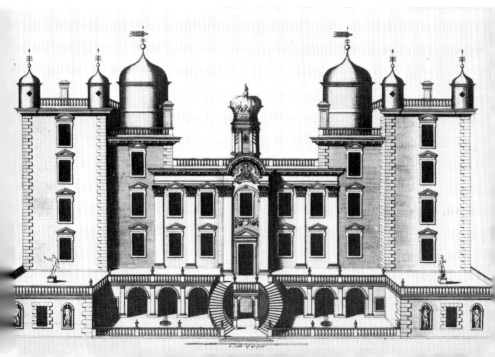

The name of Inigo Jones has been mentioned in connection with both Heriot's Hospital and Drumlanrig Castle, which are both courtyard structures with turreted corner towers and both arcaded in the classical style. The roof of Heriot's has a steep, almost Scandinavian look wholly lacking at Drumlanrig, and there are other strange details that may or may not have some connection with Jones, since we know he was sent to Denmark by the Queen to study and work under her brother Christian IV. Whether this apprenticeship, and a subsequent trip to Italy, can be stretched to explain the horseshoe staircase at Drumlanrig is another matter. Personally I discount it, for the Civil War stopped progress for twenty years and operations were not re-started until 1679, when Inigo Jones had died and the entire fashion had changed from Jacobean to late Stuart. The staircase, which does resemble one at the Queen's House at Greenwich designed by Jones, probably came from an architectural copy book which James Smith had; but what a pity he was not able to achieve the same propitious effect with the rest of the show front, which is drawn from too many divergent sources and almost barbaric in feeling. It has to be seen at a distance when it becomes a *coup de théâtre* worthy of a Donizetti opera. The other three sides are as plain as the front is ornate, and here we do have Smith controlling affairs. Robert Mylne, Bruce's mason at Holyroodhouse and at Thirlestane, worked at Drumlanrig before and during Smith's time as building supervisor; and this accounts for the repetition of certain features from Holyrood in the castle, the Ducal Crown on the cupola over the main entrance, for instance, which replaces the Royal one; and a great deal of the masonry is moulded and cut in imitation of what Bruce normally specified in chimney stalks, balustradings and window surrounds.

William Adam, father of more famous sons, is said to have been apprenticed to Sir William Bruce, and in his *Vitruvius Scoticus* there appear drawings and plans not only of Holyroodhouse but of Kinross and other Bruce designs. I do not think this proves anything, as Adam himself worked at Holyrood and completed or enlarged a number of Bruce buildings; and in any case he was only twenty-one years of age when the former Architect Royal died, in 1710, and was still unborn when Kinross was begun. He did, however, carry on at Hopetoun House, in West Lothian, after Bruce, and there was not such a tremendous break with tradition there in outward form or detail. A lot of unkind things have been said about William Adam, and although it has to be admitted that he was no genius and certainly never learnt how to make a decent plan, he had a flare for the overall effect, and in his larger designs, such as the main front at Hopetoun, and at Duff House, near Banff, he does achieve what whoever was ultimately responsible for Drumlanrig Castle failed to do. He himself said that what chiefly mattered was the immediate impression, and indeed there is much to be said for first impressions in architecture, so long as once inside a building things work well. William Adam rarely made things work well, he lacked Bruce's gift for being both down to earth and imaginative at the same time; but he did make a considerable success of his career, of his several careers, as architect-cum-mason, engineer, land specu-lator, pit-owner, Dutch tile manufacturer, farmer, timber merchant and the importer into Scotland of strong ale, or barley-bree, from Holland. He would not have been admitted to the register of the Royal Institute of British Architects had it existed then but his many non-professional activities did at least pay for the education of his celebrated sons, sent Robert on the 'grand tour' with the Earl of Hopetoun's heir and set up an office in London. The sons worked with their father learning in a practical way their art and although they grew out of his restricted background they can never have failed to look back to him with respect and gratitude, three of them combining to produce a design for his neo-classical tomb in Greyfriar's kirkyard in Edinburgh.

There is another important thing to be said about William Adam. He was the last truly Scottish architect, by which I mean he worked in the native tradition even when screening his buildings behind pseudo-baroque façades; and all his work was done north of the Border. He thus deserves a place in this narrative other than merely as the father of John, Robert, James and William, to give the Adam Brothers their order of seniority; and in taking over from Sir William Bruce at Hopetoun he can be said to have followed in that great man's wake in a literal sense. The elder Adam was very much a

personality on his own, no slavish copier of Bruce, though
influenced to some extent by Vanburgh, whose principal
works he viewed in the company of Sir John Clerk, second
Baronet of Penicuik, who took him south on one of his trips
to London and showed him some of the better known architectural sights of England. There is also a possibility, not
proved conclusively but generally accepted by art historians,
that William Adam and Vanburgh were concurrently engaged
on the building of Floors Castle, near Roxburgh, before 1718;
but if this is true it does not seem to have had much effect on
Adam's design for Hopetoun which followed in 1721 and which
is purely Roman Baroque in taste. The other suggestion is that
he also studied the works of James Gibbs, from Aberdeen, the
completer of Wren's City Churches and a consummate prac-
titioner in the Roman style. One thing is certain, his tour of
the south with Clerk took place in 1727 and work began on
Hopetoun six years earlier, so that whatever influences were
involved there they did not derive from things seen on that
particular journey. The full effect of seeing Castle Howard or
Blenheim had yet to come.

Thus we have a Scotsman with a flair rather than a genius
for amassing baroque detail against native backgrounds and
convincing well-off patrons that that was what they wanted.
This is what happened at Hopetoun, where a completed
country mansion, Bruce's most accomplished design for a
private client, was masked behind a 'Versailles' front, all
columns and pilasters, urns and balusters, which turned a
gentleman's residence into a Roman palace. One can see
exactly what occurred by walking round to the garden side
where Bruce's house remains, unaltered, the skyline only
seeming odd since William Adam's 'pots' and balustrading
rise above the original roof. Adam used the giant Corinthian
Order on his new façade, not sparingly as Bruce did at Kinross
but heavily and frequently, and not so much like Vanburgh
as in imitation of a Palladian grid design that was 'doing the
rounds', so to speak, at the time. This had been produced in
1719 by one Alessandro Galilei for Castleton, in County
Kildare, but which was not built exactly as drawn. The sketches
made for Castleton show eleven bays of a façade not unlike
that finally erected at Hopetoun, while the curved wing walls

(*above*) Hopetoun House, West Lothian: the Bruce front. (*below*) Duff House, Banff

there are almost identical to those at Hopetoun except for the use of the Ionic Order in place of Doric. Adam also changed Bruce's colonnades to concave. Later, when he came to design Duff House for the Earl of Fife he incorporated the main outlines of the same Italian grid pattern in his new design only this time adding handsome pediments and a horseshoe staircase like the one at Drumlanrig. Duff House is thought to be William Adam's masterpiece. It is certainly more Scotch than many contemporary structures, being foursquare, with corner towers, but not turreted in the baronial manner, instead capped with small domes; a traditional medieval keep in a baroque disguise. To say it in any way resembles the Villa Borghese in Rome, as has been suggested, is quite erroneous. That villa, which Sir John Clerk knew and was the home of his friend and patron Cardinal Borghese, is as plain and un-adorned as could possibly be, and the very antithesis of Duff House, which looks Roman and Jesuitical in the manner Gibbs favoured and of which Bernini was the master. The idea of creating a Scottish laird's tower in the image of Bernini may seem grotesque but it is very nearly what has happened here.

With William Adam one normally comes to the end of the story of Scottish buildings as such. The eighteenth century saw the standardization of classical Georgian architecture throughout Britain. Robert Adam, 'Old Stone and Lime's' brilliant second son, being the best known and most proficient purveyor of that mode in these islands. MacGibbon and Ross include The Drum, a Palladian mansion built by William Adam at Gilmerton, near Edinburgh, after 1730, in their *Castellated and Domestic Architecture of Scotland*; so we might as well say a few words about it here. The main interest lies more in the interior of this comparatively modest mansion than in its exterior, which displays the rustications, Venetian-windowed centrepiece and ceremonial staircase one would expect of the period; but within is some of the most elaborate plasterwork remaining in Scotland. Some of it was done by plasterers employed at Holyrood both before and after William Adam's engagement there. In the hall one meets a riot of 'umbrella-stand' features, trophies and swags, this probably being the work of Thomas Clayton whom Adam used on several occasions, notably at Pollok House near Glasgow which was, until it became a beautiful art gallery and museum, the home of Sir John Stirling Maxwell. Not all the plasterwork at The Drum, however, is by the same hand, and besides Clayton itinerant Italians may also have played a part in decorating the house, not to mention Flemings who worked at Arniston nearby. One can see the differences in the various rooms quite easily, the dining room, for instance, contains plasterwork reminiscent of that done earlier for Bruce at Holyrood; the hall is florid in the extreme and a little exotic; while upstairs the ceiling of the saloon is refined to a degree showing an expert, possibly foreign hand. There is not much else one can legitimately relate to Scottish precedent at The Drum; but the cultural links between past and present as exemplified here are significant since they demonstrate how certain standards of craftsmanship were maintained through more than one century and with different men and styles operating.

There already existed the beginnings of a new house at The Drum when William Adam came to built it, and at Arniston, a few miles to the south, there was a whole laird's tower still inhabited to contend with. Unlike Bruce he did not attempt to repeat this in order to produce symmetry but incorporated it entire in the new mansion he erected, which, however, is very Bruce-like in other ways. It is approached by side wings and pavilions and enjoys splendid long-distance vistas, or rather did until the garden and park was re-arranged in the eighteenth century. Whilst working for Sir John Clerk at that Baronet's own house at Mavisbank Adam had been let into the secrets of landscape gardening in the grand manner, which Clerk had studied abroad and in England; and at Arniston he was given his head by his Dundas patrons, members of a distinguished family of lawyers who in the collateral line included the first and second Viscounts Melville, the former of whom founded the Indian Civil Service and became known as the 'Uncrowned King of Scotland' on account of his power to dispense government posts. Adam laid out the park at Arniston in an interesting combination of schemes in which the older formal patterns of paths and parterres merged with less rigid ones and finally with the adjoining fields and woods, much as Sir Robert Lorimer advocated over a hundred and fifty years later. All the French tricks were employed, such as the use of brick chippings, pieces of coal, sand and other coloured objects on the paths and between the hedges, and the garden was bounded by low, false bastions, another French device whereby the unwanted and truncated towers of medieval castles were retained and romanticized by the owners of Renaissance châteaux. Practically all this was rooted up or otherwise destroyed under the influence of 'Capability' Brown, and today there are no cascades or canals, no formal patterns, only the remains of two vistas and a lot of grass and forest trees.

A similar fate befell the gardens at Yester, near Gifford, in East Lothian. These were not the work of William Adam but of his patron the Earl of Tweeddale, who first engaged James Smith on a mansion in the Bruce style, then Smith's partner MacGill, and finally the Adam family, William and his sons. The work went on for nearly a century, as at Hopetoun, and the result is not entirely satisfactory. Only one of Smith's ogee-roofed side pavilions has survived, and only on the garden side can one of his plain but nicely-proportioned elevations be seen, albeit with an Adam top-piece. William Adam's plans for Yester appear in *Vitruvius Scoticus* and show a not un-mannerly adaptation of the older house with a grandiose central feature on the main front that improves rather than spoils Smith's and MacGill's unfinished work. Unhappily the elder Adam died in 1748 with this feature incomplete, when his son Robert changed the design and in doing so changed the whole character of Yester. The result is disrespectful both of his father's ideas and those that went before, though Robert and his brothers did stick to the original Roman Baroque decor for the Grand Saloon, which makes a most interesting contrast with his own elegant sitting room next door. The latter is utterly charming and a particularly good example of Robert Adam's almost feminine gift for interior decoration which here virtually presages the Regency style in its delicacy and refined use of neo-classical motifs.

Robert Adam died in 1792, the year in which Louis XVI was dethroned but not beheaded, so that he did not live to see the 'Terror' in France, far less witness the Napoleonic era or the Regency; yet many of the ideas he developed towards the end of his life are far in advance of what anyone else was doing in this country and did look forward to the Greco-Egyptian modes of Napoleon and George IV, and especially to the romantic revival of Gothic architecture. In this, however, he differed considerably from his contemporaries, and in his immediate successors, in that he genuinely went back to the medieval past, as he had done to ancient Rome when in search for neo-classical perfection; and thus he built castles which were, in effect, not revivalist Gothic in the accepted sense but quasi-authentic reproductions of defensive buildings of the Middle Ages adapted to eighteenth-century use. It is here that we return to Scotland and Robert Adam's peculiar contribution to our native architecture. His country houses in the north are no different in most particulars from those he designed in the south, except perhaps in scale, but when we come to his castles, all of which he built in Scotland, then we have something worth examining in the present context. Curiously enough the best of these, Culzean, Seton and Airthrey, do not resemble the older kind of Scottish castle, they are not classicised laird's towers like Duff House either, but unique interpretations of Italian castles in the Roman Campagna put in Caledonian settings. What makes them Scottish is not their architecture so much as their backgrounds and sites, which had to be in Scotland, for at that time, the second half of the eighteenth century, the Jacobite saga was at its height, James MacPherson was writing, or collecting poems for *Ossian*, and Scottish scenery, song and dance was fashionable all over Europe. Scotland had become the land of romance, the Scottish myth was in the making, the myth that led in the nineteenth century to the covering of every available craig or evocative bend in a Highland river with a turreted edifice, a folly or hermitage, rustic hunting lodge or whatever could be afforded or devised, and the adoption of more than two hundred tartans invented by the self-styled Sobieski-Stuart Brothers for the centenary of the Forty-five rebellion as the official tartans of Scotland.

Robert Adam would have either laughed himself silly or turned away in disdain from such antics, for in the days before the French Revolution and Sir Walter Scott, romanticism was an aristocratic, refined, almost dilettante form of expression, appreciated only by the *cognoscenti*, and particularly those who had made 'the Tour' and were rich and discerning enough to employ the Adam Brothers as their architects and cultural mentors. The Scottish Arts Council mounted an exhibition of Robert Adam's drawings for the Edinburgh Festival of 1972, and these showed how the setting, half-Italian, half-Scottish was what mattered, followed by the translation of a ruined medieval pile into an elegant Georgian mansion, with towers and battlements outside but furnished and decorated inside in the usual Adam manner. Whilst in Italy Robert Adam had joined forces with Charles Louis Clérisseau, the inventor of the neo-classical style, and together they dug up some of the ruins of antiquity, using real Roman remains as their inspiration rather than the baroque palaces that currently filled the streets of the 'Eternal City'. They made sketches too, many of these came back to Scotland. Adam's are mostly in the Penicuik Collection and include drawings of three important Roman castles, Bolsena, the Castello Pio at Tivoli and Bracciano, the latter being the largest and best-preserved medieval pile in Italy and as such visited by Scott in the last year of his life, when it was practically the only thing that interested him. A set of coloured drawings of Rome by Clérisseau are at Hopetoun House where they have been ever since Robert Adam and the Hon. Charles Hope returned from 'the Tour' in 1757.

Culzean Castle, on the Ayrshire coast, is the best known of Robert Adam's Scottish works and was not completed until the year of his death. The design was clearly influenced by what he had seen earlier in The Campagna, and especially at Tivoli and Bracciano; and although it is less imaginative or original than Seton, and in some ways to Airthrey, it is important for its remarkable setting, right on the edge of a cliff overlooking the Firth of Clyde. Here the climate is very mild, and the rugged grandeur of the sea side at Culzean is matched by lush greenery, even palms on the garden side, which gives the place the requisite fashionable Italian flavour. Airthrey was a development of this but inland, set against the background of the first Highland Hills where they fall majestically down into the Forth valley near Stirling. Unfortunately the castle was Scotch-baronialized in the nineteenth century by a

Glasgow businessman and since then has been incorporated within the purlieus of Stirling University, where we had better leave it, except to add that it once had a resident hermit, the post being advertised for in the newspapers. Seton Castle, on the east coast south of Edinburgh, is somewhat different. Its Italian precedent is Bolsena, to the north of Rome on the way to Orvieto, which is truly medieval, without crenellations or Gothic features, a fort, in other words: and it is a fort Adam built at Seton, a fort with outer and inner defences, arched entry, squat round towers without fanciful turrets or other extraneous decoration, and all surrounding and protecting a central redoubt, not tall enough to be called a keep but a lowish, massive building with crow-stepped central roof, lived-in and meant to be by fastidious clients.

Seton Castle replaces an older house of defence belonging to the once powerful family of that name and stands quite near Seton Collegiate kirk which I described in an earlier chapter. It does not clash in any way with this hoary remnant and may, in fact, have influenced the architect in his choice of site, the two buildings rising comfortably on either side of a wooded burn. The Castle may also derive from earlier, more purely Scottish influences, when Robert Adam's father had been Master Mason to the Board of Ordnance, in which

Seton Castle, East Lothian

capacity he had worked with General Wade in the Pacification of the Highlands after the first and second Jacobite rebellions. William Adam designed the handsome Wade Bridge at Aberfeldy, in Perthshire, dating from 1733, and was later engaged at Fort George, near Inverness, a fact referred to by Henry Mackenzie, Scott's particular friend, in his *Anecdotes and Egotisms*; a fascinating commentary on life and persons of significance in the second half of the eighteenth and first part of the nineteenth century in Scotland. Mackenzie states that as a boy staying with his grandfather at Nairn, he saw Robert Adam, who was then assisting William Adam at Fort George, and there the young architect designed a modest country house for his father, his first known plan but not actually built.

Most of the other designs by this brilliant Scotsman that matter are to be found in Edinburgh, the University, which he never completed; the Register House, which he did; and the north side of Charlotte Square, which was completed posthumously. Elsewhere his experience died with him and his castellated masterpieces were not expertly copied or understood by his contemporaries, for the Tudor and neo-Jacobean vogue that beset the country under George IV triumphed in North as well as South Britain. It has no historical place here though there are many examples of it extant. Victorian Scotch Baronial that followed has more to recommend it, especially since in some details it has its origins in Bruce's work at Thirlestane, and David Bryce's interpretations of that at Blair and in other restorations and rebuildings undertaken by him; but they are cold by comparison, very much essays in a style and not always good essays. Like the Gothic revivalists, who made little attempt to relate plan to structure but merely clothed stereotyped plans with Gothic clothes, the Scotch Baronial architects tended to add turrets and dormers, crow-steps and other quaint touches to please clients in search of status symbols. Bryce and his associates obliged, but they could equally well have done so in another style. Balmoral is perhaps an exception having been painstakingly designed by a well-meaning German Prince; but it is just as mechanical looking and new as the tartan he devised for the family Queen Victoria referred to as 'We Stuarts'.

Dunrobin Castle, Sutherland, from the east

Further north still, away up in Sutherland, we come across a different style of castle, which for me represents the very last acceptable example unless, of course, one allows for Sir Robert Lorimer's reconstructions which are a little too near our own time for an unbiased assessment to be made yet. Actually, Lorimer worked at Dunrobin, which claims to be the oldest inhabited house in Scotland, and certainly the tiny keep built by the first Earl of Sutherland in the thirteenth century survives, surrounded and hidden by successive enlargements and additions. It is hardly lived-in though, and what we see today belongs either to the seventeenth century, the early nineteenth or the first half of this. In the reign of Charles II the rather tall wimpled turret roofs were added, plus a typical ogee imitation of Thirlestane; then in the first decade of Victoria's reign Sir Charles Barry, whose scheme for the Houses of Parliament was accepted in place of one by the deceased Adam Brothers, designed a large new addition. Unlike Robert Adam who had evolved his own inimitable castellated style from mixed Italian and Highland Paci-

fication sources, Barry turned to the French idea of what a
Scottish castle should look like and in so doing followed a
somewhat more sensible line than the Prince Consort and his
imitators, for not only had Scotland been joined to France
politically and culturally down the centuries but her architecture had been greatly influenced by French ideas. Besides
this Sir Walter Scott's historical novels, and notably his
Quentin Durward, which dramatized the Franco-Scottish alliance, had just swept the Continent. In France they set the
tone for and inspired Dumas, Victor Hugo and Merimée, to
name but a few; and thus the 'Auld Alliance' took on a new
lease of life through the life and work of the Bard of Abbotsford.

Barry's castle for the Duke of Sutherland repeats the high
pointed roofs and extinguisher capped turrets of the earlier
edifice almost to the point of exaggeration, creating something
that verges on the Gibbs-dentifrice pattern, certainly something
that Walt Disney would have appreciated. This slight arti-
ficiality is heightened, as Culzean is in its own way, by the
castle's beautiful setting on a wooded site by the North Sea,
three-quarters of the way from Edinburgh to John o' Groats.
The effect of the Gulf Stream is felt here, and this, plus the
near presence of high, heather-clad Highland hills, provides
all that could be desired by way of romantic allusion and mystical
effect. In 1915 a fire occurred in the Barry part of Dunrobin,
and soon after the war Sir Robert Lorimer was called in to
repair and restore it. Happily the structure did not require
altering so that outwardly at least the castle remains as intended
in the eighteen-forties. Inside Lorimer worked very hard and
was not especially successful in what he did, being keener on
the older, stronger native idiom than its more sophisticated
latter day development; but in the drawing room he did
achieve something worthwhile, running a whole Victorian
suite into one enormous saloon and designing a plaster ceiling
that would not have disgraced some of those at Holyrood or in
his own Kellie, for it must be remembered that his father
restored Kellie Castle, in Fife, in which two Caroline plaster
ceilings of supreme beauty were installed under Bruce's aegis.
An interesting comment on Lorimer's contribution to Dunrobin is made by Christopher Hussey in his memorial to the
architect's work published in 1931, in which the author points

the difference between Lorimer's use of native woods, sycamore in the library, cedar and larch in the Duke's private suite and Scotch oak in the dining room, and remarks; 'It is amusing to contrast the method pursued here with the pitch pine and tartans of Balmoral sixty years earlier'. Indeed it is. It is also interesting to note that here we have a Scottish castle, begun in the thirteenth century, whose ancestral and architectural history has continued unabated until the present time; for after more than a century of southern-based Dukes having it Dunrobin has recently reverted to the older branch of the family and is now the seat of a Countess of Sutherland in her own right.

One of the inevitable adjuncts to a romantic Scottish castle in the eighteenth and nineteenth centuries was a folly. We have already described the Folly-gates at Traquair in detail and told their story. They belong to the Georgian era. The Hermitage at Airthrey has also been mentioned, but before either of these Bruce and William Adam had built 'seats' and 'temples' for their clients, Bruce two for himself at Kinross. The grounds at Hopetoun have several porticoed pavilions, some ending vistas, and in the park at Craigiehall, which estate marches with Hopetoun, there are others. The house was a Bruce one, completed for the first Marquis of Annandale in 1699, whose daughter married the first Earl of Hopetoun. The second Marquis visited Italy in 1717 and it was through his promptings that William Adam came to enlarge Hopetoun in the Roman Baroque manner; and when he died without an heir the Annandale pictures and works of art went there from Craigiehall. Fortunately Bruce's pleasant mansion on the banks of the Almond River has remained relatively intact except for some dormer windows and internal re-arrangements made when it became the Officers Mess of Scottish Command. Adam's work was almost wholly confined to the park where a round 'Temple' can be seen dominating the view from the south. The date of this is given as 1759, but the pedimented portico through which it is entered is at least fifty years older and came from Craigiehall itself, or rather from a 'seat' nearer the house. The 'Temple' is not a ruin and was actually used as a weekend retreat until recently. It belongs to the pre-Gothic tradition, the Italian period when such conceits reflected the learning and culture of their owners.

One of the first Gothic follies erected in Scotland was designed by the English architect Roger Morris for the Duke of Argyll and sited on the summit of Duniquoich, an 800 foot high hill behind Inveraray of particular charm and evocativeness. It takes the form of a watch-tower and now looks as if it has always been there. The castle below was also designed by Morris with William and John Adam as Clerks of Works, and completed by Robert Mylne, last in the long line of master masons to the Scottish Crown whose major achievement was the rebuilding of Holyroodhouse under Sir William Bruce. Mylne was London based and there is nothing at Inveraray Castle other than some latter-day wimpled roofs which were added to the round corner towers in Victorian times to make this rather English edifice look a little more Scottish. The date of Roger Morris's folly is 1746, which shows how secure the Dukes of Argyll were, being prominent Whigs and on the winning side; and work went on steadily at Inveraray while the Jacobite rebellion was in progress. Indeed, the whole village itself was demolished to make room for the Duke's Georgian-Gothic castle and a brand new village laid out by Mylne on an entirely virgin site.

In 1758 'Ossian's Hall' was built on the estate of the future second Duke of Atholl, another Whig but one with a sympathetic interest in the Highlands and a well-developed sense of the picturesque. This folly stands in a romantic site on the edge of a chasm made by Braan Burn as it forges a way through the rocks to join the Tay between Dunkeld and Birnam. It is nothing more than a delightful summer house and is in the care of the National Trust for Scotland, having been renamed 'The Hermitage'. I do not know why, for its Ossianic connotation was a good one and apposite, since it was here, amongst other places, that James MacPherson, Napoleon's favourite author by the way, used to come when writing, or collecting as he claimed, ancient Celtic verse. On the same estate, and for the same man, 'The Whim' was erected in 1768. This takes the form of a one wall thick fort that ends a vista about half a mile from Blair Castle, which, as we have seen, was then debaronialized and converted into a Georgian country house. The Dukes were descended from the Kings of Man, and old prints show The Whim gay with the three-legged flag of Man flying from the highest point. Later in the century came the age of false ruins of which Scotland can boast a few. In the grounds of Hopetoun House, for instance, stands Staneyhill Tower, which, originally the ancestral redoubt of the Shairps, or Sharps of that ilk, including Sir William Shairp who was Cash-keeper to Charles II and paid Sir William Bruce his fees at Holyrood, was adapted as a Folly in the nineteenth century, its ruined state being stratified for the purpose. Again, Hume Castle, which was originally a Border pele and partly demolished by Colonel Fenwick, Puritan Governor of Berwick, in 1651, was re-edified in 1794 by the last Earl of Marchmont and turned into the dummy castle that now crowns a commanding hillock overlooking the Cheviots and fields of England; it has been a lookout for invaders from the days of Edward I to those of Napoleon and Hitler.

Moving north again we come to Kinnoull Hill, above Perth, where the ninth Earl of Kinnoull commemorated a journey down the Rhine by building a fake fortress overlooking a dramatic turn in the River Tay. It used to be a picnic site, a place for cold collations in Victorian times, when the magnificent views all round probably did conjure up suitably Germanic visions. One is reminded, however, of earlier tastes and ideas, and of Sir Walter Scott's reaction to the Roman boast of 'Ecce Tiberis' when first they beheld the Tay:

> But where's the Scot that would the vaunt repay
> And hail the puny Tiber for the Tay?

Not quite so airily placed but more interestingly designed than Lord Kinnoull's tower is Balcarres Craig, at Colinsburgh, in Fife. It was built by another much travelled Scot, ancestor of the present Earl of Crawford and Balcarres. Again sited on a rocky outcrop above the broad champaign this 'medieval' tower with Gothic openings is almost invisible in summer, hidden by its cloak of ivy and sheltering woods, but in winter it dominates eastern Fife behind the twin Royal Burghs of Earlsferry and Elie, the latter boasting one of our most amusing follies. The Lady's Tower, as it is called, stands on a small promontory jutting out into the sea, but although it resembles an old defence tower it is really a clever disguise for a bathing

Balcarres Craig,
Colinsburgh, Fife

pavilion, having been built for Lady Janet Anstruther of Elie House in such a way as she could use it whatever the tide. This was achieved by having two platforms, one for low and another for high water, while privacy was assured by a watchman ringing a bell whenever the lady entered or emerged from the sea.

Sir William Chambers was responsible for two follies in Scotland, a neo-classical Temple at Duddington and a giant Pineapple at Dunmore, between Airth and Stirling. Chambers was the rival of Robert Adam and the favourite of the Royal Family. He was born of Scottish parents in Sweden and spent part of his youth in China, which probably accounts for his affection for Continental architecture and Chinese decoration. Nothing he did in his parent's country can be said to relate directly to his Scottish origins, and the remarkable Pineapple at Dunmore House, in which stone leaves protruding as in a real pineapple are held in position by metal stays, is about as appropriate here as a pagoda in Spitzbergen; but it is a genuine folly, a classical one despite its exotic overtures; which is more than can be said for some other so-called follies, better known and more photographed. I refer particularly to Mac-Caig's 'Folly' in Oban, which was actually intended as a library and museum and was built for that purpose, though not completed, by local unemployed. Without a roof it resembles at a distance the Colosseum, which may account for its being called a folly, but one wonders what it would have looked like, even what eventual purpose it could have served, Oban being so small and remote a place. The Wallace Memorial near Stirling is a sort of folly, certainly a very visible one, standing atop Abbey Craig and built, in its lower portions, like a laird's tower of the sixteenth century, with excessive baronial attachments above and a crown-spire larger and more ornate than that of St Giles' Kirk in Edinburgh. One might call this a 'national folly', though not a 'national disgrace', which is how the unfinished scale model of the Parthenon on the Calton Hill in Edinburgh is customarily described. Disgrace because it was never finished. It combined too many divergent ideas and would have looked so chilling and perfect in the pale Caledonian sun after Athens that it surely is better left as a half-completed monument to Scottish pride. This pagan recreation was meant to house a Presbyterian kirk; to commemorate the Fallen in the Peninsular War; Wellington's Victory at Waterloo; and at the same time to support Edinburgh's New Athenian pretensions.

V

Scottish Towns and Villages

THE TYPICAL English small town or village nestling cosily round its old church, with manor house or castle half hidden in the trees behind, is virtually unknown in Scotland, at any rate it was unknown until the eighteenth century when, following the Union of the Parliaments in 1707 and the return of peaceful conditions after centuries of internecine strife, a number of model villages and small burghs were created. The first of these was Gifford, in the County of Haddington, which today looks as Scottish as anything north of the Border, with its 'L'-shaped layout, one arm running out from the gates of the big house to the Mercat or Market Cross, the other running at right angles to it from the cross in the direction of the whitewashed parish kirk, a rather Dutch looking building with a tower in the middle of the main elevation. Gifford belongs to the reign of Queen Anne, when the big house itself was in process of being rebuilt on a new site to the plans of James Smith and his partner Alexander MacGill. This was Yester, described in our last chapter, where the Adam family came to complete the work, and which was still in progress during the Jacobite rebellion of 1745, when slaters engaged on the roof threw broken slates down onto Hanoverian troops fleeing from Prince Charlie's Highlanders after Prestonpans. The whole enterprise was somewhat ambitious since it entailed the removal of an existing village to make room for the house, the desertion of his ancient castle for more comfortable quarters by the laird himself, and a new village rising on a new site for his tenants. This was Gifford, called after the ancient family of lairds who first settled in East Lothian in Norman times and are now represented in the Scottish branch by the Marquis of Tweeddale.

A somewhat similar procedure took place at Inveraray, where, as we have seen, the English architect Roger Morris built a new 'Gothic' castle for the Duke of Argyll, which was

finished by Robert Mylne of London with the Adam family
again in attendance, as Clerks of Works. To do this another
old village had to be demolished and a new one erected on a
fresh site. Mylne was put in charge, and the present attractive
burgh of Inveraray was his creation. It would be idle to pre-
tend its buildings are vernacular in style though the setting
and the use of whitewash and Ballachulish slates does give
the place a local cachet far removed from the sophisticated
origins of its architecture. The three principal buildings are
the hotel, the Court House and Parish Kirk, the latter being
the most interesting since it provides for the needs of two separate
congregations, each entering at opposite ends of this plain,
rectangular structure by dignified pillared porticoes, Gaelic
speakers through one, English speakers through the other;
and divided inside by a solid wall. Above, to mark the division
no doubt, soars a tall, slender flèche, which was removed
during the last war as a danger to aircraft but has since been
replaced after a long wrangle over who should pay for its
restitution. As at Gifford practically the only reminders of
older days at Inveraray are the ruins of the laird's medieval
castle and the Mercat Cross, which in each case was re-erected
on a new site, it being important to re-establish the burgh's
rights and standing by retaining this symbolic object.

Mercat Crosses represent, perhaps, the most original and
antique feature of many Scottish burghs, and the fact that they
were once spelt 'croce' in the Italian or Latin way, testifies to
their religious rather than commercial significance in the days
before the Reformation. They were, in many cases, not market
crosses at all but sanctuaries such as one still sees in parts of
France and Italy, sometimes at a crossroads or near a village
church. The cross at Inveraray symbolizes both purposes,
being topped still by an ancient Celtic remnant brought from
Iona, while at Banff, which is the only cross left in Scotland
with its original crucifix, it rises stupidly beside a bus stop in
front of a Georgian Town Hall, not in the market place nor
yet near the kirk. With the triumph of Protestantism, of course,
most religious symbolism was either abolished or forgotten;
but this did not mean the abolition of Mercat Crosses the shafts
of which, at least, often continued to serve as centrepieces in
the market place, or marketgate as it was usually called in

Scotland. A few retained mutilated crucifixes on top, most with the Arms of the local laird or the King's Unicorn replacing them. One of the oldest of these spared souvenirs stands undamaged on a small green beside a few cottages at Newbiggin, in Lanarkshire, literally still marking a crossroads. The top may have once formed the basis of a medieval cross and is said to date from the thirteenth century, but today, after centuries of weathering, it looks more flowerlike than anything else and the date 1693 appears on the shaft. However, that may only recall the re-erection of this hoary relic on this particular site after having been brought here from neighbouring Dunsyre, and before that from Dolphinton, each hamlet in turn having had the right to hold a market. The story goes that the Newbiggin Cross should be at Skirling, another small village in the vicinity, but that the Skirling folk transporting it from Dunsyre were forced to leave it where it is on account of bad weather! A strange explanation for something that is probably much less complicated; and the cross may have remained stationary while only the people moved.

It is perhaps worth recalling that until comparatively modern times there were no shops in Scottish hamlets and villages, only a few in the larger burghs and these not very comprehensive. Thus the market was the place where everything that was not made 'on the premises', by an army of craftsmen working at home in the narrow closes and wynds of the towns, was bought and sold. Life was much more akin to that of the twentieth-century suburb or rural centre where today vans call bringing meat and bread, vegetables and groceries, even clothes and ironmongery, for the markets were movable both in respect of the days and places they occurred. In fact, it was considered quite a privilege to have one, and the right was eagerly sought and fought over. I am talking now of the days after the Reformation and the complete secularization of such activities. Before then fairs normally took place as part of some religious festival, as they do today in Italy and elsewhere; and a number of such movable feasts persist yet in Scotland, the Lammas Market in St Andrews is a case in point, when the Marketgate is taken over by booths and buyers and amusements in much the same way as many Continental towns are. Curiously enough, the old Mercat

Cross which once stood at the centre of all this bustle and from which Royal Proclamations were read, and to which malefactors were chained by means of iron neck-pieces, or jougs, has been removed.

A particularly fine and well preserved example of a Mercat Cross erected purely for commercial and civic reasons, and still *in situ*, is the one at Kincardine-on-Forth, which bears the Coat of Arms of the first Earl of Kincardine, who set it up in the reign of Charles I when he obtained the coveted royal authority for so doing. Another good specimen, this time with the Royal Unicorn atop as well as local and baronial heraldry below, is at Inverkeithing, in front of the Town House, or Tolbooth, itself a delightful building of the kind in which the roles of overnight prison and council chamber were combined. The outside forestair is typical too, and the octagonal turret above with ogee roof and ship-finial just right. Edinburgh boasts a Unicorn-crowned cross, raised on a shaft above a galleried platform of some magnificence. Here the accession of kings and queens and other official proclamations were announced, and on one occasion, for the Restoration of King Charles II, wine flowed from the gargoyled waterspouts projecting from the foot of the Gallery. This cross is only original as to its shaft, but a very similar one, entire in all its details, may be seen at Prestonpans, a few miles to the south; while a bare quarter of a mile away from the city centre, in the separate burgh of the Canongate, a medieval cross survives, removed for safety to the graveyard of the Canongate Kirk. To see a large municipal cross intact, or nearly so, replete with roundel effigies of all the kings of Scots from James I to James VII decorating the gallery, one must go to Aberdeen, where, however, the splendidly arched supports leave the actual platform free-standing, the spiral stair by which dignatories once ascended ...ing been removed when the cross was placed on its present

...ing the reign of James VI of Scots and to some
...the seventeenth century that Scottish com-
...d and more or less caught up with that of
...Kingdom. Trade was mostly with the
...Baltic States and there developed a
...ngly reminiscent of Flanders and

Scandinavia. This was most noticeable along the east coast but not only there. Civic pride then expressed itself in a number of significant ways, but principally in the erection and adornment of handsome Town Houses, extensions and improvements to the old burgh tolbooth, or prison-cum-council-chamber, as at Inverkeithing; and in bigger towns quite large buildings appeared. Especially evocative of the age were some of the towers added to these structures, many of them making one think of the *beffrois* of Belgium or the elaborate bell-towers of Holland. Glasgow, a city which was almost totally razed to the ground between the end of the eighteenth and the middle of the nineteenth centuries, quaintly retains three interesting memorials to this earlier and relatively prosperous era. They are the tower of the now defunct Tolbooth, which is known as 'The Cross', on account of the fact that the original Mercat Cross once stood before it; the Trongate, derived from gait, or walk, and not to be confused with a 'port' or entrance gate of which only one remains in Scotland, the West Port at St Andrews; and the Bridgegate Steeple, an isolated tower that belonged to the old Trades House, or Chamber of Commerce. This is said to have been designed by Sir William Bruce whose part, probably, was confined to an extensive restoration in the late Cromwellian period and the addition of the existing bulbous cupola. Glasgow does not boast an original Mercat Cross but a brand new one in the Jacobean style erected between the wars to a design by the late Mrs Edith Hughes, the oldest practising lady architect at the time of her death, in 1971, and the first lady to become a member of the R.I.B.A.

The Trongate is all that remains of a former *piazza*, or arcaded space on the Continental model where folk foregathered to talk business or pass the time of day. Such 'piazzas' were comparatively common in Scotland, they being eminently suited to our climate, and one wonders why they have mostly disappeared and not been replaced. At Elgin, in Moray, there are still one or two arcaded stretches along the High Street and one especially fine piece at No. 7, the so-called 'Braco House'. This was built in the reign of William and Mary for Johr Duncan and Margaret Innes, his wife, whose initials and t' date 1694 are carved on the skew-putts, or corbelled projections at the foot of the gables. Later it became

(*left*) Braco's 'Banking House', Elgin, Moray—note arched 'piazza'. (*right*) Tolbooth and Town Steeple at Strathmiglo, Fife; note forestair. (*below*) Old Aberdeen: the Town House

premises of a very early bank founded by William Duff of Dipple and Braco, who was father of the first Earl of Fife and ancestor of the modern dukes of that name. The Glasgow Trongate, like many others, was the place where the 'tron' or public weigh beam was, and goods entering the city were weighed and charged duty there. It stood near the Town House which served, as we have seen, a variety of purposes, jail, council chamber and court. There are many notable Town Houses in Scotland and most still used, if not as jails at least as council chambers and sometimes as courts. An excellent specimen graces the Altoun of Aberdeen, but others worth a journey are at Stirling, by Sir William Bruce; Haddington, by William Adam; Kinross, by Robert Adam and presented to the burgh as a token of his representing it in Parliament and being the local sheriff; Berwick-upon-Tweed, which has a handsome baroque steeple designed by Joseph Dodds of Edinburgh; and Banff, by James, third son of the elder Adam.

Bruce's Tolbooth and Town House at Stirling is interesting on a number of counts. It dates from 1702, when the architect had just been released from confinement in Stirling Castle for his alleged Jacobite sympathies, and the workmen had to travel to and from Kinross to get their orders. There is a jail, of course, and above is a fine suite of rooms panelled in much the same manner as those of the laird's loft at Abercorn, some of the joiners being employed at both places. The mason here and at Hopetoun, and indeed at Kinross, was Tobias Bauchop of Alloa, who subsequently copied Bruce's tower at Stirling when he built the Midsteeple and Town House a few years later in Dumfries. There are several precedents for this particular design, the ancient belfry of the kirk of St Ninian at Leith, for example, which is Cromwellian in date, and more particularly that at Cowane's Hospital in Stirling itself, which was built in the reign of Charles I by the Royal Master Mason John Mylne. The latter was the uncle of Robert Mylne, who worked at Holyrood and elsewhere under Bruce, and the designer of a number of fine official buildings, notably the new Parliament House and the Tron Kirk in Edinburgh. Cowane's Hospital is an 'E'-shaped, crow-stepped structure, the small arm being occupied by the tower and entrance porch, which has the effigy of the founder, John Cowane, the town's Dean of Guild, set in a classical niche above the door. The tower is surmounted by an ogee lead roof with amusing iron spikelets marking the edges as at the Tolbooth.

There used to be a dignified Town House at Dundee, replete with arcaded *piazza* and Gibbsian steeple. It was the work of William Adam and was needlessly demolished in the nineteen-thirties to allow a better view of the extremely ordinary, post-1914 Civic Centre. It made a pair in respect of its Adam tower with Haddington, in East Lothian, which mellow country town has recently been the subject of a Civic Trust rejuvenation scheme. One has two thoughts about this. One, to welcome anything that improves the overall appearance of our streets, and two, doubts about the result of such standardization when it comes to using modern architectural colours, yellow, grey and khaki in place of the traditional Scottish white, orange and pink. With St Andrews and Elgin Haddington is one of the best preserved and lively of our old Lowland burghs, with a noble Collegiate Kirk, many largish town houses with Dutch gables and attractive doorways, and a wide 'marketgait' closed at one end by William Adam's Tolbooth and at the other by the Castle Hotel, a building whose owners did not join in the Civic Trust exercise and retained their brightly-painted façade which, I am bound to say, seems rather better suited to the Scottish scene than the more refined, 'non-committed' hues of much of the rest of the street.

The Tolbooth at Culross is fine, as are others along the Fife coast at Dysart and Crail; while away to the north, at Cromarty, the Court House is as douce and elegant an edifice as any of the other buildings erected there in the second half of the eighteenth century, when the little burgh was recast by an 'improving' laird. Georgian factories, warehouses, mills, breweries, houses and churches are amongst the charms of this far away model township, which until the last few years looked like being abandoned to decay. Since the discovery of North Sea Oil, however, and the development of the Inverness-Invergordon area by industry, Cromarty has become an appreciated dormitory for perspicacious incomers and its future would appear assured provided the rival claims of commerce and culture can be met without destroying either. At Culross, the outlook has been somewhat blighted by the presence of large oil refineries on the south side of the estuary, reminding one of the view of Mestre from Venice; and although this is not so bad as the salt-panning operation that formerly took place here, sending up smoke and fumes and covering the houses with black, oily soot, it can scarcely appeal to potential residents of the more discriminating type.

The special feature of nearly all Scottish Tolbooths is their towers which in many cases are veritable *pièces de résistance*. The oldest is probably at Tain, in Ross-shire, where Norse influence was strong, and indeed where the very name of the burgh derives from the Viking *thing*, or meeting place. Whether these associations were responsible for the local Town House taking the form of a strong keep in the middle of the town is not quite clear, but that is what it is, a simple donjon-like tower with corner turrets and pointed roof, and an obvious retreat, possibly redoubt, in times of trouble. It has been restored and made less 'medieval' inside, but may date from the fifteenth century in its lower portions. At Kirkcudbright, in Galloway, the Tolbooth tower also has corner turrets and a rounded, pointed roof, and again it has been restored. The really odd thing here is the way in which the Mercat Cross has been treated, the pre-Reformation top being placed on the balcony at the entrance to the Tolbooth, while the octagonal base stands below, a modern street lamp rising from its steps. The burgh is one of the bonniest in Scotland, its position on the banks of the tidal Dee, three hours driving from either Edinburgh or Glasgow, has resulted in its tranquil, unassuming character remaining largely intact. Greyfriars Kirk I have already described in a previous chapter, also MacClellan's Castle; there is not much else of great antiquity except the Tolbooth, but whole streets of pink and white houses, sometimes black ones with pale blue margins, survive, most of them dating from the late eighteenth or early nineteenth century and beloved of artists of the 'Glasgow School'. It is a backwater in many ways, but it is often in such backwaters that civilized conditions seem to subsist today.

The Tolbooth at Kirkcudbright is said to have been partly built, or rebuilt, with stones from Dundrennan Abbey, where Mary Queen of Scots spent her last few days in Scotland before throwing herself at the mercy of her cousin, Queen Elizabeth.

If so it makes the rebuilt portion quite a bit later than the rest, for Queen Mary's sojourn in the district was in 1568 and it was not until twenty years afterwards that Dundrennan, a Cistercian foundation whose mother house was at Rievaulx, in Yorkshire, finally passed to the crown, its revenues being added to those of the Chapel Royal in Stirling in 1621. At Strathmiglo, in Fife, is another Tolbooth built or enlarged from more ancient masonry, this time from the castle of Sir William Scott of Balwearie, a courtier at Falkland in the reign of James V. Strathmiglo and its neighbour, Auchtermuchty, were closely connected with the court, the royal bread being baked in the former, the royal falcons, or gleds, being kept in the latter, a fact recalled in the present Gladgate. The Tolbooth tower at Strathmiglo set a standard for several others in the vicinity, towers that seem more like the *campanile* of the Venetian *Terra Ferma* than the *beffrois* of Belgium, with their sturdy seventy or so feet crowned with open galleries and octagonal spires. They mostly date from the first half of the eighteenth century, and thus their quaint but happy blending of Renaissance and Gothic features makes them unusual, giving the small towns they punctuate personalities all their own. The tower at Kinross is of the same group but free-standing, the Tolbooth proper having been redesigned for a site opposite by Robert Adam in the severest late-Georgian manner; and there is another at Milnathort, about two miles to the north. The Strathmiglo specimen is approached by a typical Fife forestair leading direct from the street to the first floor, while at Auchtermuchty, where the Tolbooth tower is perhaps the best of its kind, the town worthies were themselves once locked up for bankrupting the burgh.

It is at Auchtermuchty that most of the surviving thatched cottages of the region are, though few remain in a decent state, many are empty and no local thatcher survives to repair those still occupied. The divots, used to line the roofs and form the roof coping, are showing through in almost all the existing cottages, which were originally thatched from reeds grown on the banks of Lindores Loch or the shores of the Firth of Tay near Newburgh. Nowadays should anyone wish to have his thatch replaced, as was done in the case of the Moncreif House at Falkland, they must go to England and employ a

Norfolk reed man. I only know of one recently re-thatched house in north Fife that was done locally, and that is at Collessie, where a former weaver's cottage was restored by an enterprising builder for his own occupation. The Tolbooth at Falkland, incidentally, is superior to all its brethren, belonging to the late eighteenth century; but it is still very Venetian in style and makes an·intriguing contrast with the twin-turreted Gothic gateway of the Palace across the road. The latter used to be cobbled in the old, rough cobble-stones one now only finds in neglected farmyards, not the regular pavé, or setts that survive in some of our city streets, but bumpy irregular stones that are very difficult to walk on and must have made travel by coach or cart most uncomfortable. The improvers might, however, have left a small token area of cobble around the Mercat Cross, which in Victorian times was rebuilt in monumental form and pompously decorated with lions and the Civic and Royal heraldry of this ancient Royal Burgh, the first in Scotland to establish a Conservation Area.

Many of the houses in Falkland are at least three hundred years old, and besides the bigger, better kept ones that housed royal courtiers and their descendants, there are rows of smaller cottages in which, as at Collessie and elsewhere, weaving was a home-industry. They frequently had forestairs to their living quarters, the lower space being reserved for stores, were thatched, though few of them are now, and later roofed in red pantiles, which came from the Low Countries in the seventeenth century and were made in Scotland by William Adam and his associates in the eighteenth. Slate arrived with the industrial revolution and the whisky distilleries that presently support many of the people. There are three distilleries in the neighbourhood and many more throughout Fife, most of them making what is called 'Grain Whisky', which is not quite the same either in process or content as the old Malt Whisky, being a mélange of maize and barley and continuously distilled in a patent still. Before the mid-nineteenth century barley alone was used and the whisky made from malt dried over peat sods in 'pagoda'-topped kilns; the flavour was inimitable and the shape of the kilns an integral part of the Scottish architectural scene, as traditional in some lowland districts as in the Highlands. On a smaller scale, but not entirely

Falkland, Fife: Old Wheelhouse, with Parish Kirk (right)
and Palace (left)

different in purpose or design, are the numerous modest grain
mills whose drying kiln hoppers still dot the countryside; they
are driven by water power and I know of one miller who uses
his mill rather cleverly to make electricity and so take advantage
of both worlds. Besides water, of course, motive power was
provided on the farm by animals, oxen and horses, as witness
the octagonal sheds known as 'horsegangs', with a central
wheel for threshing the corn and performing other agricultural
labours. There is a particularly good example, and in complete
state of wholeness, in a farmyard at the southern end of
Falkland, within sight of the Palace and the Parish Kirk.

Despite a few notable exceptions few of the old private houses
in Scotland, even in a burgh like Falkland, date from before
the Jacobean age, which begins in the north with the accession
of James VI to his mother's throne in 1567, not in 1603, as in
England. Stirling boasts two pre-Jacobean houses in its
Spittal group, one of them bearing the inscription;

THIS HOVS IS FVNDIT FOR SVPORT OF THE PVIR
BE ROBERT TAILLOYOVR TO KING JAMES
THE 4 IN ANNO 1530,

which if genuinely referring to the existing structure would make it the oldest inhabited town mansion of its kind in Scotland. The property was certainly bought in 1521 by Robert Spittal, who was Court Tailor to James IV and died in 1550, having founded a hospital for the poor in 1530. The existing house may not actually have been this hospital, however, and the date stone placed here afterwards; but in any event it belongs to the sixteenth century and stands next to another and better preserved building of the same period, Darrow's Lodging, which retains its semi-circular stair turret on the front and some original fenestration. The windows are now sashes, not casements as originally, and this makes one wonder why, when restoration work is undertaken on such properties, the casements are not put back, or if sashes are repaired they are not given thick astragals with small panes instead of the wafer-thin variety and big rectangular panes introduced in the late Georgian and early Victorian eras. The Spittal group at Stirling is probably contemporary with John Mossman's House in Edinburgh, erroneously but irrevocably associated with John Knox, though built for and lived in by the man who recast the Crown of Scotland for James V and was jeweller to Mary, Queen of Scots. He was a well known Roman Catholic and his initials and armorial device appear on the house.

Adjoining John Knox's House is another survivor of the sixteenth century in the attic of which George Jamesone, the 'Scottish Van Dyck', Limner in Scotland to Charles I, once had his studio. The building undoubtedly owes its continued existence to the proximity of its apocryphally named neighbour and it is interesting for another reason, its main saloon is decorated in the style prevalent in the reign of Charles II, with richly moulded panelling and ceilings. In Perth there is the house called the Fair Maid's, which is partially late medieval but very much restored. Its ancient purpose is still evidenced by a tiny niche at one corner wherein stood the statue of St Bartholomew, patron saint of glovers. It was, in fact, the headquarters of the Perth Glovers' Guild and features as such in Sir Walter Scott's novel. Not far away the Kinnoull Dower House, later the Gowrie Inn, was demolished in 1967. It was the last half-timbered house left in Scotland outside the capital and should never have been allowed to go. Another irreparable loss was George Jamesone's father's house in Schoolhill Aberdeen, which with its corner turrets, high roof and elaborate corbelling was not unlike a smaller version of one of the famous Aberdeenshire castles, Craigievar or Crathes, in which its begetter is said to have had a hand, he being an architect-cum-mason of repute.

Still with us, fortunately, is the tiny town-castle that gaily ornaments the crossroads in the middle of the Banffshire village of Fordyce. This 'toy' was built in 1592 for Provost Thomas Menzies of Aberdeen when he retired, and although small in scale is perfect in every detail. It epitomizes its kind, displaying in miniature a true Jacobean fortalice, corner turrets, crow-stepped gables, swept-dormers, a marvellous projecting stair turret in the re-entrant angle with cable-ringed corbelling, carved monograms and inscriptions, shot and shut-holes and a fine nail-studded oak door. Grander but not more delightful is Provost Skene's House in Aberdeen city, which is a lucky surival of the Jacobean age now crowded in by bad-mannered neighbours in the form of modern skyscrapers and a pretentious granite college. Its interior is particularly interesting since it contains rooms decorated at different periods including one with some notable wall paintings of a religious nature completed just after the Reformation. Provost Skene's House is furnished and run as a municipal museum. It is matched by a near contemporary, Provost Ross's House, which again looks rather lonely in its 'cleared', re-developed setting, on the way down to the harbour where the Provost had ships and could see them berthing and sailing from his upstairs windows.

The transition from town-castle to town house took place in the reign of Charles I, when a number of small mansions were built in Scottish burghs which did not sport the usual corner turrets and tall roofs of their immediate predecessors. One of the best of these was erected by a Senator of the College of Justice, Lord Magdalens, at Prestonpans, where a few years earlier, having obtained Royal permission to hold a regular fair, he had built the dignified Mercat Cross, with tiny lock-up below. His new house, known nowadays as the Hamilton Dower House on account of its owner being a Hamilton of Preston, forms a double 'L' on plan, with one arm rounding

(*left*) Jacobean mercat cross at Prestonpans, East Lothian. (*right*) Eighteenth-century Town House and green, Culross, Fife

the street corner and the other protecting a small courtyard facing the road. It is white and was probably once pantiled, though now slated and with modern sash not the older casement windows. It has no fake baronial ornament and only one minute stair turret, and some gaily painted Hamilton heraldry to recall Jacobean antecedents. 'Magdalens' was the first building of its kind to be rescued from decay by the National Trust for Scotland and restored, before the war, by Mr Robert Hurd. The house supplanted the Hamilton of Preston's crow's nest of a tower that still stands in gaunt vacancy in a field behind, together with a double doocot, which provided winter food and the status-symbol of a Bonnet Laird, or non-titled gentleman. Dr Douglas Simpson describes Preston Tower in detail in his *Ancient Stones of Scotland*, amplifying his description with a sketch and a whole page of plans and a section. The lairds evidently made some attempt to improve its comforts before finally deciding to move, for above their five storeyed eyrie they added a further two floors, a sort of

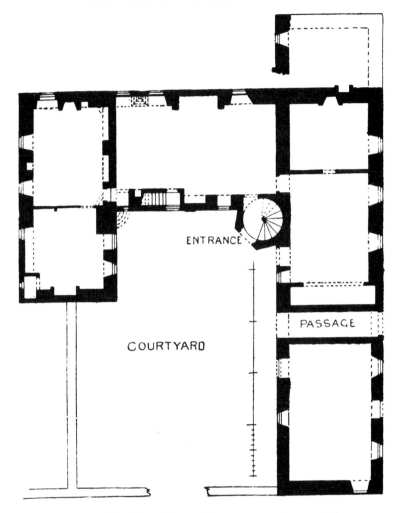

Magdalens, the Hamilton Dower House: plan of ground floor, before removal of stables (bottom right).

Renaissance 'penthouse' which looks most odd.

Prestonpans has other attractions, and within a stone's throw of the Hamilton Dower House is 'Northfield', home of Joseph Majoribanks, a Burgess of Edinburgh who was married to Lord Magdalens' sister in 1607. No two houses could be more different in architecture and appearance, 'Northfield' having been built while the Jacobean taste for high sweeping roofs and bulging corner turrets was still in vogue, and but for a lengthening of the original building seems as tall and perky as any other late sixteenth-century laird's tower. Within are notable painted ceilings, a feature of the period and largely resulting from trade with Scandinavia and the Low Countries. These were revealed when the house itself was renovated by Mr Schomberg Scott, formerly architectural adviser to the National Trust for Scotland. Renovated is his own word, not restored; and there is quite a difference, indeed, many buildings 'restored' by the Trust and others could more accurately be termed rebuilt; which may have made them convenient for modern living, and may also have saved them from complete demolition, but as historic buildings some are now no more authentic than an antique chair with new legs. Renovation suggests, quite rightly, that the house has been repaired where necessary, redecorated and made comfortable without reducing its antique properties. The beehive doocot that once pertained to 'Northfield' now stands without the garden wall on a municipalized green beside some expensive looking Council Houses, becoming in the process more of a monument than the resort of doves, and might, but for the excessive mortaring of the masonry, be a cairn commemorating the famous battle that took place here in 1745.

The hero of the Battle of Prestonpans was not Prince Charlie, nor yet the Hanoverian general who ran away with his soldiers at the first charge of the Highlanders, but Colonel James Gardiner, a veteran of Marlborough's campaigns and a stout defender of George II. Though retired and suffering from old wounds he stayed his ground when his dragoons fled, resisting the enemy single handed until finally struck down, when he was carried off the battlefield and died near his own house. This beautiful late-Stuart mansion, with curved central pediment and Dutch gables, has twice been gutted by fire but remains capable of renovation. It is approached via a broad tree-lined avenue and has in front of it an obelisk commemorating the only real hero of the fight in which such interesting persons as Lord Provost Drummond, the man who founded the Georgian 'New Town of Edinburgh', was a volunteer on the Government side, and the future Dr Alexander Carlyle of Inveresk, who as a young man was also a volunteer, watched the battle from the safety of the kirk tower. I mention this because it shows how dispersed the typical Scots village was, even a small town like Prestonpans, where half a mile of fields lay between the church and 'Magdalens', and nearly as much between it and Colonel Gardiner's Bankton House, while the Mercat Cross is nowhere near any market. The Church is actually in the Seatoun, where once there was an oyster war between Preston and Newhaven, and where, before that, salt had been dried in big iron pans on the seashore, the second-grade coal fires used spluttering and steaming and creating at least as great a pollution hazard as Cockenzie Power Station.

Salt panning was a major industry along the shores of the Firth of Forth, more on the northern side than the southern, hence the greater number of small but prosperous burghs, and possibly King James VI's reference to Fife being 'A Beggar's Mantle lined with gold', if that is what he did say. Some records word it as 'Silver buttons on a serge mantle', which certainly describes the position of the coastal burgh's *vis-à-vis* the country areas at that time. So far as buildings are concerned it has been said that the coast road from Culross, in the extreme west of the kingdom, to St Andrews, in the north-east, contains more of interest in the native style of architecture than any other single stretch in Scotland, and this is probably true. Fife was, until the latter day development of the central belt between Glasgow and Edinburgh, the most populous part of the country, separated to some extent from the rest by its geographical position on a large peninsula, with no linking bridges before the building of the Forth and Tay railway and road bridges, and spared, thereby, much of the internecine strife that characterized life elsewhere; and it was more open to overseas influences. Sir George Bruce of Carnock's ships, for instance, sailed for Norway and the Hanseatic ports, to Holland, to Belgium and to France, carrying coals for export and bringing in salt from Portugal for curing Scottish fish.

We have already seen how prosperity was brought to Culross largely by Sir George Bruce's new drainage machinery whereby coal seams under the Forth could be tapped, and how the burgh became one of the most active and rich in the whole of Scotland. His 'palas' was not at all like the little turreted buildings of old Aberdeen but much more akin to burgher's dwellings in Bruges or Antwerp, with their pantiles, dormers, stepped gables, lattice windows and wooden shutters. Inside too there were barrel-vaulted rooms lined with painted boards, some of which have survived exposure and are now restored and protected by the Department of the Environment, acting for the owners of the house, the National Trust for Scotland. In the same Forthside Royal Burgh are numerous other buildings of the Jacobean or Caroline periods, mostly white or pink harled and roofed with red pantiles, while a few of the rough cobbled causeways, or narrow alleys that passed for streets 300 years ago, have been kept in their characteristically bumpy state. The old Tolbooth, with ogee-roofed tower, is entered via an external staircase as are several of its neighbours, and this, plus the crow-steps and Dutch gables elsewhere, makes Culross a virtual dream town so far as recreation of an ancient Scottish burgh of the seventeenth century is concerned.

Amongst the most photographed of the old houses is the one known as 'The Study', on account of its supposed association with Bishop Leighton of Dunblane, afterwards Archbishop of Glasgow, whose Lodgings have been nicely renovated recently. He is said to have retired to the top room of 'The Study' to meditate and to compose his sermons. Be this as it may, this small town tower is one of several in similar vein built along the Fife coast in or around the year 1590. They are all 'L'-shaped structures, tall, with tiny rooms and typical corkscrew-stair turrets; and all have been added to later on. 'The Study' was made more comfortable in 1626, when the large room at present used as an office and meeting place by the local representative of the National Trust, who lives with his wife in part of the building, acquired its beautiful panelling, and more recently had its painted beams restored and repainted. Those responsible had the good sense to eschew harsh modern colours and try to match the mellower shades of the past.

Of 'The Study's' more obvious and important architectural companions The Abbot's House at Dunfermline has been briefly mentioned before. Further along the coast, at Inver-keithing, No. 4 the High Street, almost opposite the old Tolbooth and handsome Mercat Cross, is a particularly in-teresting specimen of the period since it retains a fine mullioned window, a rare thing in Scotland and sure evidence of the approaching union with England. 'The Towers' at Dysart, recently restored as an Old People's Club, dates from 1587, while beyond, at Elie, the house known as 'The Castle' repeats at its western end the usual 'L'-shaped tower, then carries on with a Charles I wing and a William and Mary extension, when the original turnpike stair was removed and replaced with a scale-and-platt, or straight up to the landing and round, stair was put in. Its position, right on the shore, is most impressive, especially seen from the beach at low tide when the immense masculinity of the sea-wall protecting it is apparent. Kellie Lodge in the High Street at Pittenweem has likewise been added to in the seventeenth century, when its tall turreted stair tower proved inadequate for the lairds whose town mansion it was, and where the reception of Charles II took place in the tiny courtyard facing the street in 1651, with an out-of-doors banquet, and turkey carpets hanging from the windows. The best, or at any rate best-known and most thoroughly recorded of these small coastal *châtelets* is the former Manse of Kilrenny, which is actually in Anstruther Easter and called 'The Watch Tower'. It is the oldest manse, as opposed to parsonage, in Scotland and was built very largely by the minister himself, at his own expense but with some help in the form of materials supplied by the burgh. He had to do it himself because even then they had the sort of trade dispute we have come to expect, and if he had not turned handiman as well as preacher might not have gained entry when he did. The Rev James Melville, the minister in question, has written the whole story up for posterity, so there is no need for me to elaborate here, except to mention his receiving the Captain of a stranded ship from the Spanish Armada in 1588, which suggests that either there already existed part of 'The Watch Tower' or that the encounter took place elsewhere, since Melville only came to Anstruther in 1587 and his Manse was not built until 1590. At the top of the stair tower, in the equivalent room to Leighton's 'study' at Culross, they house what is said to be a portion of carved panelling from Senor Gomez's galleon, also the plaster cast of the murder of Archbishop Sharp taken from the van Nost-style tribute to that prelate in Holy Trinity Kirk in St Andrews.

In 1972 Scotland witnessed a spate of Conservation Area declarations, some of them to preserve old buildings which were already safe under existing orders, thus showing a misunderstanding of what was intended by the government when they introduced the appropriate legislation. The operative word is 'area', for it is useless leaving isolated buildings merely as monuments of the past, standing uncomfortably amidst twentieth-century development, or in vacant plots, like unwanted toys in the nursery when the children have grown up. A good example of what should constitute a Conservation Area, and conserved long before enlightened new laws were made, exists at Culross, and in the way practically the whole town was saved by the National Trust for Scotland from becoming a museum, or a decayed memorial to neglect of our cultural heritage. Culross was the first Fife burgh to receive 'the treatment', that is to be restored house by house and street by street. Inverkeithing has not been so treated though it would have made a rewarding successor if it had been taken in hand in time. Unhappily its centre has been ruined almost beyond recall. In the main 'square' is the over-restored and lonely-looking hulk of the former 'palas' of Queen Arabella Drummond, spouse of Robert III, whose Arms appear on the Mercat Cross. All around, until their untimely destruction, stood a number of only slightly younger buildings to which the 'palas' was itself physically joined. Old photographs show rows of them, some with wooden galleries on the first floor, the total effect being extraordinarily Continental and picturesque. They have all gone in the levelling-down process, which in Scotland applies both to people and buildings and often passes for 'progress', but which is really a pandering to the lowest common denominator and the triumph of the commonplace. The trend may have reached its climax, for some newer rebuilding plans now include the retention of older, interesting properties, and at least some last minute respect is being paid to the vernacular.

Too little and too late is certainly true of the course of preservation in Inverkeithing, but at Dysart, to the east of Kirkcaldy, the rot seems to have been stopped just in time. Here a comprehensive rehabilitation scheme in which old and new merge has recently been undertaken. There is an upper and a lower town at Dysart, a civic centre and high street area and a 'seatown'. The upper has more or less been gouged out and modernized in a mundane if inoffensive manner, leaving the Netherlandish-looking Tolbooth standing as a monument of better days and ways; and here and there a number of interesting pantiled and crow-stepped edifices have survived, one of these being 'The Towers'. Down by the harbour, on the other hand, a more sympathetic attempt has been made to rescue some very attractive seventeenth-century buildings. They are dominated by the fortified tower of the ruined kirk of St Serf, commemorating the Celtic saint and hermit who inhabited one of the local 'weems' or caves, making his retreat, or *desert* in the neighbourhood. Close by is 'The Anchorage', another little town-castle but more Flemish than French, and an old pub, the erstwhile Bay Horse Inn, which was once thought to have been a manse on account of the improving texts and effigies of a man with a ruffle and lady with a coif carved on the skew-putts. This probably merely dates the building to the second half of the sixteenth century. The harbour whence in the past so much salt was imported, and so much coal and so many nails exported, is neither deep nor big enough to take modern coasters and is now the resort of small pleasure craft and a few fishermen.

The busiest place along the Fife coast is Pittenweem, where the fish market on the quayside guarantees the fishermen whose boats fill the newly deepened harbour a good living. Pittenweem also has an older harbour lined by some of the tallest and handsomest seventeenth- and eighteenth-century houses in Scotland. They are not fishermen's houses and were not built as such but as the homes of rich merchants who made a 'bonny penny' trading in Holland, and who sat up in their top rooms watching the loading and unloading of their boats as the Aberdeen worthies did. Behind is the Priory and 'Great House', recently restored as a home for retired clergy, while at the seaward end of Cove Wynd is the entrance to St Fillan's Cave, after which Pittenweem is named and from which a 'secret' stair carved out of the rock leads up to the Priory garden. This was used by smugglers in the eighteenth and nineteenth centuries; and Pittenweem was the scene of the arrest of the two which led to the Porteous riots in Edinburgh in 1736. Pittenweem is famous for its witches, who were locked up the night before their burning in a corner of the Priory garth in a cell at the foot of the Tolbooth tower, a jolly Jacobean affair with rows of fake cannon doing service as gargoyles; and attached to it is the mutilated shaft of the Mercat Cross, chained like some unwanted animal.

Anstruther is the next town in the East Neuk, as this corner of Fife is called, then Crail, whose old church has already been described and which was created a Royal Burgh as early as the thirteenth century. Its plan in some ways resembles that of St Andrews, with two nearly parallel streets and houses with long narrow gardens behind. The Town House-cum-Tolbooth is Dutch eighteenth-century on top and late medieval below, and crowned with a fish finial. It is one of the most amusing in the East Neuk. Crail once had walls round it, and like those of St Andrews these were more ecclesiastical than secular; and it is the old Priory walls, the only defensive ones left in Scotland, that first greet the visitor approaching St Andrews from the south. They are remarkably entire and can be followed round for much of their course, the enclosed area within consisting for the most part of ruins and grave-yard, and St Leonard's Girls' School, which is situated on the site of a former University College of the same name. Near the entrance is a seventeenth-century archway which few people notice but which is all that remains of the *Hospitium Novum* of post-Reformation Archbishops, including James Sharp, and which was erected to receive Mary of Lorraine, consort of James V, when she came to St Andrews to be received in state after landing in Scotland at Fife Ness, near Crail, in June 1538.

Of all the smaller but important Royal Burghs in Scotland St Andrews retains most of the atmosphere and substance of its former self, displaying in its architecture its tumultuous history and significant role in the development of learning and culture. Today the University has been reduced in size and scope by the hiving off of several faculties to a newer and larger sister at Dundee, but what remains, the wearing of the red 'toga' by the students, and especially the ancient buildings, gives the small grey city part of its special flavour, one at once English and Scottish; English because of its greater sense of continuity as compared to so many Scottish towns, which have been desecrated in a way scarcely possible anywhere else, and Scottish in its slightly dour but doucely civilized air, which reflects the national characteristics in a natural, non-chauvinistic manner. The cathedral has gone except for a few toothy towers of the ruined, stratified masonry, the castle is little more than a collection of crumbling walls secured by the Department of the Environment and looking as much part of the rocky coast as the rugged cliffs they overhang, the Town House has been demolished and there is no longer any Mercat Cross. Down by the harbour, silted up and only used by small boats, 'progress' has been at work replacing in concreted, flat-roofed mediocrity a row of delightful red-pantiled houses in the native style, yet the frame of St Andrews is there, and the bulk of its particular form.

The West Port through which most traffic has still to pass dates from Jacobean times, and despite baronial allusions in the shape of gargoyles, shot-holes and a military-looking parapet is non-defensive in origin. Its purpose was more as a barrier against country marauders and to prevent folk entering

West Port, St Andrews, Fife

the burgh with goods without paying their dues. The Priory Walls were for defence and are medieval, while the town was adequately protected by the high stone dykes that ran at the bottom of the gardens, a system which pertained in Edinburgh and Elgin and other old towns and which can still be seen in the long narrow rigs, or strips, behind the houses. These 'back dykes' seem to have been quite efficient except when foreign invaders approached, which they rarely did at St Andrews; and the only complete system of military defence undertaken in Scotland was at Berwick-upon-Tweed where the Renaissance walls built by Italian engineers in the sixteenth century never saw a siege and are perfect to this day.

Amongst the buildings that give St Andrews its pleasant appearance and help to preserve its ancient character are, of course, its churches, and the University chapels which have been referred to in an earlier chapter; more particularly one is struck by the way the old system of wynds and closes survives so that one can walk through from, say, South Street to Market Street via narrow passages between and sometimes under the houses. Here and there trees have been planted or allowed to remain unharmed, and in the Market Place the old cobbles have been left. The centre of the town is bounded by South and North Streets and bisected by Market Street, the three running something like an arrowhead towards the ruins of the cathedral and the castle, and the harbour. They are full of sixteenth, seventeenth, eighteenth and a few good nine-teenth-century buildings, almost all of which exude charm and delight, or at least do not make one wince as so much does in other towns. What is perhaps more surprising in this moderately-sized burgh are the neo-classical quarters, which derive almost wholly from the Georgian 'New Town' of Edinburgh and the latter-day golfing ascendancy. They do not seem at all out of place, indeed help to give dignity to St Andrews on its outskirts. There are suburbs too in the 1930s style, and a few modern estates, but nothing outrageous, so that the layers of building appear like the bark of a tree and do present a fair idea of the cultural history of what is, after all, the 'Scottish Canterbury', from its Anglo-Norman beginnings until today. There is, incidentally, a first rate Preservation Society in St Andrews which does not over-restore and choses its properties carefully, one of the more recent efforts, in conjunction with the University, being the restoration of the fine beehive doocot at Bogward, on the western side of the town, which is replete again with its central potence, or movable ladder, and louvred turret for the birds to fly in and out by.

With the example set by the Preservation Trust and fewer commercial pressures put upon them the local council have, on the whole, done well by St Andrews, but it has frequently been touch and go, indeed it took quite a fight to prevent the University from getting upsides with the rest of the community when it wanted to expand and talked of pulling down a church near the middle of the town. Eventually they were persuaded to build on new land, which was better from everyone's point of view, not least their own, since it provided space around for further expansion. Now the future size of St Andrews has been decided for many years ahead, and the growth of this historic little 'city' planned in such a way that its essential character is assured for several generations. Few comparable towns in Britain are so fortunate in this respect and St Andrews probably owes its good luck to its position, well away from destructive industries and site covetousness, and to the fact that there has been no too obvious desire on the part of the burgh authorities to keep up with anyone else or follow passing trends in housing and education. This has not been the case in some other old towns in Scotland, though the battle has not always been lost to the philistines.

The first big confrontation between a thrawn, 'ding-it-doon' burgh and those people who thought something of the local character ought to be saved for posterity occurred in Banff, where, before 1960, there existed the undamaged nucleus of one of the most distinguished small towns in the country, that is until they started widening the High Street and building new premises half way along. Fortunately a number of folk with a feeling for the local tradition were alerted before the whole street was spoilt so that today Banff has, like Crail, St Andrews and Elgin and one or two other enterprising places, a thriving Preservation society which, besides saving old properties from destruction, buys them and 'does them up', then offers them for resale. Thus a great deal that is decent and good has been spared and groups of buildings have been preserved as they should be, not in isolation or 'utterly restored', nor affronting their neighbours. Banff, in common with coastal burghs elsewhere in Scotland, has a lower and a higher town, but also a 'seatown' that constitutes a picturesque and unusual third quarter. The lower town has links with Banff House, the baroque mansion designed by William Adam for the first Earl of Fife, the Elgin banker whose descendants, marrying royalty, became dukes, when the little Royal Burgh acquired the status and air of a miniscule capital. It has not entirely lost that air, though much of its status, except that of County Town, went with the departing Royal Dukes in more modern times, and a new and appropriate use for their grand *palazzo* has not yet been found. It is classified as an Ancient Monument and officially, if only theoretically, protected thereby from further damage, but what to do with the interior? Perhaps Banff might organize a Northern Festival of Music and Drama, when Banff House would once more come into its own?

Banff architecture is comprehensive from the sixteenth century to the nineteenth; a turreted mini-castle rising cheek by jowl beside a Georgian house and a Queen Anne pub. Arched pends and canty crow-steps abound, simple Scots buildings with no pretensions, just well proportioned and sturdily built; while in the 'seatown' are rows of single-storeyed buts and bens, some still red-pantiled but most slated and slightly less gay than their Fife counterparts. The sea has receded and despite various attempts to reform the course of nature, including an ambitious scheme devised by the great Thomas Telford himself, the River Deveron continues to silt up the harbour and the fishermen now keep their boats at Macduff, where their masts can be seen bobbing up and down from Banff windows, much to everyone's chagrin. In the High Street stands the 'Fife Arms', well-known to a generation or more of anglers with 'rights' on the Deveron, and once an annexe of Banff House. It is built in the 'Adam style', like the Tolbooth and the Parish Kirk, and would not disgrace classical Edinburgh. Elsewhere in this extraordinary symposium of Scottish domestic architecture is Banff Castle, rebuilt in the early eighteenth century, in the patrician tradition established by Sir William Bruce and James Smith, by one of the many aristocratic families who kept a house in town as well as in the country in the days when the burgh and county were more important and lively than they are today. There is even a delightful Gothic-revival Episcopal church designed by Archibald Simpson, the best of the 'Battle of the Styles' architects in Aberdeen, and a master of granite. Here he has adopted his own earlier design for St Andrew's Cathedral in the 'granite city', but in local sandstone.

In *Burgh Architecture*, published by the Saltire Society in their Scottish Tradition series, Ian Lindsay gives a plan of a typical Scottish burgh of the seventeenth century. This does not show any particular town but combines attributes from several, with a West Port, a Mercat Cross, a Tolbooth, Castlegait and so on. In fact, it seems based on a broad mixture of St Andrews and Elgin, but smaller and more diagrammatic than either. Amongst the items marked are the communal doocot and Bow butts; the latter, an archery field, recalls James I of Scots' encouragement of the art after he had seen English archers decimate the French cavalry at Agincourt. The king made football illegal on Sundays, substituting archery, and establishing wappinschaws, or arms contests, not unlike those pertaining in modern Switzerland except that there they show off their guns and here it was bows and arrows. Montrose won a silver arrow on the butts at St Andrews; and these butts are still remembered in the local street nomenclature, as they are in the village of Ceres, in mid-Fife and in other Scottish towns and villages. There is also a communal watermill and burgh bridge shown on Mr Lindsay's plan; and water, of course, was very important in Scotland, it being one of the country's principal assets in the days before steam.

Scotland played its part in the agricultural and industrial revolutions in the building of factories, warehouses, cottages, bridges and canals much of which was scarcely different from that in other regions of the United Kingdom, perhaps most of it, but there are some things which are particularly Scottish. As early as the first years of the reign of Charles II, for instance, the seventh Earl of Eglinton, with Sir William Bruce advising, had the idea of turning Monk's Citadel at Ayr into a model industrial estate with factories and houses altogether, thus providing for the poor of the town in a novel way for those days; while a later scion of the same lordly house actually introduced tartan weaving into the country on a commercial scale, exporting it to Northern Ireland where his family, the Montgomeries, had family connections. In fact, the Mongomeries were amongst the first Lowland clans to adopt the plaid, not the kilt which belongs properly and only to the Highlands; and they did so more as a demonstration against the Act of Union of 1707 than anything else. The Montgomerie tartan is, therefore, one of the oldest authenticated setts, for most others, including many of the Highland ones, derive either from military sources or were invented for the visit of George IV to Scotland in 1822; further extensions to the tartan dictionary being added by the Sobieski-Stuart brothers, alias the sons of Third Lieut. Thomas Allan, R.N., in *The Costume of the Clans*, published in 1845.

The twelfth Earl of Eglinton created a new Eaglesham, a late eighteenth-century model village for cotton weavers, complete with factory and houses round about; but the contrast between this and its counterparts either in Northern England or even neighbouring Lanarkshire, where Robert Owen's socialist experiments in communal working and living took place, is startling. Eaglesham consists of two long streets, with a single row of houses, each facing a wide triangular green down the centre of which runs a burn, the necessary motive power for the cotton mill. The site slopes from an open moor at one end to a broad, green oasis at the other, where the main road to Glasgow crosses and where the pub, older than the village, and the church are. The latter was rebuilt in the severest 'reformed' manner, all white and classical, octagonal and fronted by a 'Venetian' steeple crowned with an eagle, the heraldic allusion being obvious. What makes the village so different architecturally, not to mention scenically, from other settlements of weavers north or south is the variety and interest in the buildings, which are all sizes and heights, not built in a line, many with gardens, and all displaying indigenous touches either in detail or colour. Fortunately Eaglesham has been taken over by Glasgow suburbanites with enough money and appreciation of what they have got not to spoil the place by too much modernity or brash over-development; and they have given the village a new lease of life.

I mentioned Thomas Telford a little earlier, that famous

Wade's Bridge, Aberfeldy, Perthshire, designed by William Adam

Scottish engineer, bridge-builder and planner of the Caledonian
Canal. Like William Adam, whose post as Master Mason to
the Board of Ordnance led him to design bridges and forts as
part of Marshall Wade's Pacification of the Highlands pro-
gramme, Telford's work in the Highlands had a social and
political purpose, his 'prefabricated' kirks and manses bear
this out, and certainly his bridges do. Let me first, however,
say a bit more about the best of William Adam's bridges, which
was built in 1733 over the Tay at Aberfeldy. Its begetter clearly
saw himself as the successor to Caesar, or at any rate one of
Caesar's generals, in his taming of the wild Highlands by
building roads, bridges and forts. The Aberfeldy bridge has
faint suggestions of one by Vanburgh in the park at Blenheim,
but only faint, and one likes to think that the elder Adam
managed to design this on his own, even to the two obelisks
at either end. These are probably a further allusion to Roman
precedents, as the inscription to Wade undoubtedly is, referring

as it does to his troops as legionaries and himself as prefect. The other inscription, to George II and William Adam, is less effusive and more pacific, speaking of linking the peoples and trading towns of the Highlands and Lowlands. The bridge is symbolic as well as handsome, for within sight of it is a romantic memorial to the Highland Volunteer Companies, ancestors of the present Highland Regiments. These were raised as part of the pacification policy, it being realized that a Highlander is nothing if not warlike, and like most warriors not so very worried about who he fights for so long as he is paid and allowed to fight in his own way. The statue recalls the raising of six independent companies which, because they wore predominently sombre tartan, became known as the 'Black Watch'; they fought for George II on the Continent and during the Jacobite rebellion.

Bridges have always played a major part in the furtherance of trade and the maintenance of law and order, and several fine early specimens have already been referred to, the Guardbridge over the Eden near St Andrews, the Brigs o' Balgownie

Fifteenth-century Stirling Brig

and Dee at Aberdeen. Of much the same vintage as these is Dervorguilla's Bridge at Dumfries, named after the last Princess in the native Scottish line, who married John Balliol, father of Edward I's puppet King of Scots and founder of Balliol College, Oxford. Dervorguilla built Sweetheart Abbey, near Dumfries, in memory of her husband, and the bridge over the Nith has long since been swept away, it being a wooden structure. The present one has six arches with intermediate buttresses and is not later than the fifteenth century in date, which makes it contemporary with the more beautiful four-arched bridge over the Forth at Stirling. The latter is often erroneously associated with another older wooden bridge which gave its name to the battle in which Sir William Wallace, called in at the last moment to assist, led the Scots to victory against the English in 1297. The celebrated fifteen-arched bridge over the Tweed at Berwick is late medieval also, but often repaired and strengthened, notably in 1611 after James VI's shaky passage over it a few years before.

Throughout the history of Scottish bridge building the name of Mylne frequently occurs. We saw how Alexander Mylne, Abbot of Cambuskenneth and first President of the Court of Session, built the first bridge over the Tay at Dunkeld in his capacity as Master Mason to James III. This, like others, was afterwards replaced, and here by one designed by Thomas Telford, who managed to combine a remarkable gift for engineering with a genuine understanding of architectural principles, especially of scale and proportion. One of his most famous bridges spans the valley of the Water of Leith on the north side of Edinburgh, its four 60-foot rounded arches supporting the roadway being paired by four lighter eliptical ones under the pavement, current architectural and structural expressions being happily matched thereby. The Dean Bridge, as it is called, dates from 1831 and was copied, only with five 48-foot spans over the River Tyne at Pathhead, near Dalkeith, in the same year, but because of the cleaner country air the warm, brownish stone remains untarnished with soot and grime, and completely unworn, so that the Pathhead bridge looks almost as if it is new. Another Mylne, Robert Mylne of London, designed two bridges at Inveraray which have an Italian quality rarely seen in Scotland and would not disgrace

the Grand Canal, in Venice, especially the single-arched one over the Shira; light and elegant it nevertheless is humped, for it was not until the days of Telford and John Rennie that bridges were built with flat carriage-ways. Rennie's bridge over the Tweed at Kelso was, of course, the model for the old Waterloo Bridge, in London.

The crossing of the Tay at Perth has several times been undertaken, and notably by John Mylne, Master Mason to Charles I; but Mylne's bridge was washed away and eventually rebuilt to a design by John Smeaton in the mid-eighteenth century. Smeaton was English, but with Telford and Rennie worked both on our canals and bridges. His Perth bridge is almost identical to one over the Tweed at Coldstream and both are less elegant than Robert Mylne's bridges at Inveraray and less sympathetic to their natural environment than Telford's at Dunkeld, where the keystones to the arches are strongly emphasized and the semi-circular buttresses romanticized in the Adam castellated style. Dunkeld almost certainly presages Telford's more daring and more imaginative concept at Craigellachie, where he designed a cast iron bridge spanning the River Spey in a single, graceful arch of 150 feet, the ends terminating in amusing Gothic abutments that seem to fore-shadow the Wagnerian approach to Highland architecture that developed after his death, in 1834. Craigellachie dates from 1815.

Canals are not exactly architecture, and this may not be the place to go into detail about the works of Smeaton, Rennie and Telford in that field, but one must draw attention to the latter's splendid Caledonian Canal, which in its day had much the same significance and aroused as much public interest as the cutting of the Suez and Panama Canals in theirs. It carved a way from the North Sea to the Atlantic through some of the grandest scenery in these islands and with such skill that its under-use today as a commercial route seems a tragedy of the first order. A particularly difficult but successfully accom-plished feature was the building of a lined canal trench out into the sea at the Inverness end to obviate the problem of high and low tides in this flat area; while the construction of the eight locks known as 'Neptune's Staircase' at the Atlantic exit of the canal, in successive falls of eight feet, provoked the

Telford's Dean Bridge spanning
the Water of Leith

poet Robert Southey into comparing the Pyramids unfavour-
ably with Telford's achievement here. 'A panorama painted
in this place would include the highest mountain in Great
Britain', a reference to Ben Nevis, 'and its greatest work of
art', he declared. A clear overstatement but symptomatic of
the enthusiasm generated then by engineering enterprises of
this sort.

There had actually been previous schemes for canals in
various parts of Scotland, a country which, apart from its
central plain, does not readily invite a comprehensive system
of inland waterways. Still, in the year 1515, a retired Scottish
admiral, Sir Andrew Wood, built what must be our first
canal, about a quarter of a mile long, between his medieval
tower house and the Parish Kirk of Upper Largo, along which
he was rowed in an eight-oared barge to church. The course
of this early waterway can still be made out, straight from the
old man's tower, which survives in part, to the existing kirk.
More important were the schemes drawn up in exile of the
Jacobite Earl of Mar for the improvement of Edinburgh, which
included the construction of a Forth to Clyde Canal with its
eastern basin where Princes Street Gardens are now. Details
of these proposals are contained in *The Earl of Mar's Legacies
to Scotland and to his son Lord Erskine*, an edited version of which
has been published by the Scottish History Society. The Forth
to Clyde Canal was actually begun by John Smeaton in
1768.

While the great Caledonian Canal was being built, between
1804 and 1822, the development of Scottish Lighthouses was
proceeding apace. A Bill went through Parliament in 1786
establishing the Northern Lighthouse Commission, which took
in the Isle of Man as well as Scottish waters, and between that
date and 1820 a whole series of Lights were planned and lit.
D. Alan Stevenson, descendant of Robert Stevenson, one of
the first Commissioners, has listed them in his *The World's
Lighthouses Before 1820*. As early as 1797 the famous Cloch
Point Light was set up on its dramatic site on the Firth of
Clyde south of Greenock, and not long afterwards work began
on the most famous of all Scottish Lights, that on Inchcape,
the Bell Rock of legend, on which it is said the Abbot of
Aberbrothock placed a bell to lure shipping to its doom and

his enrichment. Bell Rock was the work of Robert Stevenson, with Sir John Rennie being consulted from time to time, and is the masterpiece of that family of engineers and lighthouse-builders of whom Robert Louis, Robert's grandson, has written. Sir Walter Scott was one of the original Commissioners and it was he who saved from demolition the first Scottish Light-house, the so-called 'House o'Lights' on the May Isle, erected in 1630 by order of Charles I. It was converted into a castellated folly at the Bard of Abbotsford's suggestion and may be seen yet, painted white! Elsewhere, at Kinnairds Head, near Fraserburgh, the ancient castle of Sir Alexander Fraser of Philforth, founder of the town in 1546, was incorporated in the first of the Lights erected by the Northern Lighthouse Com-mission in 1786; and throughout their work there is a distinct attempt to adapt modern requirements to traditional tastes and natural settings. Cloch Point, for example, is crow-stepped and turreted, while later lights show an acquaintance with contemporary trends which, if not entirely qualifying as architecture very nearly does. In fact, Robert Stevenson, in common with many of his contemporaries, was both skilled engineer and architect, town-planner and consultant, the man who designed the crane that enabled Lord Melville's Column to be raised in St Andrew Square, Edinburgh, from one devised for the Bell Rock Lighthouse; and he advised the architect William Burn on the column's foundations. Together with Archibald Elliot he was responsible for the layout of the ceremonial eastern approach to Edinburgh via the Calton Hill and Princes Street, thus making his contribution to the shape of the 'Athens of the North'.

VI

The Building of Edinburgh

CAPITAL CITIES are built or developed for a variety of reasons. Rome had legendary beginnings, Paris and London commercial origins, Brasilia and Canberra were planned as administrative centres but Edinburgh was purely strategic, and for hundreds of years was no more than a fort. Its founders did not have any idea of making it the capital of anywhere, merely of protecting themselves and their possessions from warring tribes and the vagaries of political change. The city which is now the pride and joy of Scotland, its capital and its principal tourist attraction, though not as commercially important as Glasgow and no longer the significant administrative centre it was, did not officially acquire its present status until 1633, in which year King Charles I came north for his Scottish Coronation at Holyrood; and even then there were folk who thought he should have chosen Leith instead! The rivalry between Edinburgh and its nearest port has been continuous and is not yet dead, though the matter should have been settled in the twenties of this century when Leith lost her civic independence and was formally joined to the capital by Act of Parliament. I shall have more to say about Leith, for without it Edinburgh could not have advanced as it did, the city being neither on a navigable river nor the sea. In ancient maps the site is recognisable by its *Castrum Puellarum*, the wooden fort on the castle hill in which Pictish kings are said to have kept their daughters for safety, the *Château des Filles* of later cartographers. As for its name this may safely be ascribed to the first christian king of Northumbria, Edwin, whose capital, or at any rate northern redoubt it became in the seventh century, being known then as Edwinsborough. The Celtic version of this, Dunedin, in no way invalidates King Edwin's part in its founding, though it does confirm his loss of the place and its subsequent demoting. For 300 years Edinburgh returned to purely fort status, and thus it remained until the arrival of Queen Margaret, whose tiny chapel on the highest point of the castle rock is also our oldest stone building still in use. The Saxon Margaret, however, and her Scoto-Pictish husband, Malcolm Canmore, had their real capital at Dunfermline, in Fife.

In the twelfth century St Margaret's most pious son, David I, founded the Abbey of the Holy Rood right at the foot of the long hill stretching down from the castle eastwards for about a mile, the future Royal Mile, within which the old city of Edinburgh began to grow. The legend of the Holy Rood perhaps needs some explanation, not only because it has subsisted until today but also because in the middle of the fourteenth century it was completely altered. King David's original intention had been to honour the memory of his sainted mother and provide sanctuary for an ebony crucifix containing a piece of the true cross which she had left him. This 'Holy Rood' became the religious talisman of the whole Scots nation; it went with the Scottish army on its campaigns into England and was taken south by David II, Robert Bruce's unsatisfactory son, to the Battle of Neville's Cross, in 1346. Here it was lost, when the monks of Holyrood Abbey saved the royal face by inventing a brand new story based on the legends of Saints Eustace and Hubert, both of whom seem to have gone hunting on the sabbath when they should have been in church, and coming across a white stag with a crucifix between its antlers repented. The monks turned David I into Eustace, or Hubert, the patron saint of hunting, and Holyrood Park the scene of his vision; and thus the myth has stuck and still sticks. When James VII and II wanted the restored kirk of Holyrood for his new Chapel of the Thistle, in 1687, he built another church in the Canongate and placed on the top of its baroque front a set of antlers in commemoration of the ancient link; while in more recent times these antlers were replaced with new ones from Balmoral by King George VI.

The setting up of a Royal Abbey at one end of the street with a strong castle at the other did not, at once, make Edinburgh the most important place in Scotland, far less its capital. Perth remained pre-eminent until after the murder of James I of Scots there in 1437, when future kings made their capital wherever they chiefly resided. Perth was near Scone, the traditional centre of Scottish history, whence the 'Stone of Destiny', thought by some to be Jacob's Pillow and now under King Edward's Chair at Westminster, was handed over at the point of the sword. Because of this age-old connection Scone retained its special position in the Scottish consciousness for many years after the Royal Stewarts moved to Stirling, and the spiritual comfort of Cambuskenneth, and eventually to Edinburgh and an enlarged Holyrood Abbey. It was James III who finally effected this change, he disliking war and preferring the company of ecclesiastics and using the Abbey as an alternative residence to the castle. His son, James IV, went further, laying the plans for the present Royal Palace, which plans, albeit with a Palladian façade instead of an early Renaissance one, were carried out by Sir William Bruce for Charles II between 1672 and 1679.

Taking the castle as our starting point, the oldest Edinburgh building after Queen Margaret's Chapel is the battlemented Banqueting Hall in the Castle, erected at the end of the fifteenth century for James IV. King David's Tower, dating from a hundred years before, is now hidden under the Half-Moon Battery, and the King's Lodging, as the 'palace' within the castle was designated, has been so altered down the years that

Edinburgh: view from Randolph Crescent showing dome of St George's Kirk and the Castle

what one sees today is largely the rebuilding done for James VI's homecoming in 1617. The Banqueting Hall, on the other hand, makes up for many things, being not too dissimilar from the slightly earlier example at Stirling designed by Robert Cochrane for James III and preserving its unique hammer-beam roof. One could claim with some justification that a number of the details here, especially the carvings on the stone corbels at the ends of the beams, are the first signs of the Italian Renaissance in Scotland. The pre-war guide to Edinburgh Castle was prepared by Dr James Richardson and is a model of its kind. In it mention is made of the use of the fleur de lis, cherub's heads and the head of James IV set against a leafy background, of the Sun-in-Splendour emblem with the monogram I.H.S., and the thistle and the rose, symbol of the king's marriage to Margaret Tudor, rising together from a vase. The best view of the Banqueting Hall is from the Grassmarket, to the south, and indeed the best view of the castle itself is from there, beside a short run of the town wall, built in a hurry after Flodden, which lines one side of a narrow vennel near Heriot's Hospital.

The Half-Moon Battery, sometimes also known as 'Mylne's Battery' because Robert Mylne, afterwards Master Mason to Charles II, rebuilt and heightened it in 1662, was largely the work of Regent Morton in the reign of Mary, Queen of Scots. It forms the principal object in the backcloth to the celebrated Edinburgh Tattoo, with the turreted King's Lodging behind. In the latter the first King of Great Britain was born in 1566, in a tiny room now called 'Queen Mary's' which was repanelled and painted by John Anderson for her son almost exactly fifty years later. In another small room the 'Honours of Scotland' are housed, the Crown of Bruce, enlarged and arched by John Mossman for James V, the Sword of State and Sceptre presented to James IV by the Pope, and various other intriguing items including the ring worn by Charles I at his Scottish coronation and the original ensigns of the Orders of the Thistle and Garter taken abroad by James VII and II when he went into exile in 1688; all of which were bequeathed by the last of the Royal Stuarts, Henry, Benedict, Cardinal York, Prince Charlie's brother, to George III. It is a pity that practically none of the furniture or decoration formerly in the Royal Apartments has survived intact. Records speak of fine panelling and a number of elaborate plaster ceilings, some of the moulds being brought from Kellie Castle, in Fife, where a contemporary ceiling does survive. We are told the plasterers came from York, no doubt sent to Scotland at the king's express command. Other amusing innovations concern the merry-making ordered by James for his 'salmond-like' homecoming, such as Morris dancing, fireworks, music and the firing of cannon, and a boy with his hobby-horse who came from Berwick.

The exterior of the King's Lodging is much as the Royal Mason, William Wallace, left it in 1617. He was a well known and proficient sculptor who began Heriot's Hospital, the finest Renaissance building in Edinburgh and the ancestor of Drumlanrig Castle; and amongst his works here, but mutilated by Cromwell, are the Royal Arms of Great Britain, plus representations of the Scottish Crown, Sword and Sceptre set in richly carved panels. It is interesting to note the sources

Heriot's Hospital, begun before the Civil War and completed afterwards

of some of the materials used in this rebuilding and restoration, stone from Craigleith, the same quarry as the famous 'New Town' of Edinburgh was built from, and timber from Orpington and Danford in England, brought by 'Sir George Bruce's grit schip'. A great deal was for show, as the castle had ceased to be a Royal Residence, even in cases of emergency, when King James mounted the throne of the Tudors in 1603. Charles I used Holyroodhouse, Charles II never visited Edinburgh after 1650, and James VII and II only did so as Duke of York, when he was the first and last Stuart monarch to inhabit the Palace built for his brother in 1679. 'Mons Meg', a curious old cannon still to be seen on the battlements of the castle, burst whilst firing a salute at his departure in 1683.

The fact that Edinburgh was not officially declared the capital until 1633, and had no cathedral before that date, confirms its peculiar history and late development; a situation epitomized in the story of the High Kirk of St Giles, whose characteristic crown-spire rises evocatively in the view looking eastwards from the castle. If the reported remark of a visitor, 'what a pity it isn't a church' may seem a little unkind, there is some truth in it, for the status of this big, square structure has always been a little dubious. It is certainly not a cathedral, for to hold that position presupposes its being the seat of a bishop, which it has not been since 1690, and then only that of a Caroline prelate, not one in the pre-Reformation descent. It is not a parish kirk in the old sense, nor even quite collegiate, though once a bit of both, having enjoyed direct papal protection in the Middle Ages. Architecturally the High Kirk, which began life as a normal medieval church of cruciform plan, became in time wider and squarer as numerous private altars and chantry chapels were added, each with its relic and endowment for prayers to be said in perpetuity for rich burghers and other high-heidians. The first of these chapels, and still retaining much of its fabric and carving, is the Prestoun Aisle, which was founded to house the relic of St Giles himself, a small piece of the saint's arm bone which came from Bruges in the fifteenth century. With the statue that went with this, and which was ignominiously ducked in the 'Nor' Loch' at the Reformation, the St Giles relic has been lost for ever, but the

Arms of James II of the 'Fiery Face' and his Flemish Queen, Mary of Gueldres, plus those of Sir William Prestoun himself, are still there, together with other souvenirs of the pre-Reformation era. The building was subdivided in the seventeenth century, with three churches, a police-station and a prison incorporated. An earlier attempt to tidy things up provoked a riot; and before St Giles' was thoroughly taken in hand in the nineteenth century, the remaining unoccupied part had become a meeting place, with shops and coffee houses attached to its exterior. Eventually the restorers got busy, too busy in the event, leaving only the beautiful spire unharmed externally, and opening up the interior, which today has become the pantheon of Scottish heroes and worthies, though not Robert Burns, and virtually non-denominational in ethos. Hence, the visitor's comment anent a church. It is the place where Her Majesty the Queen worships when she is at Holyroodhouse, where the Edinburgh Festival is opened by a service and where, since 1911, the Most Ancient and Noble Order of the Thistle has had its chapel.

Immediately behind St Giles' is Parliament Close, with a lead equestrian statue of Charles II almost on the spot where John Knox is supposed to have been buried when there was a graveyard there; and behind that, enclosing the courtyard, is Parliament House, the neo-classical façade of which masks the old Hall of the Scottish Parliament, designed by John Mylne for Charles I. The chief glory of this immense and inspiring interior, wherein advocates walk either in consultation or in the hopes of obtaining commissions, is the timber roof made up of myriads of pendant-keys, arches and beams in the French late-medieval manner, the finials being carved and gilded. At the far end is a stained glass window recalling the setting up of the Court of Session under James V, with Alexander Mylne, Abbot of Cambuskenneth and First President of the Court, receiving the requisite Papal Bull. Nearby the old Tolbooth used to stand, but was removed in 1817 because it was said to incommode the traffic. Its site is marked on the road by a heart worked in the setts; this is Scott's 'Heart of Midlothian' into the centre of which all good Edimbourgeois should spit as they pass, though if they do so nowadays they are likely to be stared at by the ignorant.

Crown spire of St Giles' High Kirk,
with statue of Charles II in foreground

John Mylne was also responsible for the unusual design of the Tron Kirk, erected shortly after Parliament House and remarkable for its merging of Gothic and Renaissance detail in which the style and feel of the church of St Eustache in Paris is vividly recalled. It is unfortunate that the spire, which was in the same form as that of Stirling Tolbooth, was burnt down in the nineteenth century and replaced by an inferior Victorian version. The future of this kirk, against whose walls the breaking of bottles used to resound at Hogmanay, is in doubt. It was sold for a commercial use, then the purchasers were prevented from doing anything with it. Now it stands empty, isolated in the middle of the street with no obvious purpose except, apparently, to impede impatient bus drivers. Near it, in College Wynd, Sir Walter Scott was born, his family then still living in the Old Town but shortly to move to George Brown's Square, the first example of eighteenth-century planning in Edinburgh, and the first stage in the eventual removal of many of the inhabitants to the New Town. George Square, as it is now named, was also the first to become the subject of a bitter environmental argument when the University wished to expand into it and pull down all but one side. This they succeeded in doing despite the protests of the citizens and promises made over many years that this would not be allowed. The only consolation is that the side they did keep contains the house in which Scott was brought up; but that, of course, is simply another case of sentimentality versus aesthetics. One other result of the defeat of those trying to preserve George Square was the formation of the Scottish Georgian Society, which was able, with the co-operation of the Civic Trust, the Cockburn Association and others to save Randolph Crescent, in the New Town, when it was similarly threatened in 1958; and this time amenity won.

Ian Lindsay, whose *Old Edinburgh* and *Georgian Edinburgh* have yet to be bettered either in coverage or accuracy, suggests that out of all the picturesque houses that line the Royal Mile between the Castle and Holyrood not more than about a third are of any great antiquity and most are restored or much altered. One that is original, however, is Gladstone's Land, in the Lawnmarket, which retains its arched 'piazza' on the ground floor and outside stair to the main rooms above, some of the latter possessing fine painted ceilings. The building dates from the late Jacobean period and was restored by Mr Robert Hurd for the National Trust as the headquarters of The Saltire Society. A walk through a nearby pend brings one to James Court, where Boswell lived and entertained Samuel Johnson, and the site of the Palace of Mary of Guise, which was demolished in the nineteenth century to make room for the present Church of Scotland Assembly Hall, a building in Cambridge-transitional Gothic. The terms court, close and wynd, incidentally, are not exactly interchangeable, the closes and wynds are not so different, they being narrow alleyways, or vennels and small backyards, but a court is something else. In fact it is a building enclosing a 'square'. James Court is one of these and dates from the eighteenth century. The earliest is Mylne's Court, which Robert Mylne, mason under Bruce at Holyrood and nephew of the famous John Mylne, erected in 1690 as a speculation. He had other properties of this kind, notably in Leith.

Mylne's Court rises to more than eight storeys on the north and six on the south, and has recently been carefully and expensively restored by the University as a students' hostel, perhaps in mitigation of what they have done in George Square? I wonder if the amorphous society that presently inhabits the place appreciates its restored panellings, shutter-board windows, old doorways and other nicely preserved features? It was the first tall tenement, or 'land', to be built round an open space and is the architectural ancestor of all those lesser 'skyscrapers' that were built throughout Scotland in the eighteenth and nineteenth centuries, but more particularly here in Edinburgh, where the restricted site on the ridge of a long narrow hill had the same effect on planning as that of the Island of Manhattan on the development of New York. The houses, in effect, were vertical instead of horizontal, with each floor being reserved for a specific class, porters at the bottom, fishwives at the top, gentry on the main floor and burghers in between; each having his proper place yet passing the time of day with the other on the Common Stair; and the curious thing is that so well did this system work that when the movement to the New Town occurred the Common Stair was transplanted there too, though the heights of the buildings were reduced to a maximum of five stories, with basement.

Almost opposite Mylne's Court, at the corner of Castlehill and the Lawnmarket, is the big nineteenth-century church of Tolbooth St John which, while not coming directly within this review, is interesting on account of its steeple, which is said to have been sketched by A. W. Pugin for the Scottish architect, James Gillespie Graham, whilst surveying the city from a rowing boat on the Firth of Forth! Gillespie Graham was responsible also for some of the sternest Doric erected in the New Town in the second decade of the nineteenth century. From here a short lane which quickly dissolves into steps is all that remains of the West Bow that formerly swept round and down to the Grassmarket, the 'Place aux Herbes' of romantic early Victorian prints and international stage scenery. A few old houses survive there, amidst the depradations of the post-war era, when a number of buildings have been demolished to make car parks, and one side has been ruined by the erection of what can only be described as a Mussolini-style monstrosity that replaces the handsome Italianate Corn Market. This is the corner of Edinburgh which, before its despoliation, promoters of the Edinburgh Festival thought might make an excellent cultural centre.

The Cowgate enters into the Grassmarket at its south eastern end, running almost parallel to the Royal Mile to Holyrood. It was once residential, with back-gardens and even farmyards attached; hence the name. Here too was the palace of Cardinal Beaton, which was still there, at the foot of Black-friar's Wynd, turrets and all, when it was photographed just over a century ago. Today hardly a building of note remains in the Cowgate except St Patrick's neo-classical church, at the foot, St Cecilia's erstwhile music-hall, about half-way up, and the Magdalen Chapel, at the Grassmarket end. This was founded in 1541 as part of a Hospital attached to the Hammermen's Guild, and is at present half-buried below the bridges and high level roads of the late eighteenth and nineteenth centuries. It is recognizable by its Jacobean steeple, and note-worthy for containing the only complete window of pre-Reformation stained glass in Scotland, which bears the Arms of Mary of Guise, and the founder and his wife, Michael Macquhen and Janet Rynd. St Cecilia's Hall was the hub of civilized society in the city in the days before its flitting, and as late as 1802 was the headquarters of the Musical Society of Edinburgh. It was designed by Robert Mylne of London, in 1763, supposedly on the model of the opera house at Parma, in northern Italy, though which opera house is difficult to say as it bears no resemblance to any extant. The shape is a pleasant oval roofed with a low dome, pilasters having been added round the sides to improve the accoustics, a point over-looked by modern restorers who, however, are to be con-gratulated on rescuing the place from decay, and arranging within a modern annexe a permanent exhibition of historic musical instruments.

Candlemaker's Row rises from the same Grassmarket exit and leads to Greyfriar's Kirk, a largely eighteenth-century building but erected on older foundations and well known for the fame and number of those whose tombstones fill its grave-yard, the Adam family and the Mylnes being notable in the architectural line and designed by themselves. The church in its present form is barn-like and has an interesting curvilinear gable to the west, finished with quaint Renaissance finials. The date is 1721.

From here it is but a stone's throw to the University the existing buildings of which were begun by Robert Adam in 1763 on the site of older quarters dating from 1580 and founded by James VI. The façade onto the South Bridge, that is, the main road out of Edinburgh, is the best and wholly Adam. It was intended as the centrepiece of an ambitious overall scheme for the opening out of the area between here and Holyrood and creating a ceremonial entrance onto the city from the south. Indeed, Robert Adam's plans for Edinburgh, especially for the Old Town, were greatly superior to anything devised or undertaken in the much vaunted New Town, the tragedy being that so little of it was achieved. The colonnaded quadrangle of the University Court was completed by the architect William Playfair, better known for his design of the Scottish National Gallery and some of the more obvious pseudo-Athenian allusions on the Calton Hill, including 'Scotland's Disgrace'. This was in 1834, and the dome is modern. The buildings back onto the southernmost extremity of the Flodden Wall, which ran from the castle, to encompass Heriots and

Greyfriars, past the University and the back of the Cowgate to end at the Netherbow Port. It did not go any further because there existed here, as in other Scottish towns, high garden walls and long rigs behind the houses, and these still form the basis of that intricate pattern of narrow closes and wynds which is such a feature of Old Edinburgh and which never ceases to amaze and intrigue visitors.

The original Mercat Cross of Edinburgh was demolished after the 1745 rebellion because, it has been suggested, the Jacobites had proclaimed James VIII and III from it. Whatever the reason it went, and only the shaft survived as a folly on the front lawn of Lord Somerville's mansion at The Drum, Gilmerton, whence, in this century, largely at the instigation of W. E. Gladstone, who was at one time M.P. for Midlothian, it was brought back to the city and placed beside St Giles', facing the City Chambers. A new platform was erected and a new unicorn surmounts the shaft, but there it is, restored in fact and favour after a period in the shadows. The City Chambers are interesting because the building began as the Royal Exchange, supplanting St Giles' as a mid-morning rendezvous in 1753, when the present elegant Palladian structure with 'piazza' was put up. It is one of the many classical and neo-classical structures of the Old Town, where most of the better examples actually are, despite the larger area of the Georgian suburb that arose after 1767, when the architect James Craig won the competition organized by the burgh for an extension north of the Nor' Loch.

The new suburb was never intended to be what it has since become, the principal shopping and commercial part of the town, it was simply a long last breakout from the confines of the Flodden wall and the strait-jacket imposed by history and geography; at first it had no shops, no markets and for a while no church, and architecturally represented no more than a repetition of the same kind of house that had already gone up in George Brown's Square and his brother James's in the Old Town. I mention this specifically because people are apt to think of the Georgian New Town of Edinburgh as a separate development, which it was not, but a natural and logical re-drawing of existing boundaries once the restrictions of the past had been overcome. It was planned in the reign of Charles II,

when Sir William Bruce designed a bridge to span the eastern
end of the Nor' Loch, and James, Duke of York granted permission for the Royalties, or boundaries of the city to be
extended. What held things up was the fall of the House of
Stuart in 1690, and the subsequent disruption of trade which
was not properly settled until after Culloden and the defeat
of Prince Charles Edward in 1745; but one must not forget
that Lord Provost Drummond, as he laid the foundation stone
of the eventual North Bridge in 1763, said it was 'all due to
the Duke, afterwards James VII, who first thought of the idea'.
A striking tribute coming from a confirmed Hanoverian who
fought against the Duke's grandson at Prestonpans.

The real difference between the Old and New Towns, and
the only one that need concern us here in any detail, lies in the
layout of the latter, which was extravagant with land and
regular in the classical manner, even boring, with long straight
parallel streets, few squares and hardly a bend anywhere.
Indeed, the inhabitants went specially to stare and wonder at
Abercrombie Place, which was built with a curve in 1804.
Lord Cockburn, who lived through the uprooting and settling
down again that took place at the end of the eighteenth and
beginning of the nineteenth centuries, and has recorded the
whole process in his *Memorials*, described Princes Street as 'the
most tasteless and clumsy line of shops in the island of Great
Britain'; while Ruskin, never an admirer of neo-classicism,
thought the portal of St George's Parish Church, in Charlotte
Square, 'ghastly and oppressive'. He might not have been
quite so hard on it if Robert Adam's more refined design had
been carried out and not cribbed by an unfeeling inferior,
Sir Robert Reid, who rejoiced under the titular title of Master
Mason to the Crown; a post theatrically recreated as part of
the charade when George IV descended upon the capital in
1822 in the wake of the Romantic Revival and Scott's world
wide reputation. What does make the New Town unique is
largely fortuitous, in that its regimented layout collapses on
a non-flat site, so that many of the places and crescents possess
an accidental attraction not conceived by the architects, and
the fact that being comparatively late in time practically all
of it has survived. Melville Street, for instance, which was not
completed before 1840, is Georgian in layout and detail down

to its wrought-iron door furniture, lamp-snuffers, arched light brackets and railings; though before it was finished they were putting in plate glass windows instead of small-paned ones. There are literally miles of pseudo-Georgian terraces and rows stretching from Leith to the western suburbs, encompassing an era the original planners cannot possibly have envisaged.

Historically speaking the New Town, despite the quality of its inhabitants, many of whom were the *savants* and *literati* of the 'Golden Age', was a place in which nothing very exciting happened in the contentious context usually associated with a nation's history, and the new quarters were never really accepted as part of the historic capital. A little cold and forbidding, and relatively dull, they nevertheless represent the biggest exercise in urban planning in these islands and retain to a remarkable degree the douce, 'east-windy, west-endy' atmosphere of their begetting and development. Control of heights and window sizes, population and the use of buildings remained until late-Victorian times, when commercial interests were influential in having the regulations modified, and up went the big shops and hotels, Forsyths and Jenners, then Woolworths and Marks and Spencers, and finally the new, New Club, which has to be seen to be believed. Only now, almost at the last moment, have the authorities taken fright and clamped down again on heights and proportions, insisting on some unity of design in Princes Street. George Street, which was meant to be the main thoroughfare and is rather better maintained, is also controlled, so that we may have by the end of this century an even more unique city than we thought, for most of the Georgian parts are now incorporated within a Conservation Area, with doors, paintwork, balconies and pediments all subject to restrictions which have been made to try to preserve some of the dignity and character of Edinburgh in a swiftly changing world.

If we want history with our buildings, however, we must inevitably return to the Old Town, than which there is no other with so much crammed into so small a space and with so much to show for it in Britain. The North and South Bridges, by which the Old and New Towns are linked and crossed, form a continuous street that leaves the lower part of the High Street partially divided from the upper, making it into a sort of 'place', with John Knox's House and Moubray House closing it. It was here that the painter George Jamesone and the poet William Drummond of Hawthornden planned the Coronation festivities for Charles I and viewed the royal procession as it passed from Holyrood to the Castle and back. Nearby are Bishop's Close and Carrubber's Close, the first recalling Archbishop Spottiswood's residence there when he came to crown the king, the second marking the place where the congregation of St Giles', until then still a cathedral, sought refuge after their minister had been ejected for refusing to support William of Orange. Their chapel in the close became a hotbed of Jacobitism, being visited by no less a person than Bishop Seabury of Connecticut, the first North American bishop and a non-juror. The reasons for this are worth a brief commentary as the facts are little known and of some significance.

The Anglican Church overseas grew in much the same haphazard way as the empire and commonwealth did, without much thought for the future or provision for changes in regime. Thus at the time of the American Revolution the church abroad had no bishops of its own and all the clergy were consecrated in England, which made things difficult when the oath to George III was abolished. Pious former colonists, however, hit on the idea of coming to Scotland, where there existed an Episcopal church which, though validly constituted, was disestablished and non-juring, owing nothing to the House of Hanover. Consequently it was in Scotland, in a room in Aberdeen near where the Marischall College now is, that three Scots bishops laid their hands on the head of Samuel Seabury, imparting the Apostolic Succession from Europe to North America thereby. It was in recognition of this friendly act that Seabury's twentieth-century successors planned to build a big new Episcopal cathedral in Aberdeen and commissioned Sir Ninian Comper to design it; but the Wall Street crash came and prevented its fulfilment. The Carrubber's Close Chapel was eventually vacated and the present church of Old St Pauls' in Jeffrey Street replaced it. The site is not particularly salubrious now, facing onto part of Waverley Station, where it has a curious and much older neighbour in the former Trinity College Kirk.

Trinity College was founded by Mary of Gueldres, consort

of James II of Scots, in 1462, and possessed above its high altar a Hugo van der Goes Triptych, of which only the folding panels remain. These were saved at the Reformation as they portrayed the king's ancestors and the founder of the College. James VI took the panels south with him in 1603, presumably to show the English he had respectable and gifted ancestors; and they were returned to Scotland by Her Majesty the Queen after having been at Hampton Court for more than 300 years. The church which they had once graced survived until 1848 when it was found to stand in the way of progress, in this case the railway, and after a protest it was removed stone by stone and rebuilt a few hundred yards away on a new site. Notwithstanding this metamorphosis and the building becoming a reading room attached to the Central Public Library, it is one of the finest examples of a flamboyant-Gothic structure in Scotland, with polygonal apse and handsome window traceries; and the story of its saving is heartening.

The old Netherbow Port which was demolished in 1764 was a twin-turreted affair of considerable charm, with a statue of James VI carved by John Mylne the elder in a niche above the archway. Beyond lay the independent burgh of the Canongate, or Canongait, whose development was bound up with the history of the Abbey of the Holy Rood whose canons owned and ruled it. Their own church has gone, except for a rather hoary and blackened ruin rising half-hidden on the north side of the palace, sad, roofless and unhallowed. In common with other Scottish abbeys Holyrood was despoiled at the Reformation, its revenues diverted to a secular Commendator who built his house in front of the west end and would not move even for the king. In due course the church was restored, but only the nave, in which Charles I was crowned, and afterwards the building became the parish kirk of the Canongate. It remained so until James VII and II arrived on the scenes, turned the congregation out and made it the headquarters of a reconstituted Order of the Thistle and his private chapel. In compensation for this he commissioned James Smith to design the existing beautiful Canongate Kirk, which is surely Smith's best building with its handsome baroque gable on the front, King James's Arms and symbolic antlers above, noble little Doric portico and expressive interior, reminding one of Holland

(left) Entrance to Moray House, Canongate, Edinburgh. *(right)* Old Tolbooth, Canongate

in its simple, clean lines, whitewash and big, clear windows. The kirk was restored by Ian Lindsay, when a tiny semi-circular apse was revealed behind the organ and brought into the church for the first time since its building in 1688. It appears that the king, who was a Roman Catholic, as indeed James Smith himself was reputed to be, planned the apse as the place where an altar would one day stand when presbyterianism was abolished and the Papal supremacy re-established in Scotland. That day never came, and the apse remained blocked up until 1950.

The Mercat Cross stands nearby, also the Tolbooth, which dates from 1592 and is easily recognizable by its big turreted tower with pend under, forestair to council chamber and prominent dormer windows. There are a number of interesting houses round about, Moray House, for instance, which is one of the few larger private mansions remaining in the Canongate. It was built for the dowager Countess of Home in 1628 and boasts elaborate plaster ceilings inside. The entrance is rather striking on account of the gateposts being topped by tall, pointed pyramids, while the iron balcony on the street evokes the days when folk of quality lived here and could be seen conversing with neighbours or friends or watching some procession pass, when carpets would hang from the balcony as in southern Continental towns today. Another interesting building is Huntly House, also a former nobleman's mansion, which stands immediately opposite the Tolbooth. It is now a Municipal Museum and with its neighbour in Bakehouse Close makes a typical group of the seventeenth century. The overhanging front is one of the few left in the street. A little further along in the direction of Holyrood was Golfer's Land, demolished suddenly and rather mysteriously only a few months after an announcement that the sum of £30,000 was to be spent on its restoration. It was built with the winnings of an early 'internation' Golf Tournament played on Leith Links between two English sportsmen and James, Duke of York and his partner Jock Paterson, who won. The gap left by the removal of this house is one of many in the Old Town which give a most erroneous impression of what life was like in the seventeenth and eighteenth centuries, when people and buildings were all crowded together in neighbourliness, and for protection against lawlessness and the weather. Opening everything out or making zig-zags in the street plan may be more hygienic but it is scarcely in keeping with local tradition.

The theatre was frowned upon by the reformed kirk and the Duke of York and his modest court had perforce to be careful how they went in this respect, for they were as fond of a good play as any in Restoration Britain. On several occasions, once in celebration of the birthday of Catherine of Braganza, when the Princesses Mary and Anne, both future queens, took part, they were severely reprimanded by the ministers, as they were also for playing tennis in the catchspiel. Eventually, however, as always when a restriction is not generally acceptable, ways were found of getting round the ecclesiastical displeasure, and in the eighteenth century, which was a great theatre-loving age, plays were performed in public in what is now called Playhouse Close. The trick was to advertise a concert and present a play during the interval. Playhouse Close is one of those which have been restored, and one should go through the pend from the Canongate and take a look at the round, conically capped stair turret with its seventeenth-century inscription. The double row of dormers on the street side is also interesting, being very Continental in feeling, and the finials to some of the dormers are carved with stars, thistles and roses, fleurs de lis and other emblems.

There are several eighteenth-century buildings in the Canongate that deserve special mention, two of them restored since the war. The first is Chessel's Court, which dates from 1748 when it was built as a superior block of 'flats'. It stands behind the street and resembles a modest country house with its central pedimented chimneypiece, elegant Georgian windows, some with rounded frames, and the walls white harled except for the stone margins. Chessel's Court was one of the last things done by Robert Hurd in 1964. The second interesting building of the period, and again set back from the road, is the present Manse of the 'Radio Padre', Ronald Selby Wright, who in 1972 was Moderator of the General Assembly of the Church of Scotland. Originally known as Reid's Court it is white and plain and has side-wings, having, as Mr Lindsay remarks, 'more the appearance of a farm-house than a town mansion'. A somewhat large farmhouse but certainly a country building not a town one. We are now approaching the Abbey Strand and the precincts of Holyroodhouse, where there are more interesting buildings including the most obviously engaging one, with timber covered outside stair, right at the palace gate. This was restored by the late first Inspector of Ancient Monuments in Scotland, Dr James Richardson. Until 1972 there used to be an old pub opposite where they claimed to have Lord Darnley's waistcoat. Behind is Whitehorse Close, one of the most attractive of the recently rehabilitated properties and dating in part from the seventeenth century. What we see today is younger and recalls the eighteenth-century inn where the London coach began and ended its journeys and Dr Johnson got annoyed with the waiters and the flies, from both of which he was rescued by a thoughtful 'Bozzy'. Whitehorse Close has been converted into a group of private dwellings by the burgh, whose architect has retained the crow-stepped roofs and most of the red pantiles, forestairs, double-dormers and projecting gables supported on wooden corbels. The whole is set back from the road and the buildings range round a cobbled yard.

The Palace of Holyroodhouse is amongst the most homogeneous, and for its size, beautiful royal palaces in Europe. In general appearance it resembles one of the bigger French *châteaux* with its twin turreted wings and dignified Palladian entrance. It is almost entirely as Sir William Bruce made it for Charles II, when a modified version of the plans approved by Charles I and halted by the Civil War was completed. In origin, as we have seen, Holyrood was ecclesiastical, and James IV was the first of the Stewarts to enlarge the Hospice alongside the Abbey and create a secular palace. His scheme was for two turreted wings in a slightly less restrained style than those actually built, and an amusing, to us, early Renaissance entrance rich with strange carving and Florentine allusion, as in contemporary work at Stirling and Linlithgow. The mason employed then was Walter Merlioun, a Frenchman, with a member of the Mylne family in attendance, and progress went as far as the new entrance, when the king was killed at Flodden. His son, James V, anxious to impress his French

Holyroodhouse with old tower of James V (left) and Bruce's main elevation, *circa* 1679

queen, planned to carry on with the southern wing, but in the event all that was done was the complete redecoration and furnishing of the existing interior in the current Continental manner, with blues and gold and coffered ceilings, panelling and tapestries. A certain amount of this has survived, and a little from the time of Mary, Queen of Scots, whose cypher, with that of the Dauphin François, her first husband, is evident, together with fleur de lis, thistle and rose motifs. The actual position of these has, on the other hand, been altered, since Bruce changed the floor and ceiling levels, heightening the tiny sixteenth-century rooms to bring them up to seventeenth-century standards.

The old part of the palace, which is wholly within the northern, James IV wing, is the best known because it is associated with Mary's tearful meetings with the Rev. John Knox and the murder of her Italian secretary, David Rizzio, by a jealous husband and his friends, in 1566. In my father's day they showed you Rizzio's blood, which was repainted each year for the tourists. Today this has been discontinued and a brass plaque marks the supposed site; but of course with the floor level changed it is only approximate. Queen Mary's bed is another favourite object here, but the Queen Mary in question is Mary of Modena, consort of James VII and II, who came to Holyrood with her husband when he acted as Charles II's 'viceroy' in Scotland. The bed has the added but dubious distinction of having been slept in by the Duke of Cumberland, brother of George II, Prince Charles Edward's vanquisher at Culloden. Since then the palace has remained in the care of the Dukes of Hamilton, Hereditory Keepers, who have furnished both their own apartments and the historical north wing, the rest being mainly empty except for a few court stools and a throne until this century, when first the late Queen Mary, and latterly Queen Elizabeth the Queen Mother, took the place in hand and rendered it more comfortable and 'lived in'. The overall feeling inside the Royal Apartments now is much the same as that outside, that is of a moderately grand French *château*, and there is a considerable homogeneity in the furnishings which nicely match Bruce's Restoration panelling and rich plaster ceilings. The cleaning of the exterior has transformed Holyrood from a gloomy, black pile into the most handsome example of Scots Palladian-ism. The stone is a warm fawn, and when the evening light is on it this fine building, the first in Scotland in which the three orders of architecture, Doric, Ionic, and Corinthian were used, makes a fitting memorial to the monarch by whose command it was completed in 1679; Charles II, the 'Merry Monarch', in whose veins ran the blood of Marie de Medicis, Henry of Navarre, Anne of Denmark and the 'Wisest Fool in Christen-dom'.

Charles I, with his usual perspicacity and taste, employed his Master Mason, John Mylne, to build a palace with three courtyards, much in the mode of Whitehall and in the purest Palladian of Inigo Jones. Had repleted finances and war not prevented it Holyroodhouse would have been unrivalled amongst British royal palaces, and even as it is, it is superior to almost every other except Hampton Court. It is a master-piece of correct proportion and scale such as the connoisseur king himself would have appreciated, and the standard of workmanship is likewise very good. John Mylne lived to start work on the modified plan after the Restoration but died before much had been done, when he was succeeded as Master Mason by his nephew Robert, who with Bruce created what we see today, his initials appearing on a column at the foot of the stairs leading to the historical wing. In place of Charles I's triple courtyard only one was built, but it is here that the Royal Architect showed his mastery of the Palladian manner, and knowledge of existing models, and in particular of the Gaston d'Orleans block at Blois, in which the 'orders' and arcading are plainly reflected in the Holyrood courtyard. The first pedimented centrepiece in Scotland will also be found there, opposite the entrance. The latter is interesting because Robert Mylne made it according to explicit instructions from Charles II and carved the Royal Achievement above from a drawing by de Wet made on a big wooden board.

Full details of the building of the Palace of Holyroodhouse are recorded in the Mylne Papers, now in the Register House in Edinburgh. De Wet's name occurs frequently, and especially for his *trompe l'oeil* work and inset panels of 'celestial scenery' painted to complement George Dunsterfield's and John Halbert's fretwork ceilings. I have mentioned their work at

Royal entrance to the Palace of
Holyroodhouse

Thirlestane, Balcaskie and Kellie, but at Holyrood these 'gentlemen modellers' excelled themselves. Today their ceilings of intricate plasterwork are painted white, but in the seventeenth century they were painted in bright colours, which must have made the rooms a little gayer than now, even after a twentieth-century clean-up. Some impression of what they were like may be gained from the effect of the restored Long Gallery, where the dark stained woodwork is radiant in new blue-green and gold, which sets off the hundred or more portraits on the walls and the old furniture nicely. The gallery leads to the State Apartments which run round the courtyard from room to room without corridors, as in most royal palaces. There is no longer any chapel, the Abbey Kirk being in ruins and the bodies of Scotland's kings and queens scattered by the mob in 1690. James VII and II, who was the last Stuart monarch to live here is also the last to be represented on the walls of the Long Gallery, all the portraits being painted in about six months by de Wet. The faces of the later rulers, from James IV onwards, are more or less recognizable, but when one gets to Macbeth and the Ferguses authenticity seems remote if not impossible! It used to be thought that the artist himself was the model for some of these mythical and near mythical personages, but in fact they were copied by him from a set of kings painted for Charles I's Coronation by George Jamesone, and which came up for sale in Edinburgh, in 1971, having hung undisturbed on the walls of Newbattle Abbey, in Midlothian, since the middle of the seventeenth century.

The windows at Holyrood were originally casements with leaded lights on the front, and the architect did not introduce sashes until half way through the work and then only on the Palladian 'palazzo' he built behind the French-*château* façade. The fountain in the forecourt was copied for Queen Victoria from the more ancient one at Linlithgow, dating from the reign of James V, and the sundial-cum-lamp standard in the courtyard is a copy of the one in the Queen's private garden, which was made by John Mylne and bears the monograms of King Charles I, Queen Henrietta Maria and Charles, Prince of Wales, the future Charles II. It is one of the few things at Holyrood known to be the work of that excellent Master Mason. The façade of the Abbey Kirk, ruined though it is, was restored and improved for King Charles by, it is said, Inigo Jones, but there is no proof of this and very likely John Mylne did it himself. The formal gardens which existed in the seventeenth century and are shown on old prints have completely disappeared as has the catchspiel where James, Duke of York and his court played 'real tennis' and performed their amateur dramatics. The odd little building with several turrets and a most peculiar shape known as 'Queen Mary's Bath' may have been a pavilion or some other adjunct of the catchspiel; it certainly dates from the sixteenth century and looks for all the world like the home of a witch in its isolated position. Behind are modern flats, and on the other side of the palace breweries and more flats. Yet, despite these encroachments and the all-pervading smell of beer when the wind is in the west, the park remains an oasis of green and rocky grandeur where one can hide from the city if one knows where; a mountain and a couple of lochs are set here in the midst of urban development, a romantic ruin and a real one, and the source of the water which Bruce found and used in the building of the palace and which he subsequently incorporated in his scheme for the burgh waterworks.

When work on Holyroodhouse was practically finished Sir William Bruce was dismissed and Lord Hatton, Lauderdale's brother and heir, made Royal Surveyor in his place. Shortly after this, however, Prestonfield House, the home of the Lord Provost of Edinburgh, Sir James Dick, a prominent Roman Catholic and personal friend of the Duke of York, was burnt down in a student riot, when Bruce was re-called to rebuild it. Treasury funds were diverted to the purpose and workmen formerly engaged at Holyrood, including masons, joiners and plasterers, converted the building into a finer mansion than it had been before, though retaining such original features as Jacobean buckle-quoins and Dutch gables. Prestonfield was altered again in the eighteenth century, but retains its Restoration furnishings, which were saved from the fire and include remarkable leather-hangings, painted panels and portraits. It has stayed in the Dick family ever since. Sir James Dick, returning with the king's brother by sea from London, helped to save the future James VII and II from drowning. The ship carrying the royal party ran aground off Yarmouth, when the crew took to the boats and the Duke of York and his suite would all have perished but for the swift action of some of the Scots gentlemen in his entourage of whom one was Sir James Dick, who survived, and Charles Hope, father of the first Earl of Hopetoun who drowned. The Duke's gratitude was shown in the rebuilding of Prestonfield and in the posthumous earldom conferred on Charles Hope's two-year-old son.

Almost contemporary with Prestonfield is Caroline Park, on the seashore at Granton. This also has connections with Holyrood since it was built by workmen from the palace and again partly with government money. It was the 'country cottage' of Sir George Mackenzie, Lord Justice General and first Earl of Cromartie, a notable 'trimmer' and not to be confused with his namesake, Sir George Mackenzie of Rosehaugh, Lord Advocate and a friend of John Evelyn. Mackenzie of Rosehaugh was the very opposite of a 'trimmer', the man who founded the Advocate's Library and earned the hatred of the Covenanters, who called him 'bluidy Mackenzie' on account of his literal interpretation of the laws against violence and sedition. Bairns playing in Greyfriar's kirkyard are said to have taunted the dead Mackenzie in his handsome Renaissance tomb, which is an object worth looking at in its own right, the design being derived from the base of the Mercat Cross at Prestonpans, with shell-niches and pilasters; but here crowned with an ogee-shaped dome and urn finial. It may have been the work of Robert Mylne and is both uniquely conceived and finely executed.

After supporting James VII and II the other Sir George, then Viscount Tarbat, managed to change his coat in time to gain the confidence of William of Orange, retaining his position and being granted an earldom under Queen Anne. His 'cottage' by the Firth of Forth has suffered many vicissitudes and several changes in ownership, the last proprietors, before it was purchased by the Duke of Buccleuch in order to save it from possible demolition, being a firm of ink manufacturers, who maintained it well until it proved too inconvenient for them. Unhappily the surroundings of Caroline Park make its future highly problematical as on one side are enormous gas works and on the other a petrol refinery. Goodness knows why something was not done to prevent this, the most interesting and complete late-Stuart house within the boundaries of Edinburgh, becoming completely otiose. No one can live there any more, and the Department of the Environment preferred to move to a modern 'hen-house' in the middle of the city when their ancient monuments and historic records offices might have made this eminently appropriate building their new headquarters.

The house is notable for its two stages of development, coinciding with the owners rise in rank and favour. The façade facing the sea, which was entered by handsome Palladian gates not dissimilar in style from Bruce's, represented Sir George Mackenzie's 'country cottage' and was known as Royston; the Caroline connotation came later, in the eighteenth century, when the Duke of Argyll, whose daughter was named Caroline, bought the estate and when the Queen of George II had the same name. This resembled the main façade at Prestonfield, with its two projecting wings with Dutch gables and lower central portico leading through into a courtyard as at Holyrood. When a knighthood turned into a viscountancy and then into an earldom a grandiose baroque façade was added to the south, facing away from the sea, with *dômes a l'Impériales*, columned entrance with richly wrought iron balcony above, rusticated stonework around the base and elaborate furnishings within, including a superb plaster ceiling in the style of the gentlemen modellers who decorated Holyrood for the King. The painted panel here, on the other hand, is not by the prolific but unimaginative de Wet, but by a Frenchman, Nicolas Heude, who was apprenticed to Verrio at Hampton Court and signed his work. The name of Sir William Bruce is often mentioned in respect of Caroline Park, but if he did have a hand in it it was only in the original cottage and in helping with the supply craftsmen and materials. The new, baroque front, though magnificent in a flamboyant sort of way, and certainly without rival in this country, is remarkably crude in its details, lacking that patrician refinement one always associates with Charles II's Architect Royal. Robert Mylne may have worked here, but the French influence is strong, reminding one vividly of the Norman Château de Camp de Bataille, itself a 'country' design by François le Vau, brother of the famous Louis, architect of Vaux-le-Vicomte.

It is possible, therefore, that neither Bruce nor Mylne had any part in the baroque façade and that French masons were brought over specially. If so their influence is particularly unusual at a period when Britain was at war with France and the more popular country in politics and culture was Holland. Caroline Park, therefore, is in a class on its own.

Not everyone was as successful as the Earl of Cromartie in maintaining their positions during the difficult changeover from late-Stuart to early Georgian regimes, and the Jacobite Earl of Mar, for example, found himself exiled in Italy after the failure of the 1715 rebellion. He was based at first in Urbino, that charming hill-town in the Marchian Apennines which in the days of Frederigo di Montefeltro and Castiglione, the 'Perfect Courtier', cradled the most civilized and cultured court in Europe, and which became, under Papal Patronage, the resort of James, the Old Pretender. The Earl of Mar spent part of his time there drawing up plans for a New Town of Edinburgh, many of them extensions of earlier schemes propounded in the time of James, Duke of York, who for all his faults, displayed the same interest and knowledge of artistic matters as the rest of his family. Mention has already been made of the Earl's proposals for a Forth to Clyde canal, with its eastern basin where Princes Street Gardens are now. The whole plan hinged on the building of a bridge over the narrow end of the Nor' Loch, which without considerable deepening could scarcely have become a fully fledged port; and presumably Leith would still have retained its pre-eminence in that respect. Bruce designed a 'North Bridge' which was never built, and the one opened by Lord Provost Drummond in 1772 was the work of William Mylne, Architect to the City of Edinburgh and a member of the same remarkable family of masons and engineers as Robert, who built Holyrood and was his great-grandfather. He does not seem to have been as good as the others though, since he misjudged the strength of the foundations at the Old Town end, which collapsed and the bridge had to be begun all over again. The present structure is not his either. It is of cast iron and crosses part of Waverley Station, where the Nor' Loch was a mere marsh until drained and an 'earthern mound' raised to dam it up for ever.

Mar's scheme for a canal was eventually undertaken but

not with a basin under the bield of the castle. Another idea of his was also taken up, and that was for the creation of Princes Street, which in the first half of the eighteenth century existed as the Lang Gait, or Long Walk, which ran along the banks of the Nor' Loch on its northern side. With the bridge at the eastern end leading to Leith an accomplished fact, and the Lang Gait becoming a proper thoroughfare, the new Georgian suburb which is now the centre of modern Edinburgh began to arise. It was many years before the people left their smelly but cosy quarters in the Old Town in large numbers, and the first buildings in the New Town were undistinguished and erected in speculative fashion, higgledy-piggeldy, with gaps between them as the plots were sold or rejected, and not in rows, one by one, as might have been expected. It was not until the west end was reached, Castle Street and Charlotte Square, that any refinements worth the name or genuine attempts to be imaginative were made. Lord Cockburn's comment anent the ugliness of Princes Street was made shortly after it was finished, in 1822, before the erection of larger commercial premises. Castle Street, where Sir Walter Scott went to live with his French wife in the early nineteenth century, was the first in which the houses sported pilasters, cornices or even separate front doors, as previously the traditional common stair with single entrance prevailed. Thus far the spirit of old Edinburgh survived the transference of folk and activity to an inhospitable, windswept site beyond the Nor' Loch. There was a fight too about nomenclature, between the king, George III, and the citizens, who wished to call the new Lang Gait after St Giles, thus retaining links with the past. When the king heard of this he shook his head and said 'Hey-hey, what's this, St Giles. Can't allow that.' The result was a compromise, with Prince's Street, as it should be written, referring either to the sons of the king or to Prince Charlie and his brother in Rome, and the royally desired George Street removed one degree north to its present position. A further muddle occurred with St George's and St Andrew's Squares. The first was eventually named after Queen Charlotte but got St George's Church, while the second was named after St Andrew but got no church, St Andrew's Church being in George Street.

The first significant movement of people and trade from

south to north occured at the end of the new bridge and the eastern approach to Princes Street, and it is interesting to note that since theatres were prohibited in the Old Town, but not in the New, one of the first buildings to go up there was a theatre, in Shakespeare Place, opposite Robert Adam's new Register House. This is one of the architect's best designs in the city. In it he used the dome of the Pantheon in Rome, which his father's mentor, Sir John Clerk of Penicuik, had planned to adapt as a Library and Turkish Bath on the estate, but which was never accomplished. At either end of the façade Adam placed slightly projecting wings, or pavilions, which he crowned with little turrets, suggesting in both the Scottish vernacular. Something similar was carried out on the north side of Charlotte Square, which is the only part he designed and which was not completed in his lifetime, where the end pavilions have a quite unusual look viewed in a purely neo-classical, Georgian context, but are wholly appropriate in a Scottish, Continental one. The 'New Athenian' town, set against its romantic Gothic background and added to by the

North side of Charlotte Square, showing Bute House (*centre*), now the residence of the Secretary of State for Scotland

Victorians and Edwardians, is not, however, our main concern, the principal features being at least as much geographical as architectural; and history lying largely outwith such exercises in the romantic juxtapositioning of Mediterranean and Central European motifs.

The development of Leith has largely taken place alongside that of Edinburgh but sometimes separately, whenever the inhabitants have managed to establish their independence, which they most recently did in the nineteenth century only to have it removed in the twentieth in one of our now fairly common regionalization programmes, this one dating from between the wars. In consequence a walk around the burgh reminds one of Edinburgh, and also of places with which the port has forged its own trade and cultural links down the centuries. Leith was, of course, the principal port of entry for goods for the whole of south eastern Scotland, but most importantly for the wines of Bordeaux which have been landed here since the Middle Ages and still come in quantity, as witness the numerous wine merchants whose warehouses line The Shore. This trade was hit hard by the arrival of William of Orange, who, to encourage the drinking of Dutch spirits, put a heavy duty on French wines, and again during the Napoleonic Wars when French goods generally were either prohibited or difficult to obtain. The name 'Italian Warehouseman', however, still seen over old established grocers in the capital, recalls the part played by Venetians and Florentines, when Marco Polo discovered the land route to China and Portuguese and Flemish ships brought wine and spices to these islands.

The port has also seen the landing on its quayside of a number of celebrated persons, of which the homecoming of Mary, Queen of Scots and the much heralded arrival of George IV are perhaps the best known. There is a plaque marking the spot where the 'wee German laddie' first put a foot on Scottish soil on Monday 15th August, 1822, having waited all Sunday on board ship for the rain to stop and made sure of a sunny welcome. Of the buildings lining The Shore then few remain in any decent state of preservation and most have been greatly altered or rebuilt, though the handsome Custom House which appears behind the platform party in the painting recording the event is still there. It was designed by Sir Robert Reid, the man who misinterpreted Adam's original scheme for Charlotte Square and who was soon to rejoice under the nominal title of Royal Master Mason. His Leith Custom House is a creditable essay in Greek Revival and typical of the way in which Leith buildings of the period tended to reflect on a smaller scale those of the neo-classical New Town of Edinburgh. One might call them 'after Edinburgh', and they include, besides the Custom House, the Old Assembly Rooms, now known as the Exchange Buildings and related to Robert Adam's Register House, and Trinity House, which is the headquarters of the Masters and Mariners of Leith and built in the dignified style that graced the capital about 1816.

Accounts vary considerably as to the warmth or otherwise of Queen Mary's reception, even as to the state of the weather, which Knox described rather gleefully as misty and wet, attributing this to God's displeasure at the Queen's supposedly wanton appearance. Others say the weather was fine and sunny and the people friendly and noisily welcoming. Whatever the truth, Mary was given hospitality in the house of a wool merchant by name Andrew Lamb, whose house has miraculously survived. It was rescued from decay by the late Marquis of Bute just before the war, when a number of demolitions took place in the vicinity, and since then has been restored by Robert Hurd as an old people's rest centre. Tall and white and crow-stepped, with corbelled projections and numerous chimney-stalks rising from gablets and gables, it is a larger version of some of the houses in Fife, and in its restoration was refurnished with shutter-board windows and symbolic weigh beams and hooks for the bales of wool. Behind Lamb's House, right on The Shore, is Leith's other most interesting secular building, 'The King's Wark', which dates in its present form from the reign of Charles II but stands on older foundations and was part of a 'complex' that included a small fort, chapel, royal mansion and tennis court. James VI sold the property at the beginning of the seventeenth century and bit by bit it has been redeveloped. The house proper, with its characteristic Dutch gables and scroll skew-putts, is now an inn, and has been restored after many years of neglect and the threat of replacement.

Mary of Guise made Leith her redoubt when the Lords of the Congregation, in league with Queen Elizabeth, drove her out of Edinburgh and she and her French supporters held the port. Her house has gone, but a stone from it bearing her Arms as Regent of Scotland is preserved in the vestry of North Leith Kirk, a plain neo-classical structure with a good steeple by William Burn, who utterly restored St Giles' in Edinburgh and more often worked in Gothic or Jacobean manner. Nearby, between the church and the Custom House, was Monk's Citadel, which covered a large area of central Leith until removed a few years ago. As late as 1969 I was able to take a photograph of one of the old 'ports', whitewashed and arched, with stairs up to a picturesque private house above, and looking almost oriental in its odd setting amidst tall stone tenements and new concrete skyscrapers.

The harbour at Leith was re-organized by John Rennie and has since been extended and modernized, but one curiosity remains at the far end of the old pier in what is called The Signal Tower, which has a long history and has not only seen many changes, and people come and go, but has itself changed in appearance and use. It had been a primitive lighthouse and a windmill, making turnip, or rape oil, when Robert Mylne, Mason to Charles II, bought it and adapted it as one of his local speculations. It is now crenellated and more like a Folly than anything else, though the lower portion is a hostel. From The Shore Bernard Street leads off irregularly and ever widening to the former Assembly Rooms, with a statue of Robert Burns in front. The entire street, more of a 'place' than otherwise, is interesting and possesses unusual scenographic qualities, with The King's Wark at the foot, and buildings of various periods all the way up. The most charming is the old Leith Bank, now a branch of the Royal Bank of Scotland. This dates from the early nineteenth century; it is more than a little reminiscent of Bélanger's 'Bagatelle', in the Bois de Boulogne, which was built for Louis XVI's brother, the Comte d'Artois, afterwards Charles X, who actually came to Scotland to escape the guillotine and stayed as a guest at Holyroodhouse for several years. It is also perhaps worth recalling that Bélanger was a particular friend of Sir William Chambers, to whom he dedicated a design in Paris, so that there may in fact be some cultural or historic association here, one which is echoed again in the design of St Mark's Church at Portobello, just along the coast, which is even more like 'Bagatelle'.

In the past Leith could count a number of medieval churches, but none remains in its original form, certainly not 'Our Lady of the Sea', the present Parish Kirk, through the roof of which an English cannon ball passed during the siege in 1559. The tower of St Ninian's Chapel is all that survives of any antiquity in the ecclesiastical line, and that, though well cared for, is attached to a mill, which, however, is a fate not wholly without point since the Water of Leith, as Edinburgh's 'river' is called, was lined with mills, many of which belonged to the Canons of Holyrood, St Ninian's being their chapel. The 'river' is short and shallow, rising in the Pentland Hills not more than thirty miles from the town so that in spate it can be quite dangerous, flooding the lower floors of houses along its banks; but the level falls quickly, usually in a day, when the Water of Leith resembles little more than a country burn. This may account for its relative unimportance to the city, which, except at Leith itself, turns its back on the 'river' reckoning the Forth more significant. The Water of Leith has, on the other hand, been a source of power, with its mills, some grain, others, in the eighteenth century, grinding snuff, and today mostly sawdust. The name Canonmills in north Edinburgh recalls the old connection with Holyrood, the mills themselves having been altered beyond recognition, having all their corners and interesting features removed, coated with cement and generally made pathetic looking.

Further up the Water of Leith is Stockbridge, which still has some of the atmosphere of a separate village, and where the painter, Sir Henry Raeburn, acting on the advice of his friend, David Wilkie, turned architect-speculator and developed the land of Ann Edgar, his wife, building and naming Ann Street after her. This is a sort of Scottish Chelsea, with attractive but poorly planned 'Georgian' houses, with front gardens, in one of which Raeburn and his family lived. Below, in a wooded glen, Alexander Nasmyth, another painter but with masonic and engineering leanings, built St Bernard's Well, a round, open pavilion, colonnaded and domed, with a statue of Hygeia in the middle. It dates from 1789 and until a few years ago one could buy a glass of chalybeate water there. Half a mile beyond, almost in the shade of the Dean Bridge, is the village of Water of Leith, or West Leith as some old records call it. Nowadays it is more often referred to as the Dean Village, but the latter actually stood above the valley where the Dean Cemetery now is, and only a couple of houses remain opposite the graveyard gate. Robert Louis Stevenson in his *Picturesque Notes* describes Water of Leith as the 'Herculaneum of the North', so that even then it had become the dreamy backwater it still manages to be; and if plans for including it in a Conservation Area bear fruit, will stay for a long time. Here the Canons had their Tolbooth and Granary, which survive in a single large building with two stair projections and crow-stepped gables, and an inscription showing how the place was rebuilt 'by the Baxters', or Bakers, of Edinburgh in 1675. The Guild of Baxters succeeded the Canons of Holyrood as feudal superiors at the Reformation, and the people's dues were paid in grain which they brought to the granary; the Tolbooth serving as a warning to defaulters and breakers of the peace, for both Canons and Baxters were responsible for maintaining order in the village.

The old bridge here once carried the main road from the north into the city, and over it rumbled the coach taking George IV to and from Hopetoun House where he stayed in 1822. Prince Charlie's Highlanders used the ford upstream because they wished to arrive unannounced and take the garrison by surprise. With the building of Telford's high level Dean Bridge in 1832 the small, single-arched structure below lost its importance, and with it the village sank into pleasant decay, with several flour mills still working, and a few weavers remaining busy in their cottages until the second half of the nineteenth century. Gradually, however, commercial activity ground to a halt and the future of Water of Leith as a living entity seemed in doubt. In reports published before the war various interested bodies showed that an unusual spirit of independence and ingenuity survived there which the more perspicacious observers thought more worth preserving even than the buildings they inhabited, many of them red pantiled and quaint in the Scottish vernacular, but one, Well Court, an essay in recreative native style dating from 1884, when the then owner of *The Scotsman* built it, partly because he did not like looking at slums and tummeldoun houses from his windows and partly as an experiment in community living. Well Court never quite achieved what was intended for it in the social field, but architecturally it is a *tour de force* in which ancient and modern merge in the most interesting manner, and innumerable and apparently accidental changes in height and shape combine to produce one of the most satisfying and successful recreative designs in Scotland.

At about the same time as Well Court was being built the old Tolbooth was purchased and restored by the Episcopal Church and converted into a caretaker's house, congregational meeting place and mission of St Mary's Cathedral, in Palmerstone Place. This cathedral is the largest ecclesiastical building north of the Border housing a bishop's 'chair', and is generally accepted as the masterpiece of Sir Gilbert Scott, who won the competition for it in 1874. It is not a Gothic-revival building but a study in original medieval style, a fact that Sacheverell Sitwell and Francis Bamford draw attention to in their book on *Edinburgh*; 'but there is, as well St Mary's Cathedral, a most extraordinary structure . . . an hour or two can be spent here, lost in wonder. For this edifice, which is in the strictest Gothic, carries no trace whatever of the Pre-Raphaelite revival. Its interior is perfect down to the smallest detail; and it must nearly be inconceivable to the present age how such a building was ever erected.' St Mary's as such lies largely outwith the present narrative, though a number of details were taken from older Scottish churches and incorporated in the design. It was paid for in a single generation by the two Misses Walker, Barbara and Mary, after whom the western towers are named and whose diminutive Jacobean manor house sits proudly beside their latter day creation.

Easter Coates House, as the tiny, turreted building is called, today shelters the only Choir School in Scotland recognized by Lyon Court, and was added to here and there by an earlier occupant, Sir Patrick Walker, who acted as White Rod during the visit of George IV to Edinburgh and set up on the exterior of his house a number of inscriptions and heraldic devices brought from the French Ambassador's residence in

Easter Coates Manor,
Drumsheugh, Edinburgh,
circa 1610

the Old Town when it was demolished. It is perhaps worth
recalling *en passant* that the office of White Rod in the defunct
Scottish Parliament survives to this day in its purely titular
form, being vested in the Walker Trust, which maintains the
Cathedral, and which in 1953 sent Bishop Warner of Edinburgh
to the Queen's Coronation at Westminster as their representative. The Walkers acquired their wealth through the feuing
and completing of this, the western end of the New Town, in
the second half of the nineteenth century, when Melville Street,
the last in the Georgian plan and still the finest, was linked
with the later Victorian quarters, which, notwithstanding their
plate-glass and Italianate suggestions, were laid out according
to an overall scheme that included control of heights and sizes
of rooms, numbers of windows, materials used and limitation
to residential purposes. Sir Walter Scott spoke of George IV
as the first monarch whom all Scots could recognize as king
because he was the first of his house to reign after the death of
the last in the native line, Cardinal York, who died in 1807.
This is an appropriate place, therefore, with the story of
White Rod and the building of St Mary's Cathedral out of

the feuing of the lands of Meldrumsheugh, in whose forest Sir Patrick Walker's 'Hunting Lodge' stood, to close my narrative.

List of Buildings Described in the Text which are Regularly or Periodically Open to the Public

Buildings under the care of the Department of the Environment (Secretary of State for Scotland)

Aberdeenshire
*St Machar's Cathedral, Old
  Aberdeen

Angus
Affleck Castle, near Dundee
Brechin, Round Tower
Claypotts Castle, Dundee
Edzell Castle and Renaissance
  Garden

Ayrshire
Rowallan Castle, near
  Kilmarnock
Skelmorlie Aisle, Largs

East Lothian
*Haddington, St Mary's
  Collegiate Kirk
Prestonpans, the Mercat Cross
Seton Collegiate Kirk

Fife
*Culross Abbey
Culross, the 'Palas'
Dunfermline Abbey, Nave
Inchcolm Abbey, near
  Aberdour
Scotstarvit Tower, near Cupar

Inverness-shire
Rodil, St Clement's Church,
  Isle of Harris

Kinross-shire
Burleigh Castle, Milnathort

Stewartry of Kirkcudbright
Kirkcudbright, McClellan's
  Castle

Lanarkshire
Douglas, St Bride's Kirk
*Glasgow Cathedral

Midlothian
Edinburgh Castle (Crown
  property)
Holyrood Abbey and Palace
  (Crown property)

Perthshire
*Dunblane Cathedral
Huntingtower, near Perth
Grantully, St Mary's Kirk
Tullibardine Chapel, near
  Auchterarder

Stirlingshire
Stirling Castle
Stirling, Mar's Wark

* Religious buildings still in use, open for services only on Sundays.

The following properties have received a grant from Public funds and are open by appointment

Aberdeenshire

Craigston Castle, near Turriff:
written application only to
Mr Bruce Urquhart

East Lothian

Northfield House, Prestonpans:
apply to Mr W. Schomberg
Scott

Haddington, The Town House.
Weekdays

Fife

Elie, The Castle: apply to
Miss Scott-Moncreiff

Pittenweem, The Great House:
apply Representative
Church Council, 21
Grosvenor Crescent,
Edinburgh 12

Kinrosshire

Aldie Castle: written
application only to Mr A.
Hope Dickson

Kinross House: written
application only to Sir
David Montgomery, Bart

Tulliebole Castle: apply Lord
Moncreiff

Midlothian

Arniston House, Gorebridge:
apply Mrs Dundas Bekker

Ford House, Ford: apply Mr
F. P. Tindall

Penicuik House, Penicuik:
by written appointment only
from Sir John Clerk, Bart

Moray

Pluscarden Priory, Elgin:
apply to the Prior

Stirlingshire

The Old Tolbooth, Stirling:
apply Town Chamberlain

Buildings and properties under the care of the National Trust for Scotland open to the public

Aberdeenshire

Provost Ross's House,
Aberdeen

Craigievar Castle, Lumphanan

Pitmedden, The Great Garden

Ayrshire

Culzean Castle

Clackmannanshire

Menstrie Castle, in conjunction
with the local authority

East Lothian

Preston Mill

Prestonpans, Hamilton Dower
House: by appointment only

Edinburgh

Gladstone's Land

Lamb's House, Leith

Fife

Culross, The Study

Falkland Palace

Kellie Castle

Glasgow

Provan Hall

Kincardineshire

Crathes Castle

Private Properties open to the public

Aberdeenshire

Balmoral Castle, Braemar,
grounds only
Braemar Castle, Braemar
Drum Castle, near Aberdeen
Provost Skene's House,
Aberdeen

Angus

Glamis Castle, Glamis

Argyll

Inveraray Castle, Inveraray

Glasgow

Pollok House
Provand's Lordship

Kincardineshire

Muchalls Castle, Stonehaven

Midlothian

Prestonfield House, Edinburgh.
Open as an hotel

*Rosslyn Chapel, Roslin

Orkney

*St Magnus Cathedral,
Kirkwall

Peeblesshire

Traquair House,
Innerleithen

Perthshire

Blair Castle, Blair Atholl
Doune Castle, Doune
Drummond Castle, near Crieff
Innerpeffray Library

Roxburghshire

Abbotsford House, Melrose

Sutherland

Dunrobin Castle

West Lothian

Hopetoun House

* Religious buildings still in use, open for services only on Sundays.

Note. The above information was correct for the summer of 1973, and can be checked from the current ABC Guide to *Historic Houses and Castles and Gardens in Great Britain and Ireland*, and from *Scottish Castles and Historic Houses* published by the Scottish Tourist Board. The Department of the Environment also publish a complete list, with descriptions of properties under their care, which may be obtained from H.M. Stationery Office; as do the National Trust for Scotland at 5 Charlotte Square, Edinburgh 2. Apart from buildings regularly open to the public a number of interesting properties mentioned, such as, Pilmuir, in East Lothian; The Drum, Gilmerton; Balcaskie and Earlshall, in Fife; Cawdor Castle, Nairn; and Stobhall, near Perth, open periodically under Scotland's Gardens Scheme; for details apply to the General Organizer at 26 Castle Terrace, Edinburgh 1.

Index

Index